Microsoft® Office Excel® 2010: Part 3 (Second Edition)

Microsoft® Office Excel® 2010: Part 3 (Second Edition)

Part Number: 091020
Course Edition: 1.01

Acknowledgements

PROJECT TEAM

Author	Media Designer	Content Editor
Tim Barnosky	Alex Tong	Catherine M. Albano

Notices

DISCLAIMER

While Logical Operations, Inc. takes care to ensure the accuracy and quality of these materials, we cannot guarantee their accuracy, and all materials are provided without any warranty whatsoever, including, but not limited to, the implied warranties of merchantability or fitness for a particular purpose. The name used in the data files for this course is that of a fictitious company. Any resemblance to current or future companies is purely coincidental. We do not believe we have used anyone's name in creating this course, but if we have, please notify us and we will change the name in the next revision of the course. Logical Operations is an independent provider of integrated training solutions for individuals, businesses, educational institutions, and government agencies. Use of screenshots, photographs of another entity's products, or another entity's product name or service in this book is for editorial purposes only. No such use should be construed to imply sponsorship or endorsement of the book by, nor any affiliation of such entity with Logical Operations. This courseware may contain links to sites on the internet that are owned and operated by third parties (the "External Sites"). Logical Operations is not responsible for the availability of, or the content located on or through, any External Site. Please contact Logical Operations if you have any concerns regarding such links or External Sites.

TRADEMARK NOTICES

Logical Operations and the Logical Operations logo are trademarks of Logical Operations, Inc. and its affiliates.

Microsoft® and Excel® are registered trademarks of Microsoft Corporation in the U.S. and other countries. The other Microsoft products and services discussed or described may be trademarks or registered trademarks of Microsoft Corporation. All other product and service names used may be common law or registered trademarks of their respective proprietors.

Copyright © 2014 Logical Operations, Inc. All rights reserved. Screenshots used for illustrative purposes are the property of the software proprietor. This publication, or any part thereof, may not be reproduced or transmitted in any form or by any means, electronic or mechanical, including photocopying, recording, storage in an information retrieval system, or otherwise, without express written permission of Logical Operations, 3535 Winton Place, Rochester, NY 14623, (585) 350-7000, (800) 478-7788. Logical Operations' World Wide Web site is located at **www.logicaloperations.com**.

This book conveys no rights in the software or other products about which it was written; all use or licensing of such software or other products is the responsibility of the user according to terms and conditions of the owner. Do not make illegal copies of books or software. If you believe that this book, related materials, or any other Logical Operations materials are being reproduced or transmitted without permission, please call (800) 478-7788.

Microsoft® Office Excel® 2010: Part 3 (Second Edition)

Lesson 1: Working with Multiple Worksheets and Workbooks Simultaneously 1
Topic A: Use 3-D References 2
Topic B: Use Links and External References 8
Topic C: Consolidate Data 15

Lesson 2: Sharing and Protecting Workbooks 21
Topic A: Collaborate on a Workbook 22
Topic B: Protect Worksheets and Workbooks 33

Lesson 3: Automating Workbook Functionality 41
Topic A: Apply Data Validation 42
Topic B: Work with Forms and Controls 49
Topic C: Work with Macros 62

Lesson 4: Applying Conditional Logic 75
Topic A: Use Lookup Functions 76
Topic B: Combine Functions 85

Topic C: Use Formulas and Functions to Apply Conditional Formatting...90

Lesson 5: Auditing Worksheets..99
Topic A: Trace Cells..100
Topic B: Search for Invalid Data and Formulas with Errors....................107
Topic C: Watch and Evaluate Formulas..111

Lesson 6: Using Automated Analysis Tools........................119
Topic A: Determine Potential Outcomes by Using Data Tables..............120
Topic B: Determine Potential Outcomes by Using Scenarios.................125
Topic C: Use the Goal Seek Feature..132
Topic D: Activate and Use the Solver Tool......................................137
Topic E: Analyze Data with Analysis ToolPak Tools..........................144

Lesson 7: Presenting Your Data Visually.............................151
Topic A: Use Advanced Chart Features...152
Topic B: Create Sparklines..161

Appendix A: Cube Functions..169

Appendix B: Import and Export Data..171
Topic A: Importing and Exporting Data..172

Appendix C: Microsoft Office Excel 2010 Exam 77-882......................179

Appendix D: Microsoft Office Excel 2010 Expert Exam 77-888...........185

Lesson Labs..189

Glossary..201

Index...205

About This Course

Clearly, you use Excel a lot in your role. Otherwise, you wouldn't be taking this course. By now, you're already familiar with Excel 2010, its functions and formulas, a lot of its features and functionality, and its powerful data analysis tools. You are likely called upon to analyze and report on data frequently, work in collaboration with others to deliver actionable organizational intelligence, and keep and maintain workbooks for all manner of purposes. At this level of use and collaboration, you have also likely encountered your fair share of issues and challenges. You're too busy, though, to waste time scouring over workbooks to resolve issues or to perform repetitive, monotonous tasks. You need to know how to get Excel to do more for you so you can focus on what's really important: staying ahead of the competition. That's exactly what this course aims to help you do.

This course builds off of the foundational and intermediate knowledge presented in the *Microsoft® Office Excel® 2010: Part 1 (Second Edition)* and *Part 2 (Second Edition)* courses to help you get the most of your Excel experience. The ability to collaborate with colleagues, automate complex or repetitive tasks, and use conditional logic to construct and apply elaborate formulas and functions will put the full power of Excel right at your fingertips. The more you learn about how to get Excel to do the hard work for you, the more you'll be able to focus on getting the answers you need from the vast amounts of data your organization generates.

This course covers Microsoft Office Specialist exam objectives to help students prepare for the Excel 2010 Exam and the Excel 2010 Expert Exam.

Course Description

Target Student

This course is intended for students who are experienced Excel 2010 users who have a desire or need to advance their skills in working with some of the more advanced Excel features. Students will likely need to troubleshoot large, complex workbooks, automate repetitive tasks, engage in collaborative partnerships involving workbook data, construct complex Excel functions, and use those functions to perform rigorous analysis of extensive, complex datasets.

Course Prerequisites

To ensure success, students should have practical, real-world experience creating and analyzing datasets using Excel 2010. Specific tasks students should be able to perform include: creating formulas and using Excel functions; creating, sorting, and filtering datasets and tables; presenting data by using basic charts; creating and working with PivotTables, slicers, and PivotCharts; and customizing the Excel environment. To meet these prerequisites, students can take the following Logical Operations courses, or should possess the equivalent skill level:

- *Microsoft® Office Excel®: Part 1 (Second Edition)*
- *Microsoft® Office Excel®: Part 2 (Second Edition)*

Course Objectives

Upon successful completion of this course, you will be able to perform advanced data analysis, collaborate on workbooks with other users, and automate workbook functionality.

You will:

- Work with multiple worksheets and workbooks simultaneously.
- Share and protect workbooks.
- Automate workbook functionality.
- Apply conditional logic.
- Audit worksheets.
- Use automated analysis tools.
- Present your data visually.

The LogicalCHOICE Home Screen

The LogicalCHOICE Home screen is your entry point to the LogicalCHOICE learning experience, of which this course manual is only one part. Visit the LogicalCHOICE Course screen both during and after class to make use of the world of support and instructional resources that make up the LogicalCHOICE experience.

Log-on and access information for your LogicalCHOICE environment will be provided with your class experience. On the LogicalCHOICE Home screen, you can access the LogicalCHOICE Course screens for your specific courses.

Each LogicalCHOICE Course screen will give you access to the following resources:

- eBook: an interactive electronic version of the printed book for your course.
- LearnTOs: brief animated components that enhance and extend the classroom learning experience.

Depending on the nature of your course and the choices of your learning provider, the LogicalCHOICE Course screen may also include access to elements such as:

- The interactive eBook.
- Social media resources that enable you to collaborate with others in the learning community using professional communications sites such as LinkedIn or microblogging tools such as Twitter.
- Checklists with useful post-class reference information.
- Any course files you will download.
- The course assessment.
- Notices from the LogicalCHOICE administrator.
- Virtual labs, for remote access to the technical environment for your course.
- Your personal whiteboard for sketches and notes.
- Newsletters and other communications from your learning provider.
- Mentoring services.
- A link to the website of your training provider.
- The LogicalCHOICE store.

Visit your LogicalCHOICE Home screen often to connect, communicate, and extend your learning experience!

How to Use This Book

As You Learn

This book is divided into lessons and topics, covering a subject or a set of related subjects. In most cases, lessons are arranged in order of increasing proficiency.

The results-oriented topics include relevant and supporting information you need to master the content. Each topic has various types of activities designed to enable you to practice the guidelines and procedures as well as to solidify your understanding of the informational material presented in the course. Procedures and guidelines are presented in a concise fashion along with activities and discussions. Information is provided for reference and reflection in such a way as to facilitate understanding and practice.

Data files for various activities as well as other supporting files for the course are available by download from the LogicalCHOICE Course screen. In addition to sample data for the course exercises, the course files may contain media components to enhance your learning and additional reference materials for use both during and after the course.

At the back of the book, you will find a glossary of the definitions of the terms and concepts used throughout the course. You will also find an index to assist in locating information within the instructional components of the book.

As You Review

Any method of instruction is only as effective as the time and effort you, the student, are willing to invest in it. In addition, some of the information that you learn in class may not be important to you immediately, but it may become important later. For this reason, we encourage you to spend some time reviewing the content of the course after your time in the classroom.

As a Reference

The organization and layout of this book make it an easy-to-use resource for future reference. Taking advantage of the glossary, index, and table of contents, you can use this book as a first source of definitions, background information, and summaries.

Course Icons

Watch throughout the material for these visual cues:

Icon	Description
	A **Note** provides additional information, guidance, or hints about a topic or task.
	A **Caution** helps make you aware of places where you need to be particularly careful with your actions, settings, or decisions so that you can be sure to get the desired results of an activity or task.
	LearnTO notes show you where an associated LearnTO is particularly relevant to the content. Access LearnTOs from your LogicalCHOICE Course screen.
	Checklists provide job aids you can use after class as a reference to performing skills back on the job. Access checklists from your LogicalCHOICE Course screen.
	Social notes remind you to check your LogicalCHOICE Course screen for opportunities to interact with the LogicalCHOICE community using social media.
	Notes Pages are intentionally left blank for you to write on.

1 Working with Multiple Worksheets and Workbooks Simultaneously

Lesson Time: 45 minutes

Lesson Objectives

In this lesson, you will work with multiple worksheets and workbooks. You will:

- Use 3-D references.
- Use links and external references.
- Consolidate data.

Lesson Introduction

Although you may be responsible for analyzing your data and then reporting your findings to others, you may not be the person actually responsible for collecting and storing the raw data itself. You've also likely discovered that making mistakes can create a lot of problems throughout a worksheet or a workbook. Especially in large organizations, you may find you need to collect raw data from a number of different sources, such as budgets or sales reports from a variety of departments, in order to paint an accurate picture of the overall organization's performance. In short, you need to be able to access data from a variety of sources to perform data analysis for the organization as a whole. You need to be able to trust the data regardless of how many people have had their hands on it.

Excel 2010 includes a number of capabilities that provide you with flexibility in the way in which you treat your raw and your analyzed data that go well beyond simply referencing data in other cells. Taking advantage of this functionality allows you to maintain data integrity while still being able to perform the calculations and analysis you need the data for in the first place.

TOPIC A

Use 3-D References

It's not uncommon for various groups of people or various departments throughout an organization to keep similar data in workbooks based on templates. For example, everyone may use the same template to track budgets or time-off requests, regardless of department. Or, you may simply track quarterly sales by using the same basic worksheet layout each quarter. Although it's useful to have your data organized by specific general categories like this, you will also likely need to see the big picture of what all of the various worksheets contain. And, you will still likely need to analyze this data to some degree, so simply adding up the totals for each worksheet in one location may not be much help.

Fortunately, Excel 2010 provides you with the ability to summarize the data from a series of worksheets by applying calculations across all of them. The ability to quickly summarize any number of worksheets in a single location enables you to collect data from a variety of sources, view and analyze that data in the same layout as the original data, and avoid the errors and extra effort associated with manually summarizing the data and re-entering it in another worksheet.

3-D References

Imagine a stack of printed worksheets, one atop the next, with all of the data on each sheet lining up with the others. The column and row labels are the same, the datasets are the same size and are in the same location, and the data entered into each cell corresponds to that of the other cells stacked above or below it on the various worksheets. Now, imagine you place a worksheet on the top of the stack with the same column and row labels, but no data in the other cells. Suppose you wanted to populate each of the empty cells in the top worksheet with a summary of the cell data from the other aligning cells? Well, in Excel 2010, you can do just that by using a powerful feature called *3-D references*. A 3-D reference is simply a reference to the same cell across a range of worksheets. For example, if you have a workbook containing three worksheets and you want to reference cell **B2** on all three of them simultaneously, you would use a 3-D reference to tell Excel to execute some function on all three instances of cell **B2**.

> **Note:** 3-D references work only on worksheets contained in the same workbook. They are typically useful only if the datasets on all worksheets are entered in the exact same location and in the exact same layout.

3-D references combine the use of a worksheet reference and the range reference operator, which you'll recall is the colon (:). So, in the example mentioned previously, if your workbook contains worksheets **Sheet1**, **Sheet2**, and **Sheet3**, and you want to reference cell **B2** in all three worksheets, your 3-D reference would be: *Sheet1:Sheet3!B2*

Sheet1:Sheet3!B3

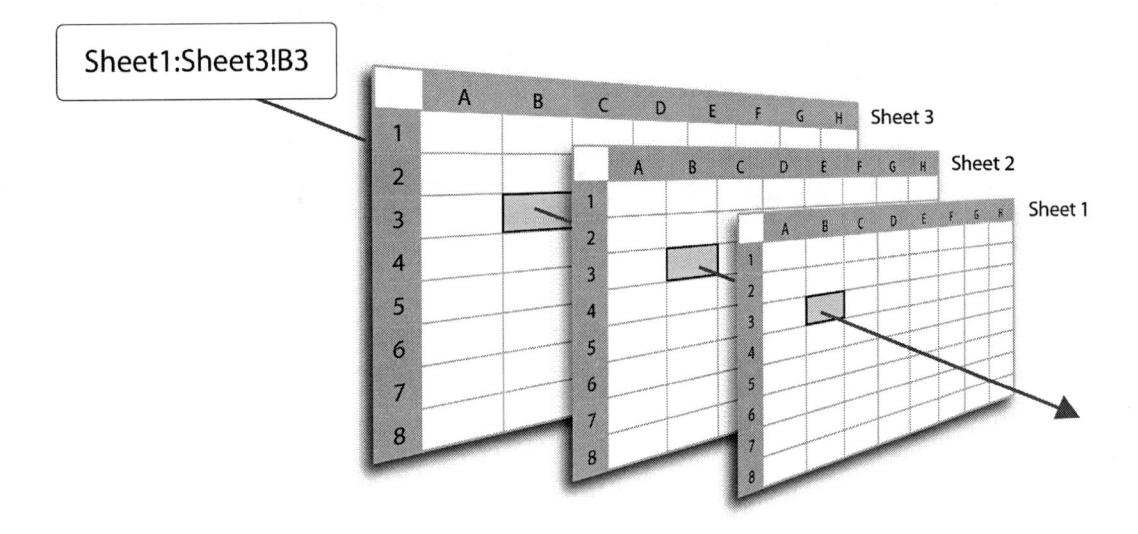

Figure 1-1: 3-D references refer to the corresponding cell values in a range of "stacked" worksheets.

3-D References in Summary Functions

You can combine 3-D references with any of the summary functions you would normally use to reference a flat, or 2-D, cell or range. So, if your goal is to add all of the values in cell **B2** on all three worksheets from **Sheet1** to **Sheet3**, you would enter the following function:

=SUM(Sheet1:Sheet3!B2)

Or, suppose you wanted to determine the average value of the values in those cells. Your function would look like this:

=AVERAGE(Sheet1:Sheet3!B2)

> **Note:** When you type a 3-D reference, you may have to enclose the worksheet reference in single quotation marks (' '), which should not include the exclamation point (!). Reasons this may be necessary include worksheet names containing spaces or a blend of numbers and letters.
> Example: *=SUM('Sales Data1:Sales Data2'!D4)*

In both of these examples, the range reference **Sheet1:Sheet3!** is telling Excel to look at the values in the corresponding cell in each of the worksheets from **Sheet1** to **Sheet3**. But, there is something really important for you to keep in mind here. The 3-D range reference has nothing to do with the sheet names. In this example, Excel will look for values in **Sheet1**, **Sheet3**, and every other worksheet physically between them in the workbook. So, if you have a worksheet in between them named **Annual Budget**, Excel will look for the corresponding value in that worksheet. But if **Sheet2** is somewhere to the right or to the left of the range referenced, Excel will ignore those values. Take a look at this image.

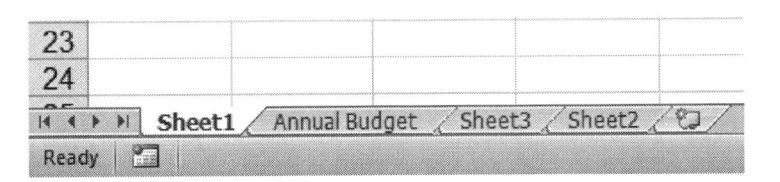

Here, the 3-D reference **Sheet1:Sheet3** would include the corresponding cell value from the **Annual Budget** worksheet, but not from the **Sheet2** worksheet.

> **Note:** You can manually select a worksheet range when entering a 3-D reference in much the same way you manually select a cell or a range reference. To do this, you select the first worksheet in the desired range, press and hold down the **Shift** key, and then select the last worksheet in the desired range.

You can also combine range references for cells and range references for worksheets to summarize a range of data on multiple worksheets simultaneously. However, remember that this will not return the summarized values for each set of corresponding cells individually. Take a look at this function as an example:

=AVERAGE(Sheet1:Sheet3!A1:D4)

Although this function will return the average of all values in the range **A1:D4** for all three worksheets, it will return that value in a single cell. You can, however, use the AutoFill feature to drag a single formula containing a 3-D reference and a relative cell reference across a range to summarize each set of corresponding cells individually. For example, if you want find the total for each set of corresponding cells in the range **A1:E10** across the same three worksheets, you would enter the following function in a single cell:

=SUM(Sheet1:Sheet3!A1)

Notice the use of a relative cell reference. Now you would select the cell you entered the function into and use the **fill handle** to drag the formula across a range that is the same size as the original ranges. Although you many want to do this in the range **A1:E10** on a new worksheet to make it easier to view and understand your data, you can do this in any range that is the correct size.

> **Note:** For more information about 3-D references and formulas, watch the LearnTO **Use Wildcard Characters in References and Formulas** presentation from the **LearnTO** tile on the LogicalCHOICE Course screen.

> **Access the Checklist tile on your LogicalCHOICE course screen for reference information and job aids on How to Use 3-D References.**

ACTIVITY 1-1
Using 3-D References

Data Files
C:\091020Data\Working with Multiple Worksheets and Workbooks Simultaneously\asian_sales.xlsx

C:\091020Data\Working with Multiple Worksheets and Workbooks Simultaneously\european_sales.xlsx

Before You Begin
Excel 2010 is installed and pinned to the taskbar.

Scenario
You are the Authors and Publications manager for Fuller and Ackerman (F&A) Publishing, a mid-sized book publishing company headquartered in Greene City, Richland (RL). F&A owns and operates offices and presses in several locations throughout the Unites States and around the world. Your company publishes books from a variety of genres, in a number of different languages, and has authors from around the world under contract.

As the Authors and Publications manager, your duties include tracking and managing the work that all authors produce for F&A. Additionally, you are responsible for ensuring that royalties, advances, and bonuses are calculated accurately and paid in a timely manner. You use Microsoft Excel 2010 to keep track of authors, publications, and payments, and have a number of worksheets that you use for this purpose.

You're working on sales projections for several of F&A's overseas markets. You have quarterly data for the various markets entered into worksheets, but you need to project total sales for each market to present at an upcoming sales meeting. As the worksheets in the sales workbooks are ordered appropriately, you realize you'll be able to use 3-D references to generate the sales totals for each region. Then you can use a simple formula to generate the sales projections for each market.

> **Note:** Activities may vary slightly if the software vendor has issued digital updates. Your instructor will notify you of any changes.

1. Open Excel 2010, open the **asian_sales.xlsx** workbook file, and then ensure that the **2012-13_Totals** worksheet is selected.

2. Use a 3-D reference to summarize the quarterly figures for China.
    a) Select cell **C4**.
    b) Type *=sum('Q1:Q4'!c4)* and then press **Ctrl+Enter**.

c) Verify that Excel returns the expected result.

	B	C	D
	Country	2012-13 Sales	
	China	$1,431,693.00	
	Japan		

fx =SUM('Q1:Q4'!C4)

3. Use the fill handle to drag the SUM function down the range **C4:C13**.

4. Use the SUM function to total the values from the range **C4:C13** in cell **C17**.

5. Calculate the 2013–2014 sales projections based on an expected 6-percent sales increase.
    a) Select cell **E4**.
    b) Type *=c4*1.06* and press **Ctrl+Enter**.
    c) Drag the formula down the range **E4:E13**.
    d) Sum the projected sales figures in cell **E17**.

Country	2012-13 Sales	Projected 2013-2014
China	$1,431,693.00	$1,517,594.58
Japan	$1,387,726.00	$1,470,989.56
India	$1,842,483.00	$1,953,031.98
Thailand	$380,884.00	$403,737.04
Pakistan	$108,535.00	$115,047.10
Vietnam	$128,534.00	$136,246.04
Cambodia	$80,212.00	$85,024.72
Philippines	$542,867.00	$575,439.02
Singapore	$79,971.00	$84,769.26
Indonesia	$746,755.00	$791,560.30
Asian Sales	$6,729,660.00	$7,133,439.60

6. Save the workbook to the **C:\091020Data\Working with Multiple Worksheets and Workbooks Simultaneously** folder as *my_asian_sales.xlsx* and leave the workbook open.

7. Open the **european_sales.xlxs** workbook, and then ensure that the **2012-13_Totals** worksheet is selected.

8. Use a 3-D reference to summarize the quarterly figures for Germany.
    a) Select cell **C4**.
    b) Type *=sum(*
    c) Select the **Q1** worksheet tab, press and hold **Shift**, and then select the **Q4** worksheet tab.
    d) Select cell **C4** and press **Ctrl+Enter**.

9. Use the fill handle to drag the SUM function down the range **C4:C14**, and then total the sales figures in cell **C17**.

10. Calculate the same 6-percent sales increase for the countries in the European market, and then total those figures in cell **E17**.

Country	2012-13 Sales	Projected 2013-2014
Germany	$1,929,486.00	$2,045,255.16
Russia	$690,905.00	$732,359.30
Italy	$1,074,308.00	$1,138,766.48
France	$907,116.00	$961,542.96
England	$761,509.00	$807,199.54
Spain	$1,334,812.00	$1,414,900.72
Hungary	$739,861.00	$784,252.66
Portugal	$851,755.00	$902,860.30
Greece	$712,836.00	$755,606.16
Ukraine	$1,285,789.00	$1,362,936.34
Beligum	$653,836.00	$693,066.16
European Sales	$10,942,213.00	$11,598,745.78

11. Save the workbook to the **C:\091020Data\Working with Multiple Worksheets and Workbooks Simultaneously** folder as *my_european_sales.xlsx* and leave the workbook open.

TOPIC B

Use Links and External References

As you've likely already discovered, introducing errors in large, complex worksheets can quickly leave you with a mess on your hands. Although you can rebuild your formulas, functions, and tables if they get too far off the right path, you may not be able to do so with your raw data. If you introduce errors into your raw data, or worse, delete it altogether, you could have a serious problem on your hands. As such, it's often a good idea to keep your raw data completely separate from the worksheets upon which you perform your calculations and analysis. But, you still want to be able to view your data. Excel 2010 enables you to link your data to other cells so that you can view the information in the raw dataset without actually having to interact with it. It doesn't take a huge leap to see that this level of data integrity can mean the difference between presenting actionable organizational intelligence and creating massive internal problems.

Linked Cells

Excel 2010 provides you with the ability to connect one cell to the data entered into another cell. When you create this connection, you create a *linked cell*. Unlike a cell reference, which merely calls the value in another cell for use in a formula or function, a linked cell behaves as if it actually contains the data in the original cell. If you update the value in the original cell, Excel updates the value in the linked cell automatically. And, as the linked cell behaves as if it actually contains the data in the original cell, you can perform any calculation on the linked cells as you would on the original cell. This allows you to take full advantage of all of Excel's calculation and data analysis functionality without having to worry about introducing errors into your raw data. And, as the linked cells update automatically, so, too, will your calculations.

> **Note:** Links do not include the formatting applied to the original cell.

You can link worksheet cells to cells on other worksheets in the same workbook, or you can link them to cells on worksheets in other workbooks. Links to other worksheets in the same workbook are known as *internal links*. Links to other workbooks are called *external links*.

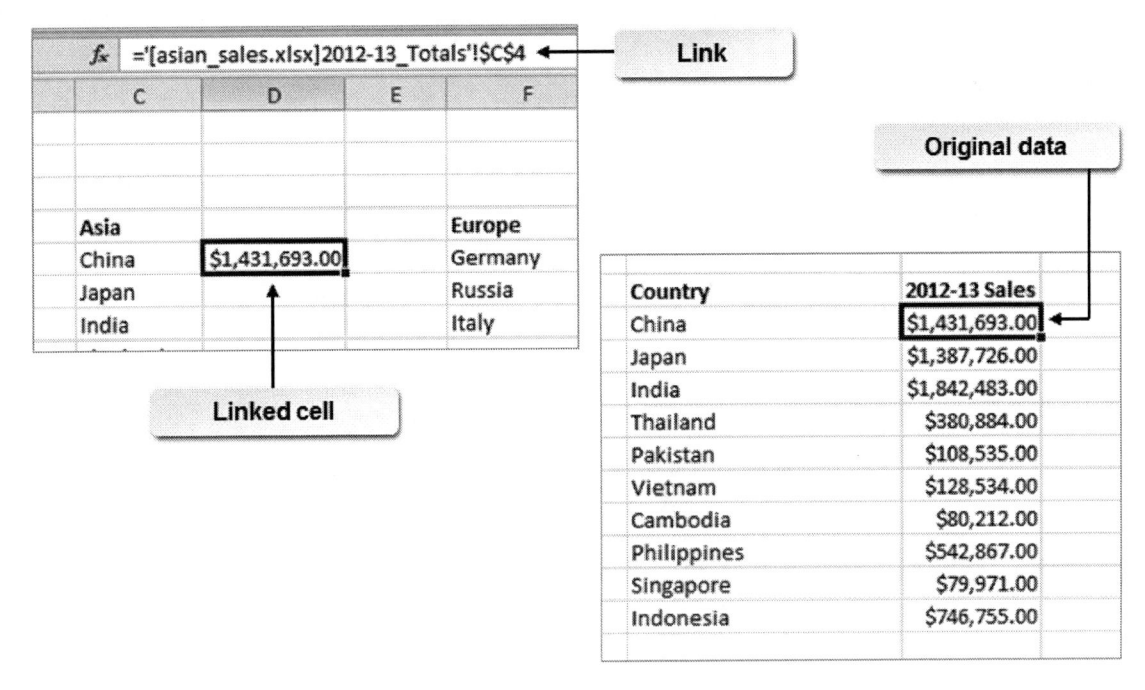

Figure 1-2: Although a linked cell behaves as if it contains the data in the original cell, it actually contains a link to that data.

Linked Cell Syntax

You create links to other cells in much the same way you enter a formula into a cell. In fact, you can think of links as a type of specialized formula. As such, with an understanding of the syntax used to create links, you can link a cell to any other cell in its workbook or in another workbook. And, you can take advantage of Excel's AutoFill feature to quickly link entire ranges of data to other ranges. If you use the AutoFill feature to create links, remember that relative and absolute references behave the same way in links as they do in formulas and functions. Typically, you will use only relative references when linking entire ranges of data.

To create an internal link, simply type an equal sign (=) into a cell as if you were typing a formula, enter the desired cell reference, and press **Enter**. If you are linking to a cell on another worksheet, include the worksheet name followed by an exclamation point (!).

> **Note:** Once you have typed the equal sign, you can also simply select the cell you wish to link to manually. This is the same as entering a reference in a formula or a function.

To create an external link, you will also have to include a pointer to the workbook that contains the cell you are linking to. To do this, simply enter the name of the workbook enclosed in square brackets ([ ]) before the worksheet and cell references. If the workbook containing the data you're linking to is open, you can simply enter the equal sign, switch to the other workbook, select the desired cell, and press **Enter**. When you use the manual-selection method to add an external link, Excel creates the link by using absolute references.

If you are creating links to cells on other worksheets or in other workbooks, you must also include a set of single quotation marks (' ') around the worksheet or the workbook and worksheet reference. The exclamation point that follows the worksheet reference must be outside the single quotes.

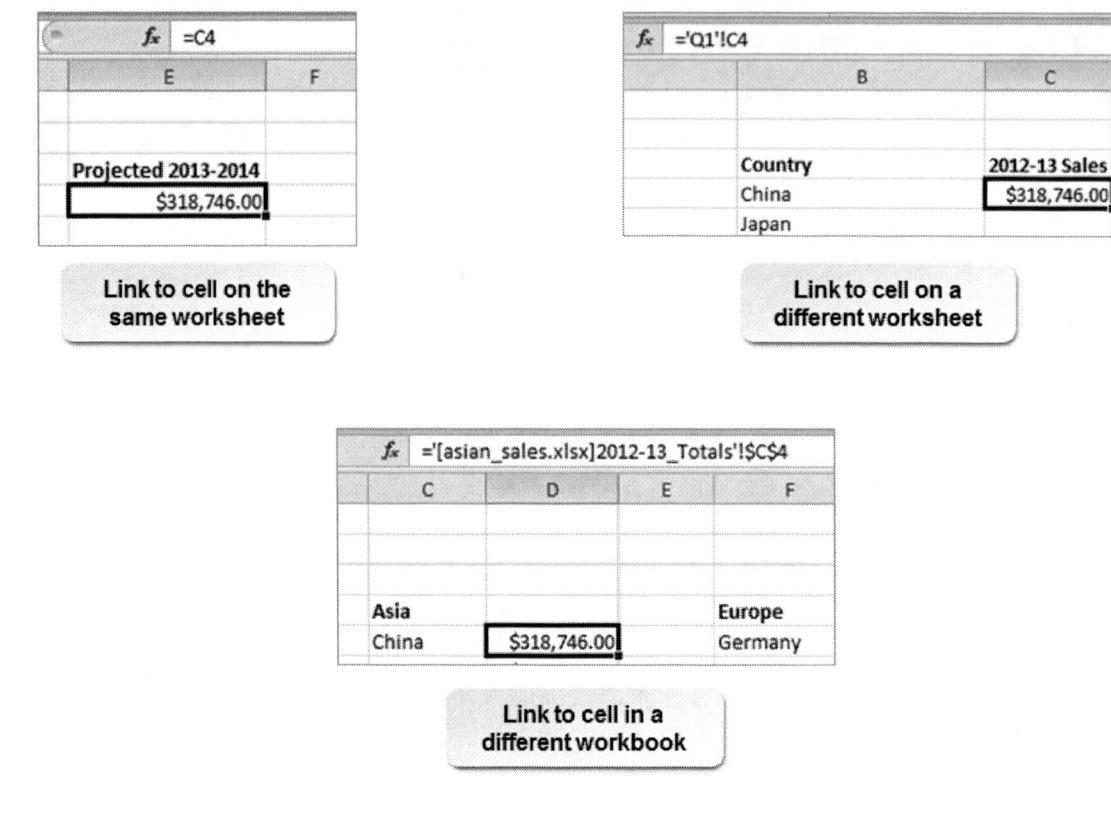

Figure 1-3: You can link a cell to any other cell in the same workbook or in other workbooks.

The Edit Links Dialog Box

You can use the **Edit Links** dialog box to manage the external links in your Excel workbooks. The **Edit Links** dialog box displays a list of all workbooks that the current workbook has links to. You can access the **Edit Links** dialog box by selecting **Data→Connections→Edit Links**; the **Edit Links** command appears grayed-out if there are no external links in the current workbook.

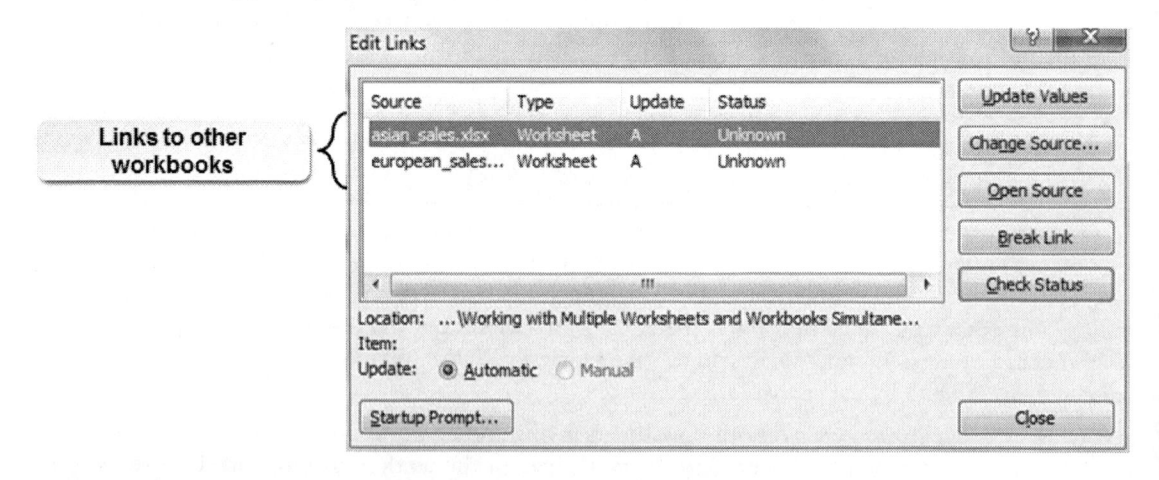

Figure 1-4: Use the Edit Links dialog box to manage external links.

The following table describes the functions of some of the elements of the **Edit Links** dialog box.

Edit Links Dialog Box Element	Selecting This Button
Update Values button	Updates the values in linked cells if changes have been made to the source data and automatic updates are disabled.
Change Source button	Opens the **Change Source** dialog box, enabling you to change which workbook the current workbook is linked to. You can change links to each external workbook separately.
Open Source button	Opens the workbook you have selected in the **Edit Links** dialog box.
Break Link button	Removes all links to the workbook you have selected in the **Edit Links** dialog box. Once you break the link to a workbook, Excel converts the data in all cells linked to that workbook to constant values.
Check Status button	Displays the status of all external links. This could, for example, let you know if you need to update values or if the source workbook is currently open.
Startup Prompt button	Opens the **Startup Prompt** dialog box, which enables you to determine whether or not Excel displays a warning message when you open workbooks containing links, and how you want Excel to treat those links.

External References in Formulas and Functions

Much as you can link cells to other worksheets and external workbooks, you can also use references to cells or ranges on other worksheets or in other workbooks to link Excel formulas and functions to those cells. This allows you to display calculation or function results in a different location than where the raw data is stored. In this way, you don't have to create a linked copy of the dataset range if you don't want to. References to cells or ranges in other workbooks are called *external references*.

The syntax for including references to cells or ranges on other worksheets or in other workbooks is the same as it is for creating links. Whenever you need to include a reference in a formula or as an argument in a function, simply include the worksheet reference and, if necessary, the workbook reference along with the cell reference. Remember that relative and absolute cell references behave the same in references to other worksheets and in external references as they do in standard references. Also, remember to include the set of single quotation marks around the workbook and worksheet references in the formula or function and to ensure the exclamation point for the worksheet reference is outside the single quotes. You can also manually select a cell to include its reference in a formula or function. When inserting external references manually, the source workbook must also be open.

> **Note:** Whenever the source workbook for an external link or an external reference is closed, Excel automatically precedes it with the file path to the saved source Excel file. Excel does not display this file path when the source workbook is open. You don't ever have to manually type the file path into links, functions, or formulas.

`=SUM('Q1'!C4:C14)`

Formula with reference to cells on another worksheet

Workbook reference | **Worksheet reference**

`=SUM('[asian_sales.xlsx]2012-13_Totals'!$C$4:$C$13)`

Formula with external reference

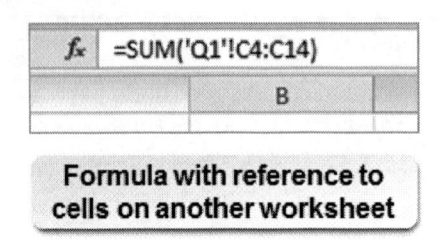

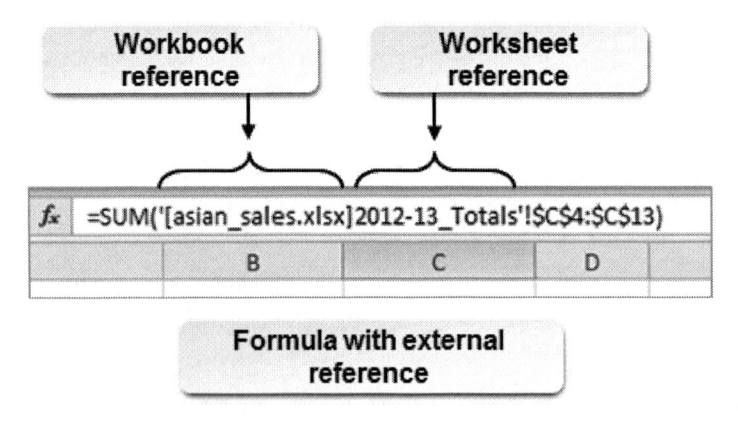

Figure 1-5: Use references to cells on other worksheets and external references to link data to your worksheet calculations.

> Access the Checklist tile on your **LogicalCHOICE** course screen for reference information and job aids on How to Use Linked Cells.

ACTIVITY 1-2
Creating External Links

Data Files

C:\091020Data\Working with Multiple Worksheets and Workbooks Simultaneously\global_sales.xlsx

C:\091020Data\Working with Multiple Worksheets and Workbooks Simultaneously\south_american_sales.xlsx

Before You Begin

The my_asian_sales.xlsx and my_european_sales.xlsx workbook files are open.

Scenario

Some of Fuller and Ackerman's regional sales managers have been asking you for the 2012–2013 sales totals so they can begin planning targets for their sales reps. As the final numbers have not yet been reviewed and approved, you don't want to share the projections information with the regional managers quite yet. Also, as the figures may need revision, you would like the numbers you share with the regional sales mangers to update if there are any changes. You decide to create a workbook with links to the regional sales workbooks that includes only the 2012–2013 sales figures for each region. You have already set up the general layout of the global sales workbook, so you're ready to create the links.

1. Open both the **global_sales.xlsx** and the **south_american_sales.xlsx** workbook files.

2. Ensure that **global_sales.xlsx** is the currently selected workbook.

3. Create external links to the Asian sales data.
   a) Select cell **D5** and type an equal sign (**=**).
   b) Switch to the **my_asian_sales.xlsx** workbook and ensure that the **2012-13_Totals** worksheet is selected.
   c) Select cell **C4** and press **Ctrl+Enter**.
   d) Ensure that Excel linked the cell as expected.

	C	D	E	F
		='[my_asian_sales.xlsx]2012-13_Totals'!$C$4		
	Asia			Europe
	China	1431693		Germany
	Japan			Russia

e) In the **Formula Bar**, place the insertion point either directly before or directly after $C$4 in the external link you just created.

```
fx    ='[my_asian_sales.xlsx]2012-13_Totals'!$C$4
```

f) Press the **F4** key as necessary until the absolute reference **$C$4** becomes the relative reference **C4** and press **Ctrl+Enter**.
g) Use the fill handle to drag the external reference down the range **D5:D14**.
h) Total the values in the range **D5:D14** in cell **D18** and apply the **Currency** number format to the range **D5:D18**.

4. Link the sales data for the European and the South American markets to the appropriate cells in the **global_sales.xlsx** workbook, and then calculate the market totals and apply the **Currency** number format.

5. Close both the **south_american_sales.xlsx** and the **my_european_sales.xlsx** workbooks.

6. In the **global_sales.xlsx** workbook, note the values in cells **D14** and **D18**.

Indonesia	$746,755.00
Asian Sales	$6,729,660.00

7. Update a value in the **my_asian_sales.xlsx** workbook.

   a) Switch to the **my_asian_sales.xlsx** workbook and select the **Q1** worksheet tab.
   b) Select cell **C13** and enter the value *165820*
   c) Switch to the **global_sales.xlsx** workbook; verify that **$763,811.00** appears in cell **D14** and that the Asian sales total is updated to **$6,746,716.00** in cell **D18**.

8. Save the workbook to the C:\091020Data\Working with Multiple Worksheets and Workbooks Simultaneously folder as *my_global_sales.xlsx* and close the workbook.

9. Save and close the **my_asian_sales.xlsx** workbook, but leave Excel open.

TOPIC C

Consolidate Data

The ability to use 3-D references to summarize datasets with identical layouts is a powerful, handy feature. What if you need to summarize data from datasets that aren't laid out in precisely the same way? Or, what if you want to summarize data from a number of worksheets in different workbooks? Life isn't always neat and tidy, and, unfortunately, the same can be said of workbook data.

The good news is that Excel 2010 enables you to summarize data from multiple worksheets regardless of whether or not the data is in the same location on each worksheet, or even if the worksheets are in the same workbook. This means you can get a birds-eye view of your overall data picture without having to painstakingly copy and paste your raw data into the same workbook and modify the layout so that it all matches.

Data Consolidation

Data consolidation is the act of summarizing data when it isn't neatly packaged in a table or PivotTable, and when it isn't necessarily entered into multiple worksheets in precisely the same location. Excel 2010 enables you to consolidate data based on either relative cell positions in the various source datasets or by categories, which are based on row and column labels. You can summarize consolidated data by using any of the summary functions available in Excel.

Although source datasets don't have to be in precisely the same location on all worksheets, or even contain the same number of columns or rows, it is a best practice to ensure your data is structured in approximately the same manner. For example, if you consolidate data by category by using column labels as the category indicators, the columns don't have to appear in the same location within the various sources and the columns don't even have to appear in the same order, but the various datasets should include the same column labels. And all data ranges that you enter into a consolidated dataset by category must be contiguous, meaning there can be no empty rows or columns. If your original data is non-contiguous, you can consolidate it by using relative cell positions as long as you enter each non-contiguous range separately.

You have the option of linking your consolidated dataset to the original data sources. In this way, your consolidated dataset will update whenever the original source data is updated. Keep in mind if you link your consolidated data to the sources, Excel automatically creates the consolidated dataset as an outline with the detail entries collapsed.

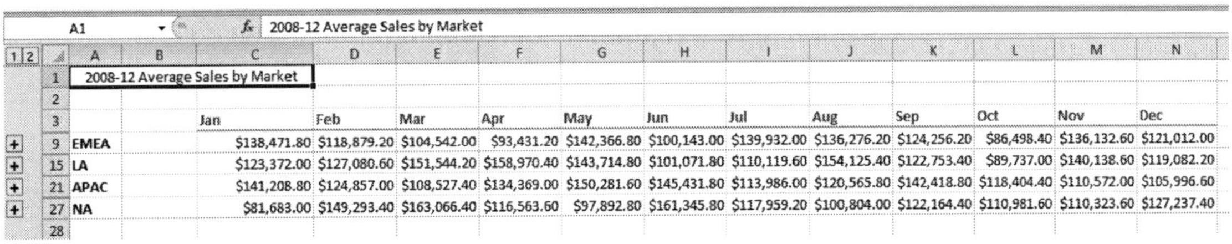
A1 | fx 2008-12 Average Sales by Market

	A	B	C	D	E	F	G	H	I	J	K	L	M	N
1	2008-12 Average Sales by Market													
2														
3			Jan	Feb	Mar	Apr	May	Jun	Jul	Aug	Sep	Oct	Nov	Dec
9	EMEA		$138,471.80	$118,879.20	$104,542.00	$93,431.20	$142,366.80	$100,143.00	$139,932.00	$136,276.20	$124,256.20	$86,498.40	$136,132.60	$121,012.00
15	LA		$123,372.00	$127,080.60	$151,544.20	$158,970.40	$143,714.80	$101,071.80	$110,119.60	$154,125.40	$122,753.40	$89,737.00	$140,138.60	$119,082.20
21	APAC		$141,208.80	$124,857.00	$108,527.40	$134,369.00	$150,281.60	$145,431.80	$113,986.00	$120,565.80	$142,418.80	$118,404.40	$110,572.00	$105,996.60
27	NA		$81,683.00	$149,293.40	$163,066.40	$116,563.60	$97,892.80	$161,345.80	$117,959.20	$100,804.00	$122,164.40	$110,981.60	$110,323.60	$127,237.40
28														

Figure 1-6: Excel creates consolidated datasets that are linked to the source data as outlines.

The Consolidate Dialog Box

You use the **Consolidate** dialog box to determine which source datasets Excel will summarize in the consolidated dataset, which summary function it will use to summarize the data, and how it will organize the consolidated dataset. You can access the **Consolidate** dialog box by selecting **Data→Data Tools→Consolidate**.

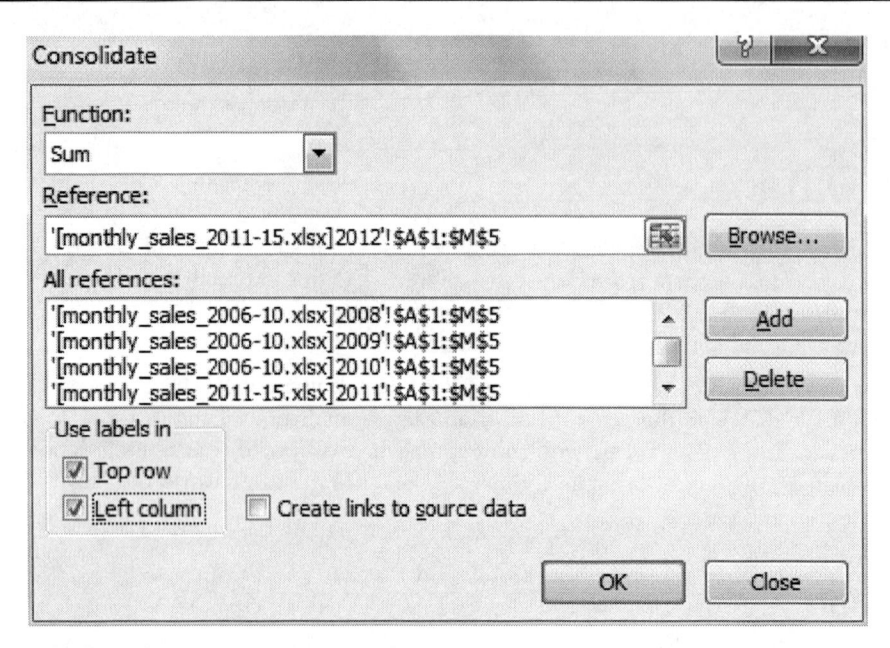

Figure 1-7: The Consolidate dialog box.

The following table describes the various elements of the **Consolidate** dialog box.

Consolidate Dialog Box Element	Description
Function drop-down menu	Use this to select the summary function Excel will use to consolidate the source data.
Reference field	Use this to enter each range of data you wish to add to the consolidated dataset.
All references list	Displays a list of all of the ranges included in the consolidated dataset.
Browse button	Opens the **Browse** dialog box, enabling you to search for workbook files that aren't currently open to include in the consolidated dataset.
Add button	Adds the range currently displayed in the **Reference** field to the **All references** list.
Delete button	Removes the currently selected range reference from the **All references** list.
Top row check box	Check this if you include column labels in your source data ranges and you want Excel to organize your consolidated dataset by category according to the column labels.
Left column check box	Check this if you include row labels in your source data ranges and you want Excel to organize your consolidated dataset by category according to the row labels.
Create links to source data check box	Check this if you want Excel to create links to the source data in the consolidated dataset. Linking the consolidated dataset automatically structures it as an outline.

Note: If you want Excel to use both column and row labels to organize the consolidated dataset by category, check both the **Top row** and the **Left column** check boxes. You must include both column and row labels in the source data ranges to do this. If you want Excel to organize the consolidated dataset according to relative cell positions within the source datasets, leave both of these check boxes unchecked.

Access the Checklist tile on your LogicalCHOICE course screen for reference information and job aids on How to Consolidate Data.

ACTIVITY 1-3
Consolidating Data

Data Files
C:\091020Data\Working with Multiple Worksheets and Workbooks Simultaneously\monthly_sales_2006-10.xlsx

C:\091020Data\Working with Multiple Worksheets and Workbooks Simultaneously\monthly_sales_2011-15.xlsx

Before You Begin
Excel 2010 is open.

Scenario
For the upcoming sales meeting, your supervisor has requested that you present average and total sales figures for each of Fuller and Ackerman's markets on a per-month basis for a period of five years. The data is stored in workbooks that cover five-year periods, with each calendar year represented on a separate worksheet. Because you're looking for the period of 2008 through 2012, you'll need to consolidate data from two different workbooks. While reviewing the monthly sales workbooks, you notice someone has apparently sorted the data on several of the worksheets by row and by column, which means you can't use 3-D references to summarize the data. You decide consolidating by both row and column labels will be your best option. As these sales figures are all approved and final, you decide not to link the consolidated data to the source data ranges; it is unlikely these will change.

---

1. Open the **monthly_sales_2006-10.xlsx** and the **monthly_sales_2011-15.xlsx** workbook files.

2. Create a new blank workbook by selecting **File→New→Blank workbook→Create**.

3. In the new blank workbook, ensure that cell **A1** is selected, type *2008-12 Average Sales by Market* and press **Enter**.

4. Select cell **A3** and then select **Data→Data Tools→Consolidate**.

5. In the **Consolidate** dialog box, from the **Function** drop-down menu, select **Average**.

6. Add the source data ranges for the years 2008 through 2012.

    a) In the **Reference** field, select the **Collapse Dialog** button.
    b) Switch to the **monthly_sales_2006-10.xlsx** workbook and select the **2008** worksheet tab.
    c) Select the range **A1:M5** and press **Enter**.
    d) In the **Consolidate** dialog box, select **Add**.
    e) In the **Reference** field, select the **Collapse Dialog** button, select the **2009** worksheet tab, select the range **A1:M5**, press **Enter**, and select **Add**.
    f) Repeat the process to add the source data from the **2010** worksheet tab.
    g) Select the **Collapse Dialog** button, switch to the **monthly_sales_2011-15.xlsx** workbook, and ensure that the **2011** worksheet tab is selected.
    h) Select the range **A1:M5**, press **Enter**, and select **Add**.
    i) Repeat the process to add the source data from the **2012** worksheet tab.

7. Consolidate the data.
   a) In the **Consolidate** dialog box, check the **Top row** and the **Left column** check boxes.
   b) Select **OK**.
   c) Select **Home→Cells→Format→AutoFit Column Width** to adjust all columns to accommodate the data.

8. Apply bold formatting to the market label text in cells **A4:A7** and apply the **Heading 3** cell style to the range **B3:M3**.

9. Review the average monthly sales data in the new workbook.

Jan	Feb	Mar	Apr	May	Jun	Jul	Aug	Sep	Oct	Nov	Dec
$138,471.80	$118,879.20	$104,542.00	$93,431.20	$142,366.80	$100,143.00	$139,932.00	$136,276.20	$124,256.20	$86,498.40	$136,132.60	$121,012.00
$123,372.00	$127,080.60	$151,544.20	$158,970.40	$143,714.80	$101,071.80	$110,119.60	$154,125.40	$122,753.40	$89,737.00	$140,138.60	$119,082.20
$141,208.80	$124,857.00	$108,527.40	$134,369.00	$150,281.60	$145,431.80	$113,986.00	$120,565.80	$142,418.80	$118,404.40	$110,572.00	$105,996.60
$81,683.00	$149,293.40	$163,066.40	$116,563.60	$97,892.80	$161,345.80	$117,959.20	$100,804.00	$122,164.40	$110,981.60	$110,323.60	$127,237.40

10. Calculate the total sales figures for the same five-year period broken out by month.
    a) Select cell **A9**, type *2008-12 Total Sales by Market* and press **Enter**.
    b) Select cell **A11**.
    c) Select **Data→Data Tools→Consolidate**.
    d) In the **Consolidate** dialog box, from the **Function** drop-down menu, select **Sum**.
    e) Select **OK**.
    f) Bold the row labels and apply the **Heading 3** cell style to the column labels.
    g) Review the total monthly sales data.

Jan	Feb	Mar	Apr	May	Jun	Jul	Aug	Sep	Oct	Nov	Dec
$692,359.00	$594,396.00	$522,710.00	$467,156.00	$711,834.00	$500,715.00	$699,660.00	$681,381.00	$621,281.00	$432,492.00	$680,663.00	$605,060.00
$616,860.00	$635,403.00	$757,721.00	$794,852.00	$718,574.00	$505,359.00	$550,598.00	$770,627.00	$613,767.00	$448,685.00	$700,693.00	$595,411.00
$706,044.00	$624,285.00	$542,637.00	$671,845.00	$751,408.00	$727,159.00	$569,930.00	$602,829.00	$712,094.00	$592,022.00	$552,860.00	$529,983.00
$408,415.00	$746,467.00	$815,332.00	$582,818.00	$489,464.00	$806,729.00	$589,796.00	$504,020.00	$610,822.00	$554,908.00	$551,618.00	$636,187.00

11. Save the workbook to the **C:\091020\Working with Multiple Worksheets and Workbooks Simultaneously** folder as *my_monthly_sales_consolidated.xlsx*

12. Close all open workbooks.

Summary

In this lesson, you worked with a number of worksheets and workbooks simultaneously in order to analyze data from a variety of sources in a single location. By taking advantage of Excel's ability to reference data from a variety of sources, you'll capture the full potential of the wide range of data available in your organization. You'll do so without the extra time and effort it would take to manually copy or move the source data, a task that could be nearly impossible in large organizations. In addition to saving time and effort, you'll also ensure that errors are kept to a minimum, maintaining the integrity of both your raw data and your analysis.

Which method of simultaneously working with multiple worksheets and workbooks do you think will help you the most with your daily tasks? Why?

Can you think of a time when having your workbook cells linked to the source data would have saved you time, effort, and hassle?

> **Note:** Check your LogicalCHOICE Course screen for opportunities to interact with your classmates, peers, and the larger LogicalCHOICE online community about the topics covered in this course or other topics you are interested in. From the Course screen you can also access available resources for a more continuous learning experience.

2 | Sharing and Protecting Workbooks

Lesson Time: 1 hour, 15 minutes

Lesson Objectives

In this lesson, you will share and protect workbooks. You will:

- Collaborate on a workbook.
- Protect a worksheets and workbooks.

Lesson Introduction

Nothing happens in a vacuum. It is a near certainty that you collaborate with a number of people in different roles fairly regularly. And it's likely that some of those people contribute to or review your work in a variety of capacities. As such, it's essential that you be able to collaborate with colleagues, provide and receive feedback on your workbooks, and ensure that everyone's input is reflected in the final version of your documents. Unfortunately, the more you share and collaborate with others, especially when they have differing levels of authority or clearance, the more you need to ensure your critical organizational data is protected. How do you balance the need to share with the need to keep a wrap on your sensitive information?

Fortunately, Excel includes a number of features and capabilities that allow you to navigate the fine balance between collaboration and security. Understanding how these features and capabilities work and how they work together will help you balance these concerns, keep your important work on track, and provide you with the piece of mind that comes with knowing your information in secure.

TOPIC A

Collaborate on a Workbook

It is likely that multiple people will have some degree of input on some of your workbooks. For example, you may be called upon to put together a sales report to present to management, but that report may have to be reviewed and approved by the sales manager first. Or, you may simply be part of a team responsible for performing some type of data analysis to present to other people in your organization. So, it's important that you be able to give and receive feedback on workbook files. Additionally, sharing workbook files back and forth via email or portable storage, ensuring that everyone who needs to contribute is able to, and keeping track of various versions to ensure that everyone's work is included can quickly become a nightmare. In short, you need a reliable method of sharing workbook files with a number of people while ensuring that the final version of that file actually includes the data it should.

Excel 2010 includes and is compatible with a number of features that allow you to collaborate on a wide scale while making sure nothing slips through the cracks. Taking advantage of this type of functionality allows you and your colleagues to work together smoothly, regardless of everyone's schedule or availability, while making sure the data and analysis you provide is complete, accurate, and up to date. With the volume of data organizations generate, and the amount of change they nearly constantly face, this level of accuracy and efficiency is a must to stay competitive in today's market.

Comments

Comments are a type of worksheet markup that allow workbook users to convey information to one another. You can use comments to provide feedback during a review cycle or to provide other workbook users with additional information about the data a worksheet contains or the type of data they should be entering. Comments appear in a pop up window that opens when you select or point the mouse pointer at a cell containing a comment. By default, cells containing comments display a red, triangular comment indicator in the top-right corner.

You can toggle the display of a single comment on or off, and you can toggle the display of all comments on or off simultaneously. You can also move and resize comment pop-up windows to better accommodate your view of either the comments or your worksheets. And, Excel enables you to navigate from comment to comment, so you can easily review all comments in large worksheets without having to hunt for them by scrolling. You can access the commands for working with comments in the **Comments** group on the **Review** tab.

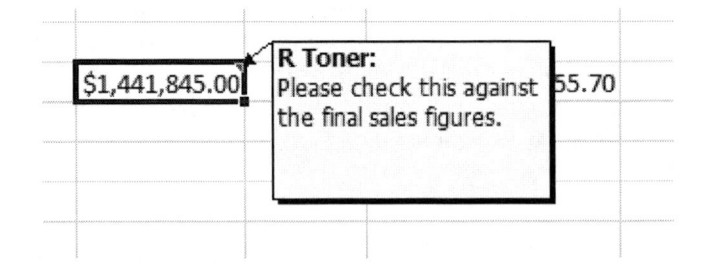

Figure 2-1: An open comment on an Excel worksheet.

The following table describes the functions of the commands in the **Comments** group.

Comments Group Command	Use This To
New Comment/Edit Comment	Create a new comment in the currently selected cell or edit an existing comment in the currently selected cell.

Comments Group Command	Use This To
Delete	Delete the comment in the currently selected cell.
Previous	Navigate to the previous comment in the worksheet.
Next	Navigate to the next comment in the worksheet.
Show/Hide Comment	Toggle the display of the comment in the currently selected cell on or off.
Show All Comments	Toggle the display of all comments on a worksheet on or off.
Show Ink	Show or hide notation markup on a worksheet. This functionality is available only on tablet or other touch-screen devices, or if you open a file that was created on one of those devices.

> **Note:** For more information about including additional information in workbooks, watch the LearnTO **Add Supplemental Information to Worksheets by Embedding Objects** presentation from the **LearnTO** tile on the LogicalCHOICE Course screen.

Shared Workbooks

Excel 2010 provides you with the ability to collaborate with others on the same workbook in ways that go beyond providing simple feedback. By creating a *shared workbook*, you activate a host of features that enable multiple users to view and edit the same workbook. You can store a shared workbook in a central location, such as a Microsoft SharePoint site or an organizational network share. From there, multiple users can access and edit the workbook simultaneously. If a SharePoint site or a network share aren't available, you can also distribute a shared workbook to multiple users, and then merge everyone's contributions in a master copy.

> **Note:** Working with shared workbooks on a SharePoint site or a network share is beyond the scope of this course. For more information on this functionality, visit Office.microsoft.com.

Although shared workbooks provide you with powerful collaboration functionality, there are a number of Excel features that are not supported by shared workbooks. Perhaps the biggest downfall of shared workbooks is that they do not support tables at all. You have to convert tables back to ranges in order to create a shared workbook. Additionally, there are several features that can exist in a shared workbook but that users cannot change once the workbook is shared. Among these are merged cells, conditional formatting, charts, hyperlinks, subtotals, and PivotTable reports.

> **Note:** Sorting and filtering in shared workbooks can cause a number of data errors, especially when multiple users are trying to sort or filter at the same time. It is generally a good idea to discourage sorting and filtering in shared workbooks.

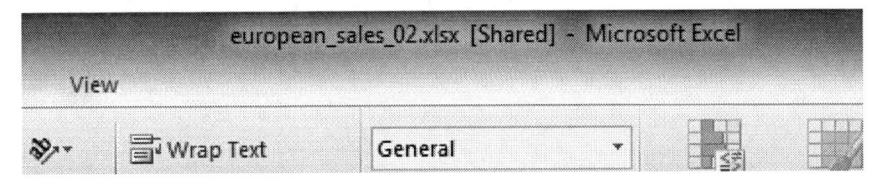

Figure 2-2: Shared workbooks display "[Shared]" after the workbook file name in the title bar.

Change Tracking

Change tracking is a feature of shared workbooks that marks up particular worksheet elements whenever users make changes to the original content. If you turn on change tracking in a nonshared workbook, Excel converts it to a shared workbook. Tracked changes help you to easily identify modifications made to the document, identify precisely what change was made, and provide you with the ability to either accept or reject the changes. As with comments, when you place the mouse pointer over a cell containing tracked changes or over other change markup, Excel displays a pop-up window containing information about the specific change.

In addition to having Excel display changes as markup on your worksheets, you can set the change tracking feature to create a list of all changes on a separate worksheet within the workbook. When you enable this feature, Excel automatically creates a new worksheet titled *History* in the workbook, and generates a detailed log of all changes on it.

Note: If you turn change tracking off, Excel deletes all markup and the record of what users have changed since you began tracking changes.

Change tracking affects some, but not all, changes made to your documents. Entering, modifying, and deleting cell data is tracked. So is adding or deleting rows or columns. But Excel does not track the following changes: revised worksheet names, inserted or deleted worksheets, changes to cell and number formatting, changes to formula results due to a change in the source data (though the change to the source data is tracked), added or modified comments, and hiding or unhiding rows or columns.

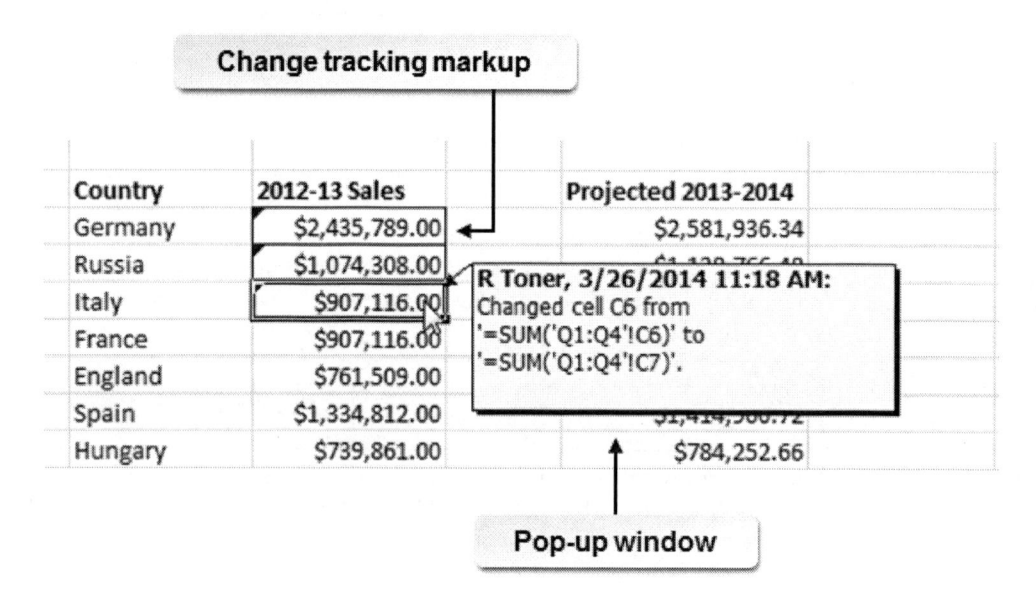

Country	2012-13 Sales	Projected 2013-2014
Germany	$2,435,789.00	$2,581,936.34
Russia	$1,074,308.00	
Italy	$907,116.00	R Toner, 3/26/2014 11:18 AM: Changed cell C6 from '=SUM('Q1:Q4'!C6)' to '=SUM('Q1:Q4'!C7)'.
France	$907,116.00	
England	$761,509.00	
Spain	$1,334,812.00	
Hungary	$739,861.00	$784,252.66

Figure 2-3: Change tracking marks up most significant worksheet changes.

The Highlight Changes Dialog Box

You will use the **Highlight Changes** dialog box to enable change tracking and to configure change tracking options. To access the **Highlight Changes** dialog box, select **Review→Changes→Track Changes→Highlight Changes**.

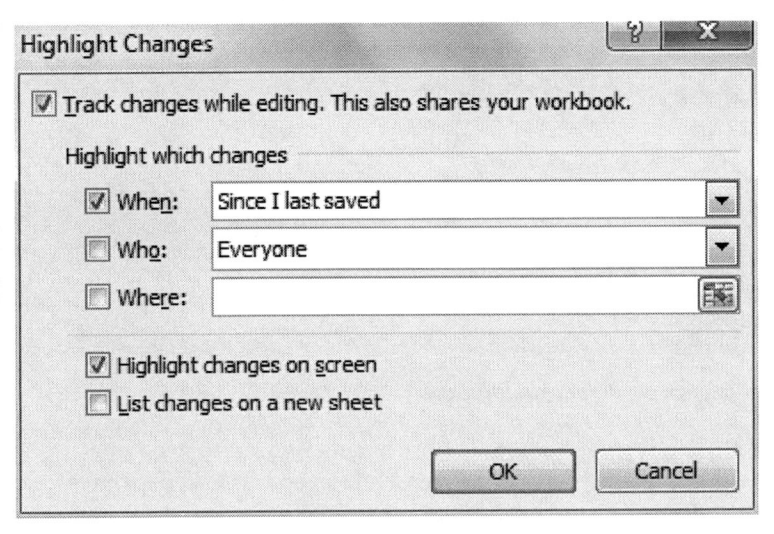

Figure 2-4: Use the Highlight Changes dialog box to specify how you want Excel to track changes to your workbooks.

The following table describes the functions of the various **Highlight Changes** dialog box elements.

Highlight Changes Dialog Box Element	Allows You To
Track changes while editing. This also shares your workbook. check box	Enable or disable change tracking.
When drop-down menu	Select which changes Excel will display based on when users make the changes. You can view all changes since you last saved the workbook, all changes made since a particular date, only changes you have not yet reviewed, or all changes since you enabled change tracking.
Who drop-down menu	Select which changes Excel will display based on who made the changes. You can view changes made by all users, any particular user, or all users except yourself.
Where field	Select the cells for which Excel will track changes.
Highlight changes on screen check box	View tracked changes as on-screen markup.
List changes on a new sheet check box	View tracked changes in a log on a separate worksheet.

The Accept Changes Dialog Boxes

There are two dialog boxes you will use to either accept or reject the tracked changes in your workbooks: the **Select Changes to Accept or Reject** dialog box and the **Accept or Reject Changes** dialog box. You will use the **Select Changes to Accept or Reject** dialog box to choose which changes to accept or reject based on when they were made, who made them, and where they appear in the worksheet. These options are essentially the same as those available in the **Highlight Changes** dialog box.

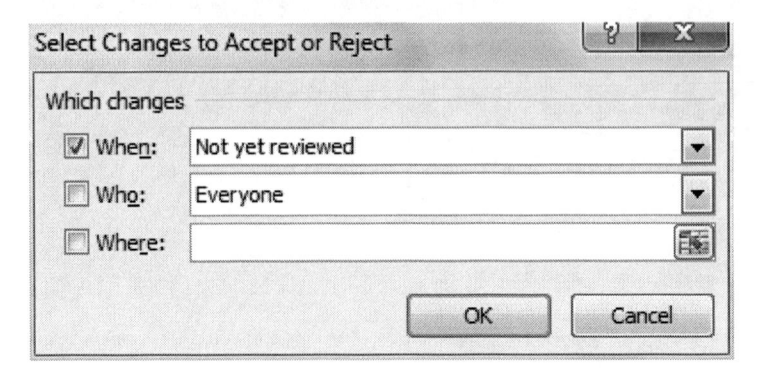

Figure 2-5: The Select Changes to Accept or Reject dialog box.

You will use the **Accept or Reject Changes** dialog box to choose whether or not to keep the changes users have made to your workbooks either one at a time or all at once. The **Accept or Reject Changes** dialog box displays information about the currently selected change, such as who made the change, when it was made, and the particular details about the change. As each change appears in the **Change *X* of *Y* made to this document** section, you can choose to accept or reject the change individually or accept or reject all changes in the selected range simultaneously.

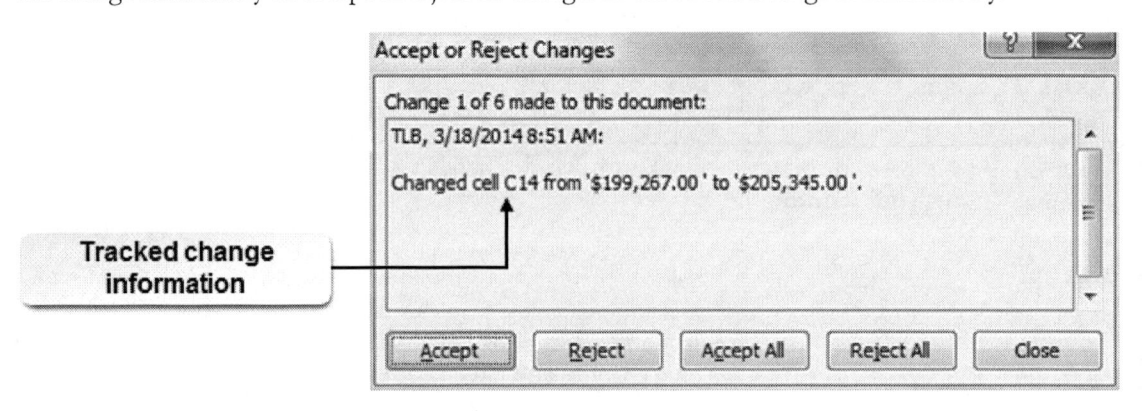

Figure 2-6: The Accept or Reject Changes dialog box.

The Save & Send Options

As you won't always need or be able to share Excel workbooks via SharePoint or a network share, you'll want to have other options for collaborating on and distributing workbooks. Excel 2010 provides you with a variety of options for doing so: the Save & Send options. You can access the Save & Send options on the **Save & Send** tab in the Backstage view.

Figure 2-7: The file sharing options available in Excel's Backstage view.

The following table describes the various Save & Send options in Excel 2010.

Save & Send Option	Enables You To
Send Using E-mail	Send a copy of a workbook to other users via email as an Excel workbook file, a PDF file, or an XPS file. You must have an installed email application to use this feature; it does not work using web-based services. This feature also enables you to send a link to a workbook stored in a shared location via email, or to send a workbook as a fax if you have an installed Internet fax application.
Save to Web	Save copies of workbook files to Microsoft's OneDrive service, which allows you to share and collaborate on documents in a web-based environment. You must have and sign in to a Microsoft account to use this feature.
Save to SharePoint	Save copies of workbook files on a SharePoint site if you have access to one.
Send by Instant Message	Send copies of workbook files across instant messaging services. You need to have an installed instant messaging application in order to use this feature.
Share Workbook Window	Screen share open workbook files with other users. You will need an installed web conferencing application to use this feature.

Microsoft OneDrive

Microsoft OneDrive is an online file storage, management, and sharing service that you can use to store, share, and collaborate on your Excel workbook files and other files. To use this service, you must sign up for a Microsoft account. If you already use one of Microsoft's other online services, such as the Hotmail email service or Xbox LIVE, you already have a Microsoft account.

One of the key benefits of OneDrive, in addition to the collaboration features, is that it enables you to access and work with your files from nearly any location on any number of devices. You can use either a web-based version of OneDrive or one of the OneDrive apps designed for a variety of platforms. Excel 2010 even includes built-in functionality that allows you to sign in to your

Microsoft account to save, share, and access your workbook files from within the Excel application. You can access OneDrive from within Excel 2010 by selecting **File→Save & Send→Save to Web**.

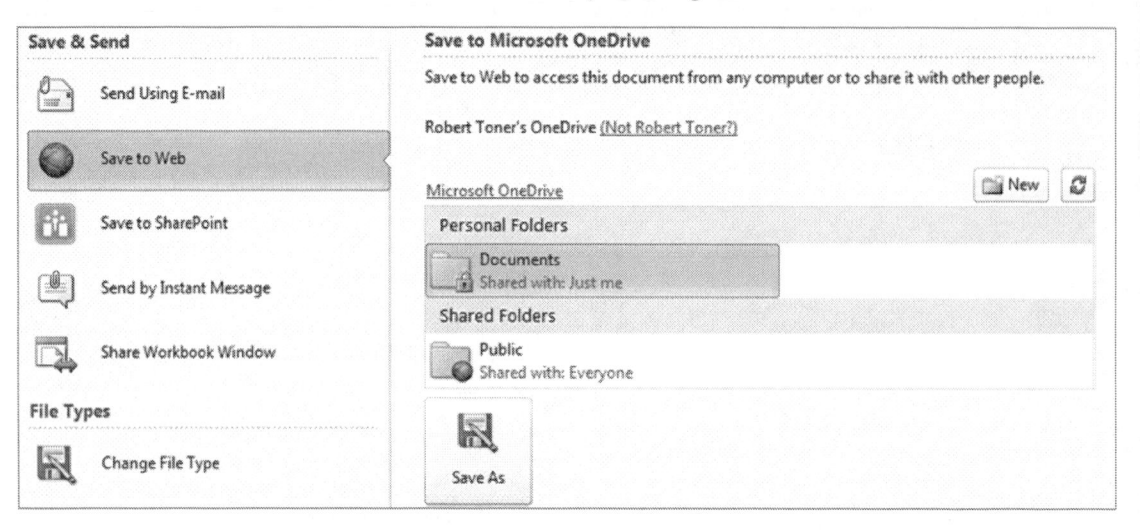

Figure 2-8: The Save to Web option in the Backstage view provides you with access to your OneDrive files.

The Compare and Merge Workbooks Command

If you are collaboratively working on a shared workbook that is not saved in a central location such as SharePoint site or a network share, you will still need to include the work other users contribute in the master copy of the workbook. To do this, you use the **Compare and Merge Workbooks Command**. This Excel feature enables you to merge two or more copies of the same shared workbook into a single file. When you select the **Compare and Merge Workbooks Command**, Excel opens the **Select Files to Merge Into Current Workbook** dialog box, which allows you to select one or more other workbook files to merge with the currently selected workbook file.

Important considerations to keep in mind when using this feature include:

- All workbooks that you wish to merge must be copies of the original shared workbook with unique file names and be stored in the same folder/directory.
- You cannot choose which changes to accept and which changes to reject when merging workbooks.
- Excel gives priority to the most recently merged workbook when there are conflicts between changes. If you merge more than one workbook into the master copy simultaneously, the one that appears last in the **Select Files to Merge Into Current Workbook** dialog box is given priority.
- If you have change tracking enabled in the master copy, Excel flags the changes in the markup or the change history.
- The **Compare and Merge Workbooks Command** does not appear on the ribbon or the **Quick Access Toolbar** by default. You must add that as a customization.

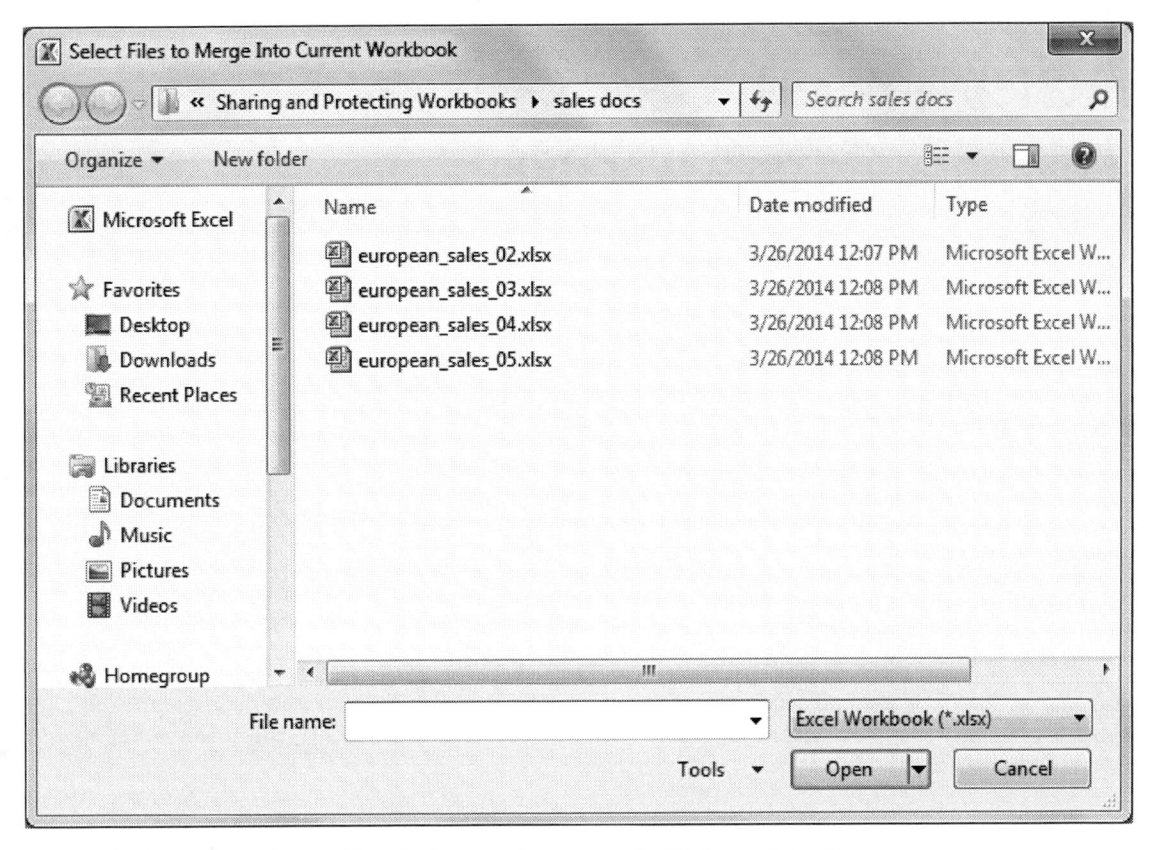

Figure 2-9: Copies of a workbook that can be merged with the original.

The PDF and XPS File Formats

Not everyone you need to share your workbook files with will always have Excel installed on their computers or have immediate access to a computer that has Excel. As people use different versions of Excel, there are sometimes compatibility issues between files and Excel versions. And you may still need your data and your workbooks to display the precise formatting and layout you worked so hard to configure in the first place. Excel provides you with the ability to publish your Excel workbooks in two particular file formats that are well suited to this need: the PDF and the XPS file formats.

PDF stands for Portable Document Format. This is an open standard for exchanging electronic documents that was developed by the Adobe Corporation. Its file extension is .pdf. XPS stands for XML Paper Specification. This is a non-editable file format developed by Microsoft that you can generate from a number of programs, but that you can only view, sign, or set permissions for in Microsoft's XPS Viewer application. The XPS file format's file extension is .xps.

> **Note:** You can access the **Adobe Downloads** page from www.adobe.com to download the free Adobe Reader application. You can download the free XPS Viewer application from the Download Center at www.microsoft.com.

These file formats allow you to easily print or distribute workbooks regardless of whether or not document recipients have access to Excel, and they give you the piece of mind of knowing your documents will appear precisely as you configured them when opened. Additionally, the PDF file format enables your workbooks to be printed by commercial printers. You can access the **Create PDF/XPS Document** command from the **Save & Send** tab in the **Backstage** view.

> **Access the Checklist tile on your LogicalCHOICE course screen for reference information and job aids on How to Collaborate on a Workbook.**

ACTIVITY 2-1
Collaborating on a Workbook

Data Files
C:\091020Data\Sharing and Protecting Workbooks\european_sales_02.xlsx

C:\091020Data\Sharing and Protecting Workbooks\global_sales_02.xlsx

Before You Begin
Excel 2010 is open.

The **Compare and Merge Workbooks** command has been added to the **Quick Access Toolbar**.

You have partnered with another student in class to perform this activity. For the purposes of this activity, one of you will continue to play the role of the Authors and Publications manager, while the other will play the role of the European Sales manager. Time permitting, your instructor may have you reverse roles and repeat the activity.

You have a valid, active email account and a web browser installed on your computer. Your instructor has provided you with your email address, user name (if different), and password. You have exchanged email addresses with your partner.

Scenario
The European Sales manager has informed you that some of the raw sales information for the European region needs to be updated before you finalize the sales projections for 2013–2014. Because you want the changes to reflect in your master copies of the European sales document and the global sales document, you decide to send a shared copy of the file to the European Sales manager with instructional text in the form of a comment. You will ask the European Sales manager to turn on tracked changes, make the necessary corrections, save the file, and send it back to you for review. Once you've reviewed the changes and are satisfied with their accuracy, you plan to merge the changes into your master copy and update the links to the data in the global sales document.

1. Authors and Publications manager (APM): Open the **european_sales_02.xlsx** workbook and ensure that the **2012-13_Totals** worksheet is selected.

2. APM: Add a comment to provide the European Sales manager with instructions to make the necessary changes.
    a) Select cell **F1** and then select **Review→Comments→New Comment**.
    b) Type the following text: *Please turn on change tracking, update the data, save the file, and send it back to me. Delete comment after reading.*
    c) Select anywhere outside the comment pop-up window to enter the comment and close the window.

3. APM: Make the **european_sales_02.xlsx** workbook a shared workbook.
    a) Select **Review→Changes→Share Workbook**.
    b) In the **Share Workbook** dialog box, ensure that the **Editing** tab is selected.
    c) Check the **Allow changes by more than one user at the same time. This also allows workbook merging.** check box, and then select **OK**.
    d) In the **Microsoft Excel** dialog box, select **OK**.

> **Note:** Sharing the workbook will overwrite the original data file. A duplicate copy has been included in the **solutions** folder for this lesson in case you wish to practice the activity at a later time.

e) Ensure that the text **[Shared]** appears after the file name in the **title bar**.

4. APM: Close the workbook, and then minimize the Excel application window.

5. APM: Email the **european_sales_02.xlxs** workbook file to the European Sales manager with the subject line *Sales projections file*

   > **Note:** Use the email address your instructor provided for your in-class partner to send the file.

6. European Sales manager (ESM): Save the **european_sales_02.xlxs** workbook file to your computer.
   a) Open the **Sales projections file** email from the Authors and Publications manager.
   b) Save the **european_sales_02.xlsx** file to the C:\091020Data\Sharing and Protecting Workbooks folder.

   > **Note:** This will overwrite the original data file, but that is okay as there is a copy of the original in the **solutions** folder for this lesson.

   c) Close the email message and minimize your web browser window.

7. ESM: Open the **european_sales_02.xlsx** workbook and, in the **Protected View** message bar, select **Enable Editing**.

8. ESM: Read and delete the comment from the Authors and Publications manager.
   a) Select cell **F1** and then select **Review→Comments→Show/Hide Comment**.
   b) Review the comment.

   > **Note:** You may have to place the insertion point inside the comment pop-up window and use the **Up arrow** and **Down arrow** keys to scroll to view the entire message.

   c) Ensure that cell **F1** is still selected and then select **Review→Comments→Delete**.

9. ESM: Turn on change tracking for the workbook.
   a) Select **Review→Changes→Track Changes→Highlight Changes**.
   b) In the **Highlight Changes** dialog box, ensure the **Track changes while editing. This also shares your workbook.** check box is checked.
   c) Ensure the **When** check box is checked and then ensure **Since I last saved** is selected in the **When** drop-down menu.
   d) Ensure the **Who** and **Where** check boxes are unchecked and that **Everyone** is selected in the **Who** drop-down menu.
   e) Ensure the **Highlight changes on screen** check box is checked and then select **OK**.
   f) If prompted, in the **Microsoft Excel** dialog box, select **OK** to acknowledge that there are currently no changes.

10. ESM: Update the quarterly European sales data.
    a) Select the **Q1** worksheet tab, select cell **C14**, type *205345* and press **Enter**.
    b) On the **Q2** worksheet tab, update the value in cell **C10** to *102987* and the value in cell **C13** to *308915*.
    c) On the **Q4** tab, update the value in cell **C5** to *213654*.

11. ESM: Save the workbook to the C:\091020Data\Sharing and Protecting Workbooks folder as *my_revised_european_sales_02.xlsx*

12. ESM: Review the changes to ensure you didn't miss any.
    a) Select **Review→Changes→Track Changes→Highlight Changes**.
    b) In the **Highlight Changes** dialog box, check the **List changes on a new sheet** check box.
    c) From the **When** drop-down menu, select **All** and then select **OK**.

d) Ensure that Excel opens a new **History** worksheet and that all four changes appear in the change history.
e) Save and close the workbook.
f) Minimize the Excel application window.

13. ESM: Email the **my_revised_european_02.xlsx** workbook file back to the Authors and Publications manager with the subject line *Revised sales figures* and then close your browser window.

> **Note:** Use the email address your instructor provided for your in-class partner to send the file.

14. Authors and Publications manager (APM): Save the **my_revised_european_sales_02.xlxs** workbook file to your computer.
    a) Open the **Revised sales figures** email from the European Sales manager.
    b) Save the **my_revised_european_sales_02.xlxs** workbook file to the **C:\091020Data\Sharing and Protecting Workbooks** folder.
    c) Close the email and then close your browser window.

15. APM: Review the changes to the revised workbook.
    a) Restore the Excel application window, and then open the **my_revised_european_sales_02.xlxs** workbook file.
    b) If necessary, in the **Protected View** message bar, select **Enable Editing**.
    c) Select **Review→Changes→Track Changes→Accept/Reject Changes**.
    d) In the **Select Changes to Accept or Reject** dialog box, ensure that the **When** check box is checked and **Not yet reviewed** is selected in the **When** drop-down menu.
    e) Select **OK**.
    f) In the **Accept or Reject Changes** dialog box, select **Accept** to accept the change for cell **C14**.
    g) Reject the change for cell **C10**.
    h) Accept the final two changes and then save and close the workbook.

16. APM: Merge the changes from the European Sales manager with your master copy of the **european_sales_02.xlsx** file.
    a) Open the **european_sales_02.xlsx** workbook file.
    b) From the **Quick Access Toolbar**, select the **Compare and Merge Workbooks** command.
    c) In the **Select Files to Merge Into Current Workbook** dialog box, navigate to and select the **my_revised_european_sales_02.xlsx** file.
    d) Select **OK**.
    e) Ensure cell **C17** on the **2012-13_Totals** worksheet displays the figure **$11,007,154.00**.
    f) Save and close the workbook.

17. APM: Update the links in the global sales workbook to reflect the European sales changes.
    a) Open the **global_sales_02.xlsx** workbook file.
    b) In the **Microsoft Excel** dialog box, select **Update**. Or, on the **Security Warning** message bar, select **Enable Content**.
    c) Ensure that cell **G18** now also displays the figure **$11,007,154.00**.
    d) Save the workbook as **my_global_sales_02.xlsx** and close the workbook.

18. Time permitting, reverse roles and perform the activity again.

> **Note:** If you and your partner switch roles and perform the activity again, some files will naturally end up being overwritten in the process. This won't be an issue, as the only original file that will be overwritten, the **european_sales_02.xlxs** file, is backed up to the **solutions** folder for this lesson. The **solutions** folder also contains a copy of the final **my_global_sales_02.xlsx** workbook file so all students can have a copy if there is no time to perform the activity twice.

TOPIC B

Protect Worksheets and Workbooks

As you share your workbooks with more and more people, or as you collaborate on workbook files with others, you face an increased risk of someone accessing, modifying, or deleting your data without authorization. Collaboration is essential, but it is critical that you be able to ensure the integrity and the security of your organization's sensitive data. Whether by accident or by malicious action, damage to your data or the acquisition of your data by unauthorized parties can have serious negative implications for your organization. As such, it is critical that you be able to balance the need to gather input and share information and the need to keep sensitive information safe and intact.

Fortunately, Excel 2010 provides you with a number of options for protecting your worksheets and workbooks from unauthorized access or changes. Taking the time to fully understand these security features means you'll be able to include everyone who needs access to your Excel workbooks without worrying about the integrity or the security of your information.

Worksheet and Workbook Element Protection

There are two general levels at which you can protect elements of your Excel files: the workbook level and the worksheet level. Workbook protection always applies to the entire workbook. At the workbook level, Excel enables you to prevent users from adding or deleting worksheets, viewing hidden worksheets, or resizing or moving worksheet windows.

At the worksheet level, Excel provides you with a number of options for allowing or preventing users from interacting with your data. For example, you can lock cells so they can't be edited or you can hide cell formulas so that document recipients can view formula or function results only. You can also enable or disable such operations as formatting cells, columns, and rows; inserting or deleting columns and rows; sorting and filtering; and interacting with PivotTables.

Worksheet-level protection works hand-in-hand with cell protection formatting, which you apply by using the options on the **Protection** tab of the **Format Cells** dialog box. From there, you control whether or not cells on protected worksheets are locked and whether or not users can view formulas and functions. Keep in mind that these options apply only once you enable worksheet protection. By default, all worksheet cells are locked, so unless you manually change this setting for cells, all cells on protected worksheets are locked.

At either the workbook or the worksheet level, you can set a required password for users to be able to edit protected elements. If you do not set a password, no users will be able to edit the protected elements. However, if you don't require a password, other users will be able to disable workbook and worksheet protection. In this case, not setting a password is best suited to preventing accidental, not malicious, modifications.

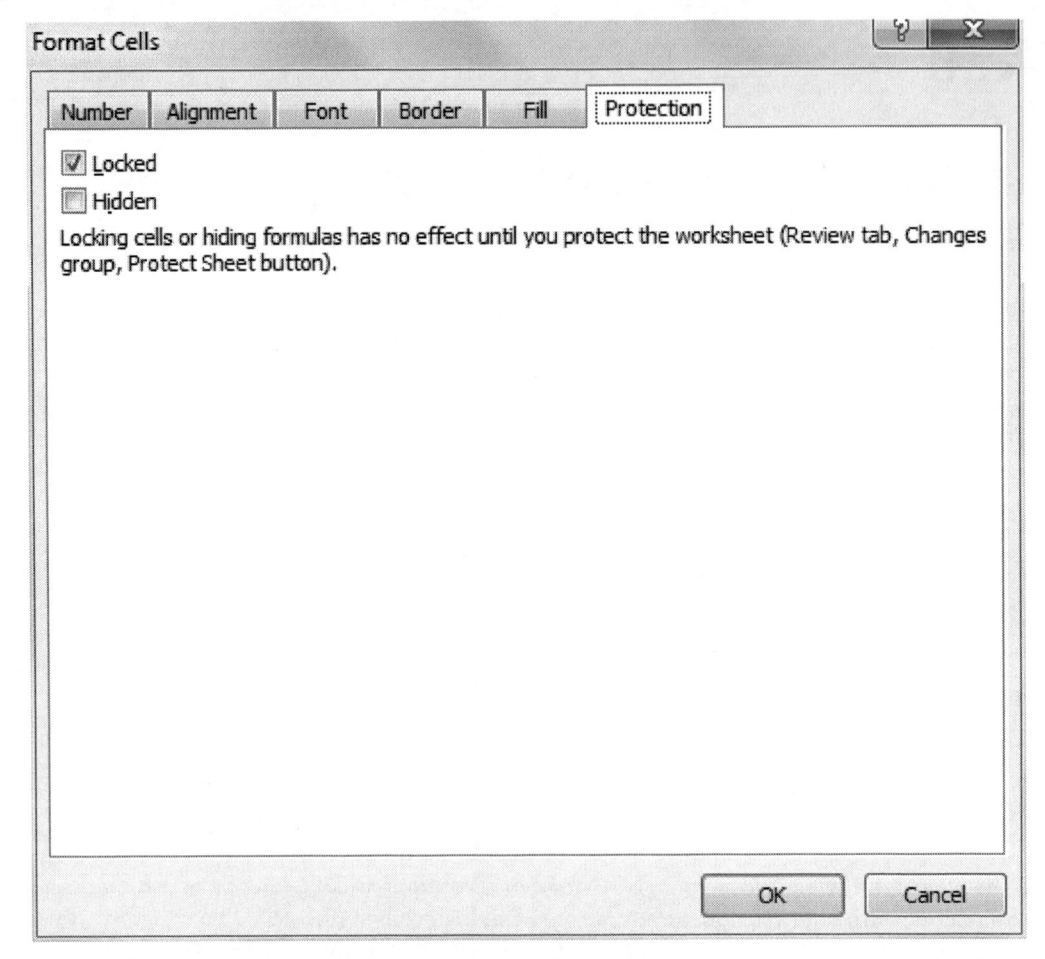

Figure 2-10: The cell protection formatting options become active once you enable worksheet protection.

The Protect Sheet Command

The **Protect Sheet** command opens the **Protect Sheet** dialog box, which enables you to select which actions workbook recipients are able to perform on a particular worksheet, set a required password for editing protected elements, and enable cell protection formatting. If you require a password for editing protected elements, you must remember the password or you will not be able to remove the protection. You can access the **Protect Sheet** dialog box by selecting **Review→Changes→Protect Sheet**.

Figure 2-11: You can determine which worksheet elements users are able to edit by checking options in the Protect Sheet dialog box.

The Protect Workbook Options

Protecting elements of your workbook may be sufficient to prevent accidental or intentional changes to your worksheet data, but there are several reasons you may want to add another layer of protection. For example, you may have workbooks that contain such highly sensitive that you don't want anyone without specific permission or authority to even be able to open and view them. In these types of cases, you'll want to add overall workbook file-level security to your Excel files.

Excel 2010 provides you with a number of options for protecting your workbook files from unauthorized access. You can access and apply these options by selecting **File→Info→Protect Workbook**.

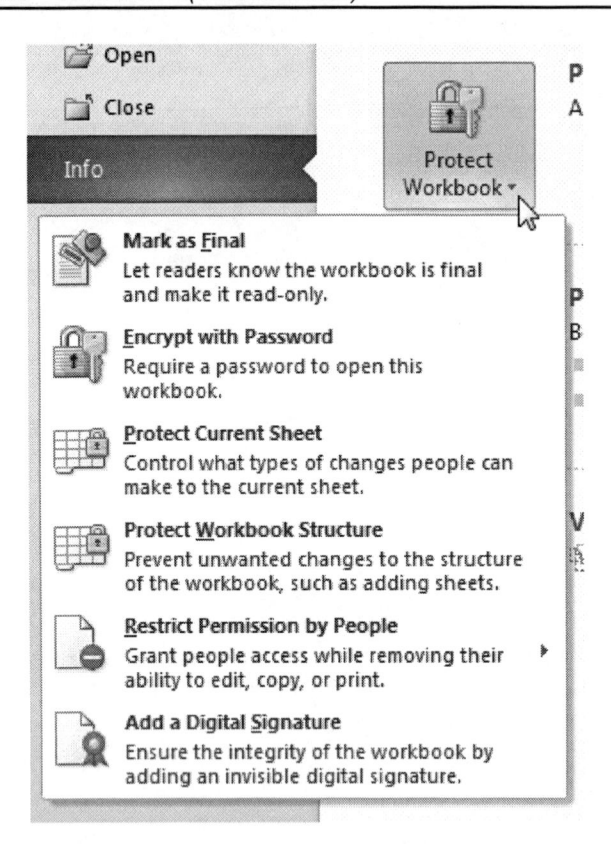

Figure 2-12: The Protect Workbook options in the Backstage view.

The following table describes the various **Protect Workbook** options.

Protect Workbook Option	Description
Mark as Final	Setting this option saves the workbook in Read Only mode, which disables editing commands and turns off proofing markup. When a workbook is in Read Only mode, the file name in the title bar is appended with the text *[Read Only]*. It is important to understand that any user can revert a workbook back to an active state by either selecting the **Edit Anyway** button in the message bar upon opening the file, or by selecting **File→Info→Protect Workbook→Mark as Final**. This option protects only against accidental revisions.
Encrypt with Password	This option enables you to require any workbook user to enter a password in order to open the workbook file. Once you set the password, only someone who knows the password can remove this requirement.
	It's a good idea to save an unprotected copy of your workbooks in a secure location before applying password protection. That way, if you forget the password, your data isn't completely lost.
Protect Current Sheet	This is simply another way to access the **Protect Sheet** dialog box.
Protect Workbook Structure	This is simply another way to access the **Protect Structure and Windows** dialog box.
Restrict Permission by People	This option allows you to restrict access to the workbook by using Microsoft's free Information Rights Management (IRM) service. A valid Microsoft account is required to use this feature.

Protect Workbook Option	Description
Add a Digital Signature	This option allows you to require document recipients to possess a digital certificate to access workbook files.

> **Note:** Digital signatures and IRM are beyond the scope of this course. For more information on digital signatures or the IRM service, visit **office.microsoft.com**.

> **Note:** For more information on workbook security, watch the LearnTO **Digitally Sign a Workbook** presentation from the **LearnTO** tile on the LogicalCHOICE Course screen.

> Access the Checklist tile on your LogicalCHOICE course screen for reference information and job aids on **How to Protect Worksheets and Workbooks**.

ACTIVITY 2-2
Protecting Worksheets and Workbooks

Data File
C:\091020Data\Sharing and Protecting Workbooks\final_global_sales.xlsx

Before You Begin
Microsoft Excel 2010 is open.

Scenario
You have finalized the regional sales information in the global sales workbook and it is ready to be presented at your sales meeting. Now that the numbers are final, you'd like to add protection to the workbook to ensure that no one with access to the workbook file can make unauthorized changes before the meeting. Specifically, you want to lock cells on the worksheet and hide formulas in all cells containing links. In this way, users can't change any information or track down the source workbooks to make changes there. Additionally, you'd like to require a password to open the workbook.

1. Open the **final_global_sales.xlsx** workbook.

2. If necessary, in the **Security Warning** message bar, select **Enable Content**. Or, in the **Microsoft Excel** dialog box, select **Update**.

3. Ensure that all cells have lock formatting applied to them.

    a) Select the **Select All** button to select all cells on the **Global_Sales** worksheet.
    b) Select **Home→Cells→Format→Format Cells**.
    c) In the **Format Cells** dialog box, select the **Protection** tab.
    d) Ensure that the **Locked** check box is checked and select **OK**.

4. Apply the hidden protection formatting to the cells containing formulas that contain external references.

    a) Select the ranges **D5:D14**, **G5:G15**, and **J5:J14** simultaneously.

Asia		Europe		South America	
China	$1,431,693.00	Germany	$1,929,486.00	Brazil	$758,200.00
Japan	$1,387,726.00	Russia	$705,892.00	Argentina	$459,244.00
India	$1,842,483.00	Italy	$1,074,308.00	Columbia	$356,863.00
Thailand	$380,884.00	France	$907,116.00	Chile	$359,630.00
Pakistan	$108,535.00	England	$761,509.00	Venezuela	$278,408.00
Vietnam	$128,534.00	Spain	$1,334,812.00	Ecuador	$343,169.00
Cambodia	$80,212.00	Hungary	$739,861.00	Peru	$664,828.00
Philippines	$542,867.00	Portugal	$851,755.00	Uruguay	$164,414.00
Singapore	$79,971.00	Greece	$712,836.00	Paraguay	$210,563.00
Indonesia	$763,811.00	Ukraine	$1,329,665.00	Bolivia	$113,421.00
		Beligum	$659,914.00		

    b) Open the **Format Cells** dialog box and ensure that the **Protection** tab is selected.
    c) Check the **Hidden** check box and select **OK**.

5. Apply worksheet protection.

a) Select **Review→Changes→Protect Sheet**.
b) In the **Protect Sheet** dialog box, ensure that the **Protect worksheet and contents of locked cells** check box is checked.
c) Ensure the **Select locked cells** and **Select unlocked cells** check boxes are checked.

d) Select **OK**.

6. Password protect the workbook.
   a) Select **File→Info→Protect Workbook→Encrypt with Password**.
   b) In the **Encrypt Document** dialog box, in the **Password** field, type *P@ssw0rd* and select **OK**.
   c) In the **Confirm Password** dialog box, in the **Reenter password** field, type *P@ssw0rd* and select **OK**.

7. Save the workbook to the **C:\091020Data\Sharing and Protecting Workbooks** folder as *my_final_global_sales.xlsx*

8. Verify the workbook is password protected.
   a) Close and then reopen the workbook.
   b) In the **Password** dialog box, in the **Password** field, type *P@ssw0rd* and select **OK**.
   c) Ensure that the workbook opens. If necessary, select **Enable Content** or **Update**.

9. Save and close the workbook.

Summary

In this lesson, you collaborated on workbooks and applied security measures to maintain the integrity of your data. The ability to work with colleagues and clients on a variety of projects is a must in today's ever-connected environment. But this level of collaboration brings with it the risk of lost, stolen, or corrupted data. Your ability to balance collaboration and security considerations means you can get the input and the feedback you need without having to constantly worry about your sensitive information.

In your current role, do you see using change tracking or merging content from shared workbooks as the best option for collaboration?

Do you feel more comfortable including sensitive information in workbooks that you need to share with other users now that you're aware of Excel's protections capabilities? Why?

> **Note:** Check your LogicalCHOICE Course screen for opportunities to interact with your classmates, peers, and the larger LogicalCHOICE online community about the topics covered in this course or other topics you are interested in. From the Course screen you can also access available resources for a more continuous learning experience.

3 Automating Workbook Functionality

Lesson Time: 1 hour, 20 minutes

Lesson Objectives

In this lesson you will, automate workbook functionality. You will:

- Apply data validation.
- Work with forms and form controls.
- Work with macros.

Lesson Introduction

Let's face it: working with large workbooks presents a number of challenges. Entering large amounts of data can be time consuming and it's prone to errors. You may also find yourself spending a lot of time and effort performing the same few tasks over and over again. And, the more people who work in the same workbook, the more these types of issues become magnified. In short, as you develop ever larger and more complex workbooks, you'll want to find ways to automate any number of tasks to save time, reduce errors, and generally make using your workbooks easier.

The good news is that Excel 2010 includes a variety of features that allow you to do just that. From ensuring that only the correct data or type of data can be entered into your worksheets to performing repetitive task so you don't have to, Excel's automation features can save you valuable time and keep your data intact.

TOPIC A

Apply Data Validation

The single most important aspect of data analysis is having accurate data to analyze. Given the large number of people who may use your workbooks, it's essential that you be able to trust the data they enter. Only a few bad entries can have a chain-reaction-like effect on formulas and tables throughout large workbooks. What can you do, short of standing over someone's shoulder as he or she enters data, to ensure your massive amounts of data are valid? This seems a near-impossible task to achieve.

Excel provides you with a robust and flexible way to make sure only valid data is entered into your worksheets: data validation. Understanding precisely what Excel enables you to control, and how to configure your worksheets to accept only correct entries, will allow you to take control of your worksheets and rest assured that you're avoiding major data errors that could take endless hours to locate and resolve.

Data Validation

In Excel, you use *data validation* to restrict data entries in worksheet cells. You can use data validation, for example, to limit cell entries to values above, below, or between particular thresholds; to only positive values; to only date values; or even to one of a selection of options from a drop-down menu. Data validation helps to ensure that your worksheet users cannot enter data that would cause unwanted results by enabling you to define restrictions on the data they enter. Data that does not meet the requirements of data validation is known as *invalid data*.

It is important to keep a few things in mind when applying data validation to your workbooks. First, data validation does not work on data that is copied and pasted or dragged to a cell; it works only on data that is manually entered. In fact, copying data to a cell to which you have applied data validation may clear the data validation from the cell. Additionally, although you can apply data validation to cells that already contain data, Excel will not notify you about nor change any existing data that does not meet the specified data validation criteria. Keep in mind that data validation is best suited for preventing erroneous data entries, and not malicious attempts to corrupt data. Use cell protection to prevent users from purposely entering bad data.

The Data Validation Dialog Box

You will use the **Data Validation** dialog box to apply validation to worksheet cells and to manage existing data validation criteria. The **Data Validation** dialog box is divided into three tabs, the **Settings**, **Input Message**, and **Error Alert** tabs, which provide you with access to the commands and functions you will use to create and manage data validation and data validation messages. You can access the **Data Validation** dialog box by selecting **Data→Data Tools→Data Validation**.

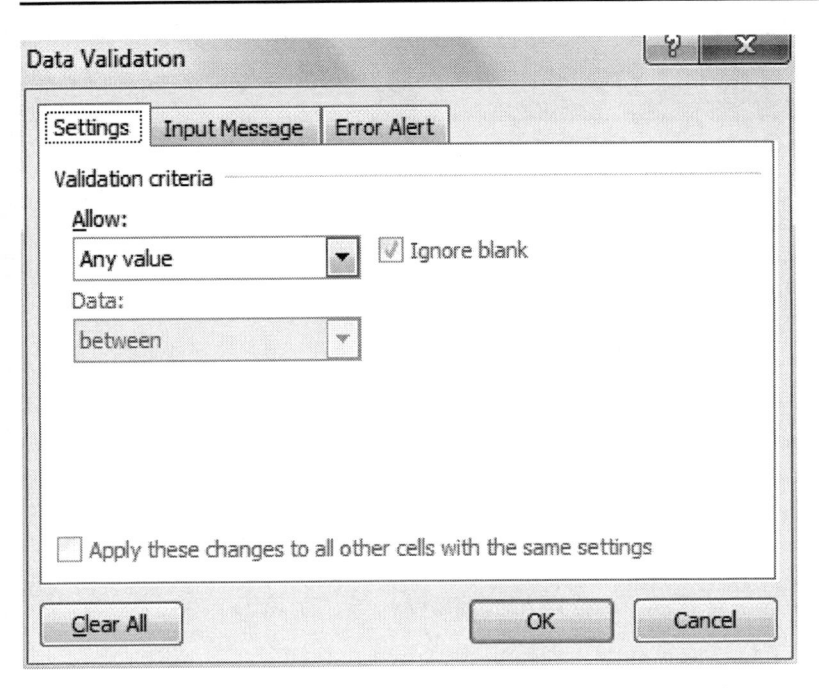

Figure 3-1: Use the Data Validation dialog box to apply and manage data validation criteria.

Data Validation Criteria

Excel provides you with a variety of criteria you can use to control what users can enter into worksheet cells. By default, you can enter any value into any cell on a worksheet. Excel provides you with six other types of data validation criteria that you can apply to worksheet cells. You can also customize your data validation criteria by using a formula. The particular options available on the **Settings** tab change depending on the type of criteria you select from the **Allow** drop-down menu.

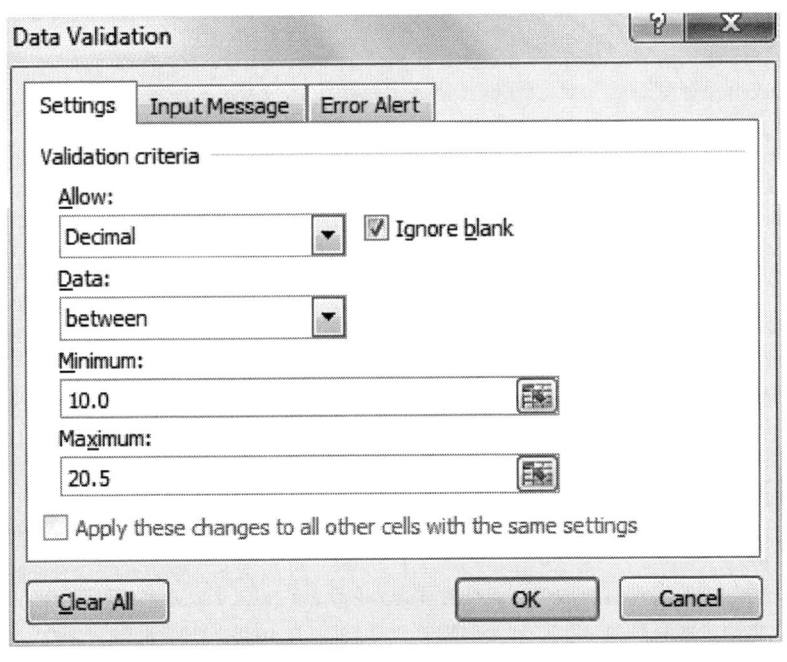

Figure 3-2: Excel provides various options for configuring data validation based on the selected criteria type.

The following table describes the various categories of data validation criteria.

Data Validation Criteria Type	Description
Any value	This is the default setting for worksheet cells. It enables users to enter any type of data in cells.
Whole number	This criteria type allows users to enter only whole numbers that meet the specified conditions, which are based on logical operators. So, for example, you can allow users to enter only whole numbers greater than 50, between 13 and 57, or less than or equal to 1,000.
Decimal	This criteria type is nearly identical to the whole number criteria type. The only exception is that it allows for values containing decimals.
List	This criteria type enables you to set a pre-determined list of options as the only valid data for the cells. You can either enter the list of options directly into the **Data Validation** dialog box, or reference a range of cells that contain the valid data. This criteria type also enables you to provide users with in-cell drop-down menus they can use to enter the data. You can also opt to allow them to manually enter the list items.
Date	This criteria type is similar to both the whole number and the decimal criteria types, but it allows users to enter only date values.
Time	This is the same as the date criteria type with the exception that it restricts data entries to time values.
Text length	This criteria type allows users to enter only values that contain a specified number of characters. The text criteria type does not limit values to only text values, you can also enter numeric or other values as long as they contain the specified number of characters.
Custom	This criteria type enables you to customize your data validation by using formulas to limit data entries.

Whereas the options that Excel displays in the **Data Validation** dialog box change depending on the criteria type selected, there are two options that always appear. The first of these is the **Ignore blank** check box. Although this check box is always available, it pertains only to criteria that is based on references to a data range; this is common when creating a list, for example. If the **Ignore blank** check box is checked and the source criteria (range) contains blank cells, then users are able to enter any value into the cells with data validation. If the **ignore blank** check box is not checked, users will receive whatever error you specified for the data validation if they try to enter a value not contained in the source criteria.

The other option that is always available is the **Apply these changes to all other cells with the same settings** check box. This check box pertains only to editing data validation. If you have a range of cells to which you've applied the same data validation, and you select only one of those cells for the purpose of editing the data validation criteria, this check box determines whether or not the changes will affect all of the other cells with the same data validation applied to them.

Input Messages and Error Alerts

In addition to specifying which types of data users can enter into worksheet cells, Excel provides you with options for prompting users with messages and warnings regarding data validation. You will use the commands and options on the **Input Message** and **Error Alert** tabs on the **Data Validation** dialog box to create and manage these messages. Input messages serve to provide the user with instructional text on what type of data he or she can enter into the cell. Setting input messages does not restrict the user from being able to enter invalid data; they simply display whatever message you specify. Input messages appear in a pop-up window that opens when users selected cells with data validation that have input messages enabled.

Data Validation

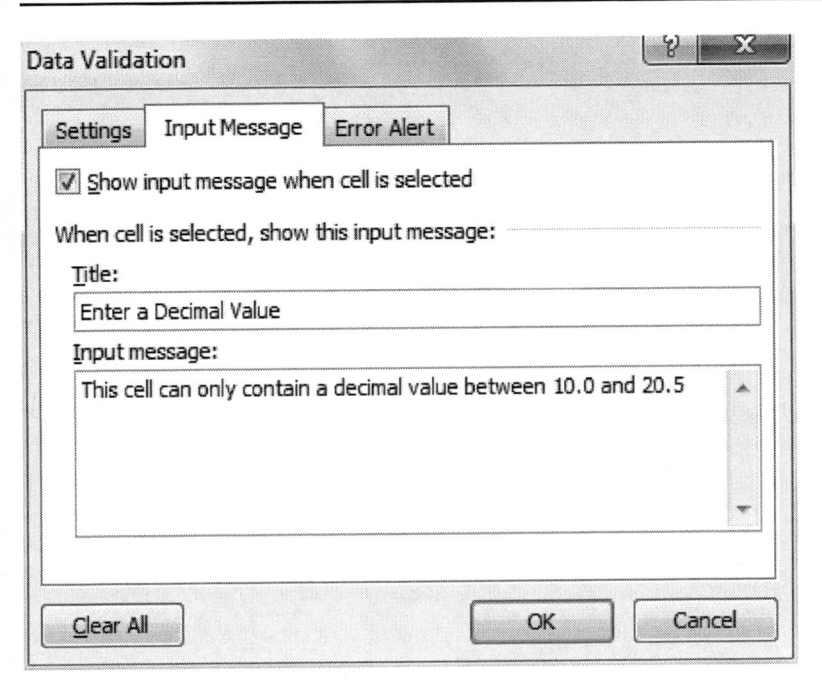

Figure 3-3: Input messages do not restrict the entry of data; they simply prompt the user to enter particular data.

The following table describes the functions of the various elements of the **Input Message** tab on the **Data Validation** dialog box.

Input Message Tab Element	Description
Show input message when cell is selected check box	Toggles the display of the input message on or off.
Title field	Enables you to enter a title for the input message. The title will appear at the top of the input message pop-up window when users select the cells with data validation applied to them.
Input message field	Enables you to enter the input message that will appear in the input message pop-up window.

Error alerts can either simply warn users they have entered invalid data or can restrict the entry of invalid data. Excel displays error alerts in a dialog box when users enter invalid data into cells that contain data validation. There are three styles of error alert you can define for cells that contain data validation: **Information**, **Warning**, or **Stop**.

Error Alert Style	Description
Stop	The **Stop** error alert restricts users from entering any invalid data. When Excel displays **Stop** error alerts, the user has only two options: to cancel or to retry the entry.
Warning	The **Warning** error alert will allow users to enter invalid data, but it first prompts them to decide whether or not they wish to continue.
Information	The **Information** error alert is the least restrictive of the three. Although it does display the specified error alert message, users can simply select **OK** to continue entering the invalid data.

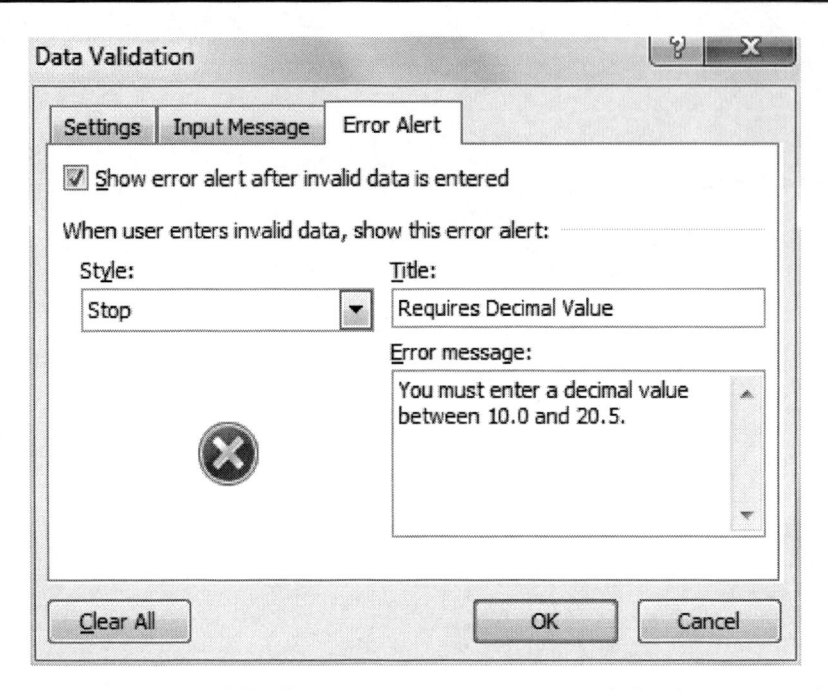

Figure 3-4: Excel displays warning messages in a dialog box. Depending on the error message level you set, Excel will either warn users about entering invalid data or it will restrict them from entering it.

The following table describes the functions of the various elements of the **Error Alert** tab in the **Data Validation** dialog box.

Error Alert Tab Element	Description
Show error alert after invalid data is entered check box	Toggles the display of the error alert on or off. As the error alert style determines whether or not Excel restricts the entry of invalid data, this essentially toggles the data validation itself on or off.
Style drop-down menu	Enables you to select the desired error alert style.
Title field	Enables you to enter a title for the error alert. The title you enter here becomes the name of the dialog box that displays the error alert message.
Error message field	Enables you to enter an error alert message.

> Access the Checklist tile on your **LogicalCHOICE** course screen for reference information and job aids on How to Apply Data Validation Criteria.

ACTIVITY 3-1
Applying Data Validation

Data File
C:\091020Data\Automating Workbook Functionality\author_master_roster.xlsx

Before You Begin
Excel 2010 is open.

Scenario
Fuller and Ackerman (F&A) recently completed the acquisition of two other publishing companies. As the Authors and Publications manager, you are responsible for ensuring the upkeep of the master roster of all authors. You have finished integrating the full roster of authors from the acquisitions into the master roster. As the number of authors under contract with F&A has grown significantly, you'd like to hand off some of the responsibility of maintaining the master roster to some of your staff members. You want to keep as much control as possible over data integrity, so you decide to take some steps to make sure other users will be able to enter only valid data in the workbook, and that the process of adding new authors and updating data is as simple and efficient as possible.

You decide to start by applying data validation to some of the columns to ensure that your staff can enter only appropriate values in them. As some of the entries on the author roster come from a predetermined set of values, you decide to add drop-down menus to prevent errors caused by typos. You have already added the possible entry options to another worksheet in the workbook. Additionally, as all agent codes fall between the values 5,000 and 5,500, you decide to restrict entries to that column to fall in that range. Your workbook already contains named ranges for some of the columns; these ranges include extra empty cells to accommodate future entries. You think it would be a good idea to apply data validation to cells in the additional rows as well to further accommodate future entries.

1. Open the **author_master_roster.xlsx** workbook file.

2. Create a drop-down list for the cells in the **Genre** column.
    a) In the **Name Box**, type *F2:F900* and press **Enter**.
    b) Select **Data→Data Tools→Data Validation**.
    c) In the **Data Validation** dialog box, ensure that the **Settings** tab is selected.
    d) From the **Allow** drop-down menu, select **List**.
    e) In the **Source** field, select the **Collapse Dialog** button.
    f) Navigate to the **Supplemental_Data** worksheet tab, select the range **M2:M7**, and press **Enter**.
    g) Select **OK**.

3. Ensure the drop-down list works as expected.
    a) On the **Authors** worksheet, select cell **F839**.

    > **Note:** Remember that you can use the **Name Box** to navigate to cells at the bottom of long columns. Also, the keyboard shortcut **Ctrl+down arrow** will jump down and select the last populated cell in a column of data.

    b) Use the drop-down menu to enter any one of the genres.
    c) Delete the value.

4. Add a drop-down menu for the state abbreviations in the range **I2:I900** by using the entries on the **Supplemental_Data** worksheet.

5. Restrict the values in the **Agent Code** column.
   a) Select the range **G2:G900**.
   b) Select **Data→Data Tools→Data Validation**.
   c) In the **Data Validation** dialog box, from the **Settings** tab, in the **Allow** drop-down menu, select **Whole number**.
   d) In the **Data** drop-down menu, ensure **between** is selected.
   e) In the **Minimum** field, type *5000*
   f) In the **Maximum** field, type *5500*
   g) Select the **Input Message** tab and then ensure that the **Show input message when cell is selected** check box is checked.
   h) In the **Title** field, type *Agent Code*
   i) In the **Input message** field, type *Enter a whole number value between 5000 and 5500.*
   j) Select the **Error Alert** tab and ensure that the **Show error alert after invalid data is entered** check box is checked.
   k) In the **Style** drop-down menu, ensure that **Stop** is selected.
   l) In the **Title** field, type *Agent Code Error*
   m) In the **Error message** field, type *You must enter a whole number value between 5000 and 5500.*
   n) Select **OK**.

6. Verify that the data validation performs as expected.
   a) Select cell **G839** and ensure the input message appears.

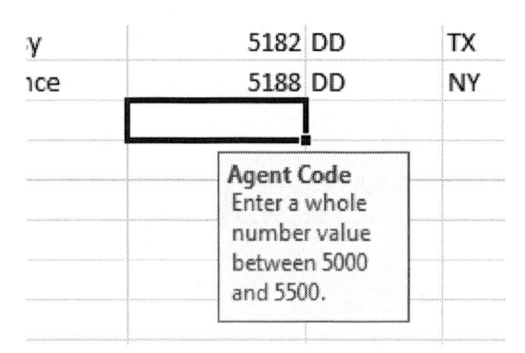

   b) Type *1* and press **Enter**.
   c) Ensure that Excel opens the **Agent Code Error** dialog box and select **Cancel**.

7. Save the workbook to the **C:\091020Data\Automating Workbook Functionality** folder as *my_author_master_roster.xlsx*

TOPIC B

Work with Forms and Controls

People use Excel worksheets for a variety of reasons. Some workbooks simply keep track of lists of information or help users track progress for projects or organizational initiatives. Other workbooks contain thousands of data entries linked by a complex series of functions and formulas. Whatever the user's purpose for the workbook, all workbooks have one thing in common: They all contain data. This means that someone has to enter that data. Although data entry in Excel worksheets is typically fairly straight forward, some worksheets require excessive scrolling for users to be able to access all cells. Other worksheets may require users to enter data that is difficult to type, such as technical jargon or complex numeric figures. Whatever the reason, you may find yourself in charge of a workbook that some users find difficult to work with. So, it would be helpful if you could include or take advantage of functionality to help those users complete the task at hand.

Fortunately, Excel 2010 provides you with a number of options for helping users enter data. Whether for saving them the time and effort it takes to navigate around large worksheets or for providing quick and easy access to the data they need to supply, your workbook users will thank you for taking the time to include this additional functionality. And you'll enjoy the benefits of managing workbooks that aren't full of errors and getting the data you need from your colleagues quickly.

Forms

Making it easy for users to add data to Excel worksheets typically involves working with some type of *form*. A form is either a physical or an electronic document that is organized for the purpose of collecting information. You are likely familiar with all manner of forms, such as those you might fill out at a doctor's office, when applying for a job, or when ordering items from a printed catalog. An electronic form is much the same as a physical form, except it exists as an electronic document, not on printed paper, and may contain additional functionality such as buttons and interactive menus, that can help you fill in the required information.

Although Excel spreadsheets are often used for storing and analyzing organizational data, they contain a fair amount of built-in functionality that also makes them suitable for creating electronic forms. For example, you can create forms that new hires might use to enter their personal and employee information. Because they would be entering that information directly into Excel, you could then take advantage of Excel's organizational and analytical capabilities to work with the information without first having to perform data entry. You can use these same capabilities to simply make entering data easier for other, more typical, workbook uses.

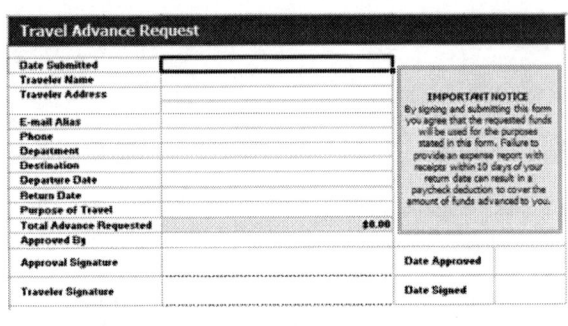

Figure 3-5: A sampling of Excel forms.

Form Types

There are three basic types of forms you can create by using Excel: data forms, worksheets that contain form controls, and VBA UserForms. Each of the form types contains varying degrees of functionality and would typically be used for particular purposes.

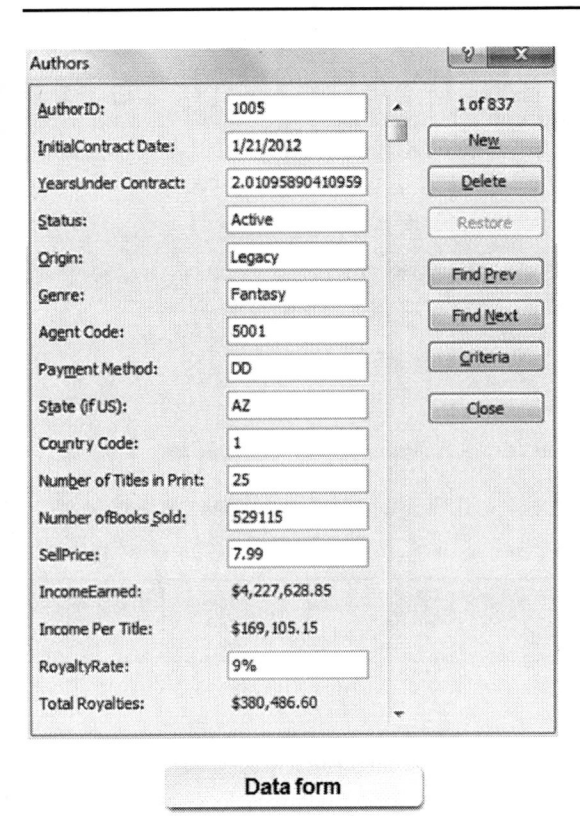

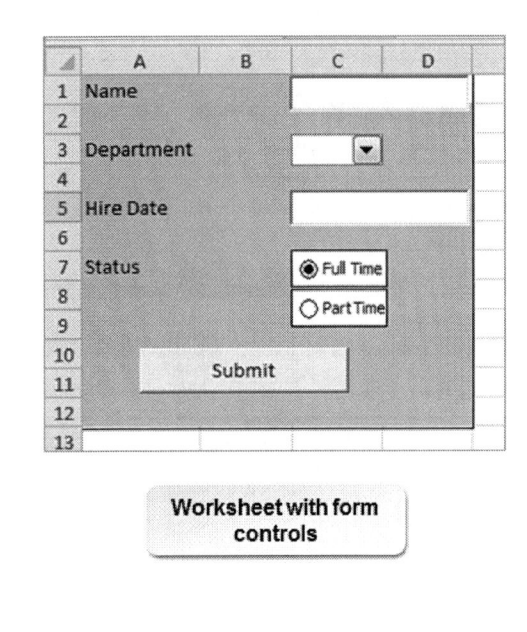

Figure 3-6: A data form and a worksheet that contains form controls.

The following table provides a brief description of the types of Excel forms.

Form Type	Description
Data forms	A data form makes entering data into worksheets that contain a large number of columns quick and easy. Excel automatically creates these forms for you based on the column labels in your dataset. The main advantages of using data forms is the fact that you don't have to scroll horizontally to enter data way at the end of long rows. But data forms also allow users to easily search for a particular entry (row) of data, view all column headers in a single window, and take advantage of simple tabbed navigation. You must add the **Form** control to the **Quick Access Toolbar** or the ribbon to generate data forms.
Worksheets with form controls	Worksheets made into forms closely resemble the physical paper forms you have likely filled out on many occasions. They are predominantly used to gather information. Text labels on worksheet forms inform users of what information to include in which cells. Additionally, you can include form controls that make it easier for the user to add particular information.
VBA UserForms	VBA UserForms are highly customized dialog boxes that can be used to enter information or data on worksheets. However, UserForms are not limited to this task. You can create UserForms to help you perform a wide variety of tasks, and they can be used in any Office application that supports apps created in Microsoft's Visual Basic for Applications (VBA) programming language. In Excel 2010, and other Office applications, you create and program VBA UserForms in the Visual Basic Editor.

The Developer Tab

In order to create forms and develop other types of additional capabilities in Excel 2010, you must first display the **Developer** ribbon tab. The *Developer tab* is included with Excel 2010, but by default, it is inactive. The **Developer** tab is divided into five groups that provide you with access to the tools and commands you can use to custom develop additional Excel functionality.

Figure 3-7: Add the Developer tab to the ribbon to access additional Excel capabilities.

The following table identifies the types of commands you will find within the various command groups on the **Developer** tab.

Developer Tab Command Group	Contains Commands For
Code	Developing and managing macros and creating applications by using the Visual Basic Editor.
Add-Ins	Managing Excel add-ins. This group contains shortcuts to the **Add-Ins** dialog box and the **COM Add-Ins** dialog box, which you can also access from the **Excel Options** dialog box.
Controls	Working with forms and controls.
XML	Accessing XML coding capabilities, developing XML code, and importing or exporting XML files.
Modify	Displaying or hiding the **Document** panel, which you can use to manage workbook document properties.

Form Controls

Controls are objects you can add to your worksheets that help users perform certain tasks, such as entering data or making a selection in a cell linked to the control. In Excel, there are two types of controls: *form controls* and *ActiveX controls*. Form controls provide you with an easy way to add functionality to your worksheets without having to use VBA code. Form controls are compatible with earlier version of Excel, dating back to Excel 5.0, but cannot be used on VBA UserForms. In addition to helping users make selections or enter content into worksheets, you can configure form controls to run either existing or new macros. To access the form controls you can add to your worksheets, select **Developer→Controls→Insert**.

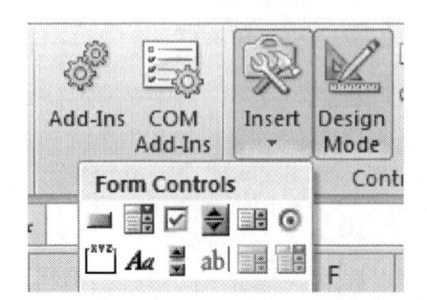

Figure 3-8: Form controls add functionality to Excel worksheets.

The following table describes the function of the nine form controls supported by Excel 2010.

> **Note:** Several other form controls appear in the **Insert** drop-down menu in the **Controls** group on the **Developer** tab, but they are inactive as Excel 2010 does not support them.

Form Control	Icon Image	Function
Button		These form controls are also known as push buttons. You can configure these to run macros.
Combo box		Combo boxes combine a drop-down list box with a text box that displays the item a user selects from the list. The list box part of a combo box is similar to the standard list box form control. But with combo boxes, the list box is minimized until the user selects the down arrow. Combo boxes return the index value of the selected item in the linked cell, so you can use them in combination with the INDEX function to return the selected item in any cell other than the linked cell.
Check box		Check boxes typically return a logical value of either TRUE or FALSE in the linked cell. This means you can use them in combination with logical functions to add functionality to your worksheets. A checked check box returns the value TRUE, whereas an unchecked check box returns the value FALSE. There is a third possible state for check boxes: mixed. A check box in the mixed state appears shaded and returns a value of #N/A. An example of a check box that might appear in this state is a "select all" check box for a group of other check boxes. If some of those check boxes are checked and some not, the "select all" check box will be in the mixed state. Users can check more than one check box at a time on a worksheet or within a group box.
Spin button		Spin boxes allow users to increase or decrease the value in the linked cell by a specified increment. You can set the minimum and maximum values, and the incremental value to suit your needs. Users are also typically able to manually enter values in the linked cell. Because spin buttons return numeric values, you can use the returned value in most formulas and functions.
List box		List boxes return the index value of the selected item in the linked cell. Unlike combo boxes, list boxes always appear full size so they can take up a lot of space. Use list boxes in combination with the INDEX function to return the selected item in any cell other than the linked cell.
Option button		These form controls are commonly referred to as radio buttons. Unlike check boxes, users can select only one radio button, within the same worksheet or group box, at a time. Radio buttons that are not grouped together in a group box will all be considered as part of the same selection. Radio buttons in a group box represent a single collection of radio buttons, meaning they represent a single decision point. For each collection of radio buttons, the selected radio button returns the index value of its place in the collection in the linked cell. So, like with other form controls, you can use the INDEX function in combination with these to return the desired option in any cell but the linked cell.

Form Control	Icon Image	Function
Group box		Group boxes provide no real functionality on their own. You use group boxes to separate individual entries (a single bit of information) on a worksheet form. Typically, you would group check boxes or radio buttons for a particular selection within a group box. Group boxes segregate the controls they contain from other controls. So, for example, radio buttons within a group only affect each other, which is important as only one of a collection of radio buttons can typically be selected at any one time. Optionally, group boxes can contain descriptive labels.
Label	*Aa*	Labels do not provide additional functionality on your worksheets. You will use labels to help users identify the purpose of the controls on your worksheets. You do not, however, have to use labels as you can also use formatted text entered into cells for the same purpose.
Scroll bar		Scroll bars function similarly to spin box form controls. Use these to return any value from a specified range, at a specified increment in the linked cell. You would use scroll bars when any of a very large number of values could be used and when calculating a precise value is not critical.

ActiveX Controls

ActiveX controls perform many of the same functions as form controls, but they are far more flexible and customizable, and they are capable of providing far more complex functionality than their form control counterparts. Like form controls, you can work with ActiveX controls directly on your worksheets without the need for VBA coding. But, unlike form controls, ActiveX controls can run on VBA applications and VBA UserForms.

Control Properties

Once you've added a control to a worksheet, you need to configure its properties. *Control properties* assign the specific functionality you desire to the control, configure the desired visual formatting options, assign the linked cell, and determine how the control interacts with the associated worksheet. You set control properties by using the **Format Control** dialog box, which you can access by selecting **Developer→Controls→Properties** when you have a control selected.

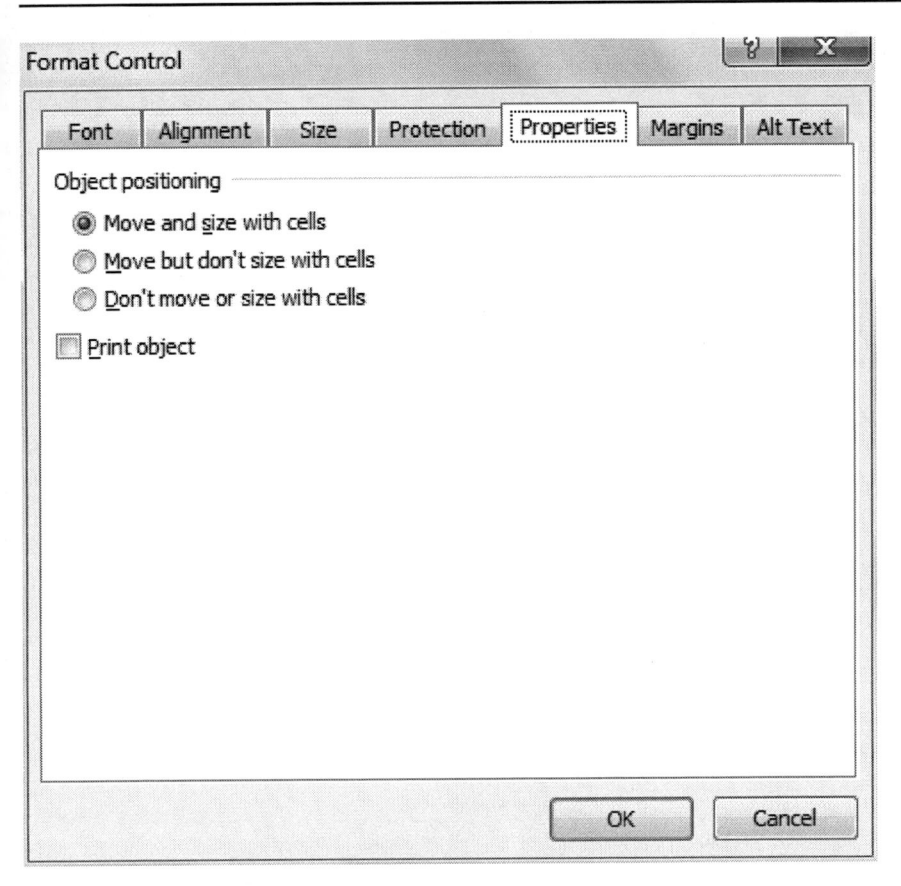

Figure 3-9: The Format Control dialog box.

The following table outlines the properties you can set from each of the tabs on the **Format Control** dialog box.

Format Control Dialog Box Tab	Contains Commands and Settings To
Colors and Lines	Format the appearance of a control. From here you can apply fill and line formatting to the control. This tab is active only for controls that you can visually format.
Size	Modify the size and orientation of the control.
Protection	Apply control protection to prevent users from making changes to your controls. As with cell protection formatting, these settings apply only if you protect the associated worksheet.
Properties	Determine how the control interacts with the cells on the associated worksheet. Although controls don't exist within cells, but rather on top of worksheets—in the way charts and other graphical objects do—you can configure them to change in size and location as you adjust column widths and row heights on the worksheet. From the **Properties** tab, you can also determine whether or not a control will appear on printed worksheets.
Alt Text	Include alternative text with worksheet controls. This can help users search for your worksheets if they are included on web pages, and it can provide assistance to users with physical disabilities.

Format Control Dialog Box Tab	Contains Commands and Settings To
Control	Determine the linked cell, establish the default state of check boxes and radio buttons, set the input range for list boxes, and set the value parameters for spin buttons and scroll bars.

> Access the Checklist tile on your LogicalCHOICE course screen for reference information and job aids on **How to Work with Data Forms and Controls**.

ACTIVITY 3-2
Adding and Editing Data by Using a Data Form

Before You Begin
The my_author_master_roster.xlsx workbook file is open.

Scenario
As other users will be adding and editing author information in the workbook, you have decided to add the **Form** command to the **Quick Access Toolbar**. Then users can manage the author roster easily and with fewer errors. As you have the workbook open, you also decide to correct some data you've discovered is incorrect and to begin adding the information for a new author to the roster.

The data that you need to correct is for author 1032. These are the erroneous entries:

- Status: Active
- Genre: SciFi
- Payment Method: Ck

---

1. Add the **Form** command to the **Quick Access Toolbar**.
   a) From the **Quick Access Toolbar**, select the **Customize Quick Access Toolbar** button and then select **More Commands**.
   b) In the **Excel Options** dialog box, ensure the **Quick Access Toolbar** tab is selected.
   c) From the **Choose commands from** drop-down menu, select **Commands Not in the Ribbon**.
   d) In the **Choose commands from** list, scroll down and select **Form**.
   e) Select **Add** and then select **OK**.

2. Locate and correct an entry using a data form.
   a) From the **Authors** worksheet, select any cell within the dataset.
   b) From the **Quick Access Toolbar**, select the **Form** command.
   c) In the **Authors** data form, select **Criteria**.
   d) In the **AuthorID** field, type *1032* and press **Enter**.
   e) Press **Tab** until the **Status** field is active and then type *Retained*
   f) Press **Tab** until the **Genre** field is active and then type *Romance*

g) Press **Tab** until the **Payment Method** field is active, type *DD*, and press **Tab** again.

Authors			
AuthorID:	1032		12 of 837
InitialContract Date:	1/6/2007		New
YearsUnder Contract:	7.05479452054795		Delete
Status:	Retained		Restore
Origin:	Legacy		
Genre:	Romance		Find Prev
Agent Code:	5072		Find Next
Payment Method:	DD		Criteria
State (if US):	ND		Close
Country Code:	1		
Number of Titles in Print:	25		
Number of Books Sold:	595341		
SellPrice:	5.99		
IncomeEarned:	$3,566,092.59		
Income Per Title:	$142,643.70		
RoyaltyRate:	15%		
Total Royalties:	$534,913.89		

3. Begin adding the information for the new author.
    a) In the **Authors** data form, select **New**.

b) Enter the following information in the fields.

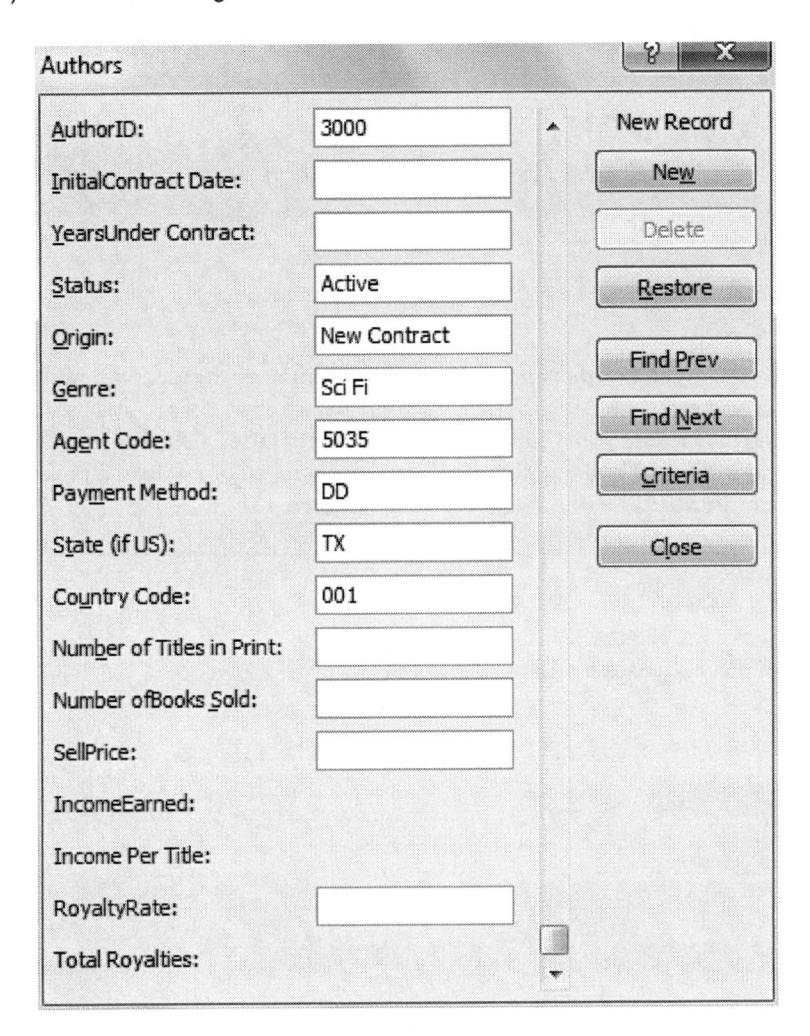

AuthorID:	3000
InitialContract Date:	
YearsUnder Contract:	
Status:	Active
Origin:	New Contract
Genre:	Sci Fi
Agent Code:	5035
Payment Method:	DD
State (if US):	TX
Country Code:	001
Number of Titles in Print:	
Number of Books Sold:	
SellPrice:	
IncomeEarned:	
Income Per Title:	
RoyaltyRate:	
Total Royalties:	

c) Select **Close**.

4. Navigate to the bottom of the worksheet, if necessary, and verify that Excel added the new record.

5. Navigate up to row **13** and verify that the entries for author 1032 have been updated.

6. Save the workbook.

ACTIVITY 3-3
Adding Form Controls

Before You Begin
The my_author_master_roster.xlsx workbook file is open.

Scenario
As the number of Fuller and Ackerman authors continues to grow, you have decided you want to create a dashboard worksheet so users can easily look up a variety of information about various authors. You know form controls include some functionality that you will find useful as you develop the authors dashboard, so you will begin building the dashboard by using a combo box that users will be able to use to select any author ID from the **Authors** worksheet.

1. Add the **Developer** tab to the ribbon.
    a) Select **File→Options→Customize Ribbon**.
    b) In the **Customize the Ribbon** list, check the **Developer** check box.

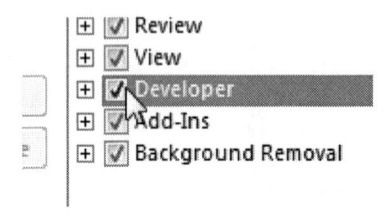

    c) Select **OK**.

2. Change the name of **Sheet2** to *Author_Dashboard*

3. Add labels for the first item in the dashboard.
    a) On the **Author_Dashboard** worksheet, add the label *Look Up Author Income* to cell **A1**.
    b) Add the label *AuthorID* to cell **A3** and the label *Income* to cell **A4**.
    c) Adjust the width of column **A** to accommodate the text.

4. Add a form control to the worksheet.
    a) Select **Developer→Controls→Insert**.
    b) From the **Form Controls** section, select **Combo Box (Form Control)**.

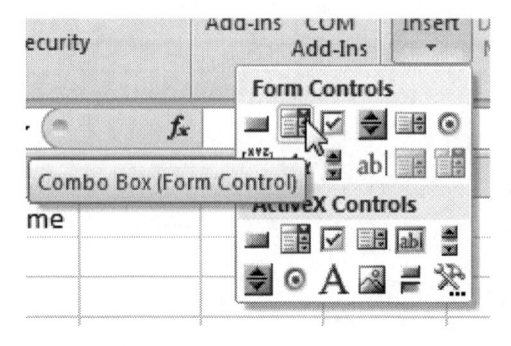

c) Drag the mouse pointer to draw the combo box on top of cell **B3**.

> **Note:** Draw the combo box so that it is the same size as cell **B3**.

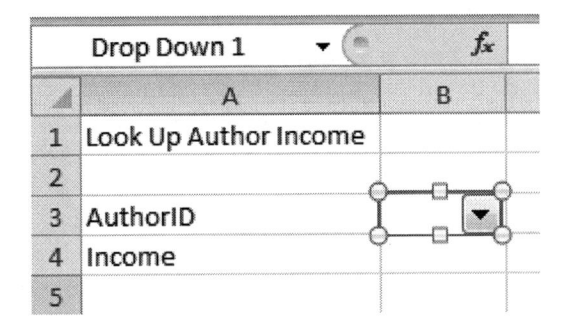

5. Configure the combo box properties.
   a) With the combo box still selected, select **Developer→Controls→Properties**.
   b) In the **Format Control** dialog box, ensure that the **Control** tab is selected.
   c) In the **Input range** field, type *AuthorID*
   d) In the **Cell link** field, enter *$C$3*
   e) Change the value in the **Drop down lines** field to *10* and then select **OK**.

6. Ensure that the combo box works as expected.
   a) Select any cell on the worksheet other than **B3** to deselect the combo box.
   b) Use the combo box's **down arrow** to select **1006** from the drop-down list.
   c) Ensure that Excel returns the value **2** in cell **C3**.

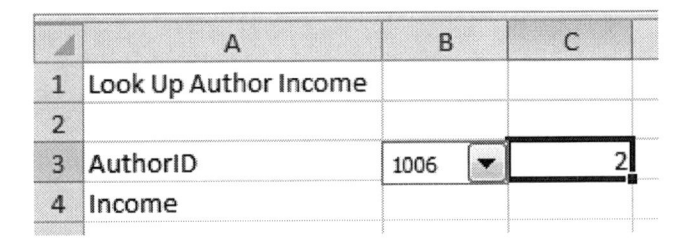

   d) Select cell **C3** and press **Delete**.

7. Change the combo box cell link so Excel hides the entry reference behind the combo box.
   a) Right-click the combo box and select **Format Control**.
   b) Change the entry in the **Cell link** field from *$C$3* to *$B$3* and select **OK**.

8. Save the workbook.

TOPIC C

Work with Macros

If you've developed Excel workbooks for any length of time, especially if you create numerous workbooks for similar purposes, you've likely found yourself performing the same mundane tasks over and over again. Perhaps you create new financial reports every quarter or period. If so, the labels, formatting, formulas and functions, and overall layout are likely the same each time. Or, perhaps you're a project manager who uses Excel to track major milestones. The workbook for each new project likely contains a lot of the same information. Whatever the reason, performing the same tasks over and over just feels like a waste of time.

If you find yourself feeling frustrated over performing the same repetitive, non-value-added tasks each time you create a workbook, you're in luck. Excel 2010 includes a powerful feature that can actually perform these tasks for you: macros. By unlocking the nearly endless capabilities macros can offer, you will not only save yourself time and effort, but also you'll begin to open up whole new worlds of automation you may have never even realized were possible.

Macros

A *macro*, in its simplest terms, is a series of steps or instructions that you can run from a single command or action. In Excel, as with some other Office applications, you can either record macros or write them in VBA code with the Visual Basic Editor. You can use macros any time you would like Excel to perform a repetitive series of steps, such as filling in commonly used labels, formatting data and graphics to suit a particular purpose or adhere to organizational branding requirements, or to enter formulas and functions that you use in multiple workbooks. There several options you can use to run macros once you've created them. These include running them from a dialog box, assigning keyboard shortcuts, and using controls. You can even create macros that run automatically when you open a workbook.

You can work with macros only in Excel workbooks that have been saved as macro-enabled workbooks. The file extension for these workbooks is .xlsm. Keep in mind that macros can be associated with security risks as they require you to run code within your workbooks. Always check with your system administrator for your organization's security requirements when working with macros.

Macro Security Settings

Although you know you can trust your own macros, that may not be the case with macros created by someone else. Macros may be convenient, but there's always a chance you will introduce malicious code to your system or network by running macros from other sources. Excel 2010 provides you with a number of options you can select from in terms of macro security settings. The easiest way to access these settings is by selecting **Developer→Code→Macro Security**. You can also access them by selecting **Trust Center Settings** on the **Trust Center** tab in the **Excel Options** dialog box.

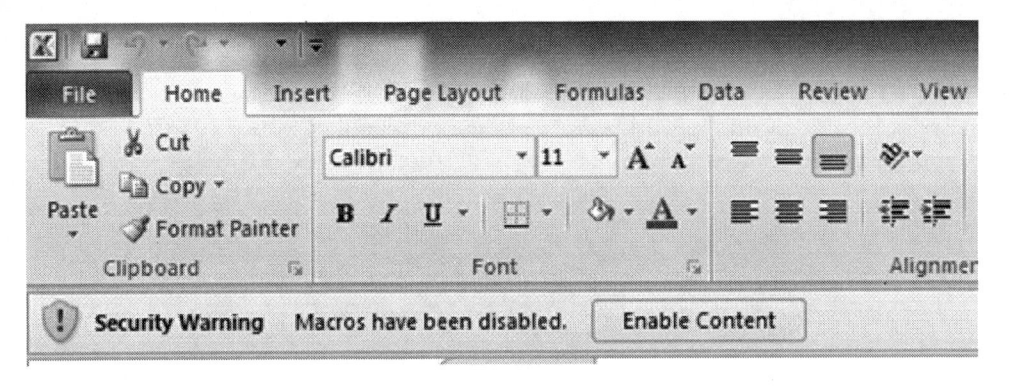

Figure 3-10: Depending on your macro security settings, workbooks containing macros may display a warning message when you open them.

The following table describes the various macro security settings as well as the additional security option for developers.

Macro Security Option	Description
Disable all macros without notification	This is the strongest security setting. Selecting this option disables all macros and any warnings Excel would otherwise display regarding macros. You can, however, establish a trusted folder, save macro-enabled workbooks in it, and still run the macros with this option selected.
Disable all macros with notification	This option enables you to decide whether or not to run macros upon opening macro-enabled workbooks. Excel will display a warning and prompt you to decide whether or not to enable macros. This is the default setting in Excel 2010.
Disable all macros except digitally signed macros	This setting is similar to the **Disable all macros with notification** option. The only difference here is that Excel automatically enables macros in workbooks from publishers you have trusted without displaying a message. If you open macro-enabled workbooks from non-trusted publishers, Excel will prompt you to decide.
Enable all macros	This is the least-secure option, which is typically not recommended. If you select this option, Excel will enable and allow to run any macro in any macro-enabled workbook.
Trust access to the VBA project object model check box	This is a separate option from the macro security settings that should be used only by developers who have extensive knowledge of the Visual Basic coding environment. Basically, this option either blocks or allows code to access Office applications at the code level for purposes of automating Office functionality.

Microsoft Visual Basic for Applications

As previously mentioned, you can either record macros or use *Visual Basic for Applications* code to write them. Visual Basic for Applications is the programming language developers use for Microsoft Office applications and other related add-ins, macros, and applications. When you record a macro in Excel, your actions are recorded as VBA code; the work is done for you. The advantage to coding your macros manually in VBA instead of recording them is that you have a far greater level of control over what the macro does. Many users don't have extensive knowledge of VBA, so they prefer to record their macros. Some experienced users often prefer to start by recording a macro and then edit the code to make small adjustments to it.

You write and edit VBA code by using Microsoft's *Visual Basic Editor*, which is included with Excel. The VB Editor is made up of several major components that you can use to navigate, inspect, and edit your macros. Saved macros are stored in folders called *modules*, which you can view in the VB Editor. Modules are saved along with the workbook file of the workbook in which you saved the macro, and they appear as part of the workbook's hierarchical structure in the VB Editor user interface.

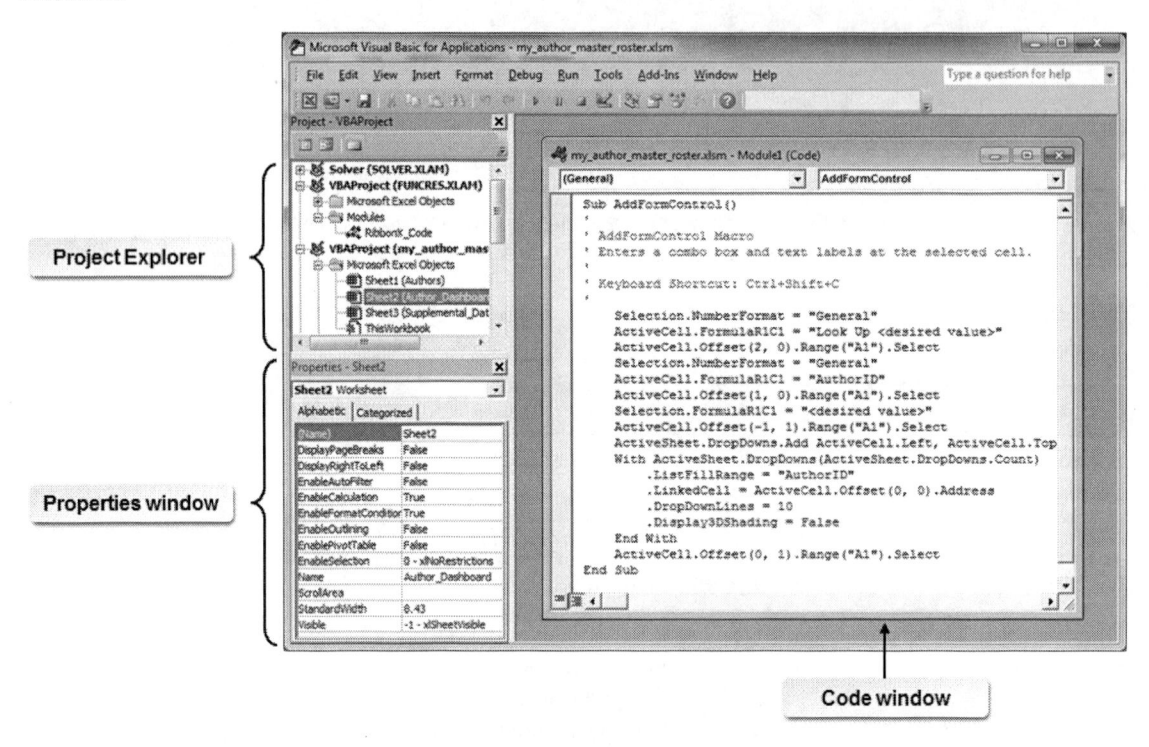

Figure 3-11: Use the Visual Basic Editor to write and edit your macro code.

The following table describes the main components of the Visual Basic Editor user interface.

Visual Basic Editor Component	Description
Project Explorer	Displays the hierarchical structure of objects in all open workbooks. This includes the worksheets in each workbook, any VBA modules, and VBA UserForms.
Properties window	Displays the properties of the object selected in the Project Explorer. The VB Editor does not display the Properties window by default. You can open it from the View menu in the VB Editor menu bar.
Code window	Displays VBA code. It is in the Code window that you can write and edit macro code.

The Record Macro Dialog Box

You will use the **Record Macro** dialog box to begin the process of recording macros. From here, name the macro and select a location to save it. Optionally, you can also assign a keyboard shortcut that will run the macro; then you can add a description to the macro to inform users of what, precisely, the macro does. You can access the **Record Macro** dialog box by selecting **Developer→Code→Record Macro**.

Once you begin recording a macro, nearly every action you perform in Excel becomes part of the code's instructions, including errors. So, it is sometimes necessary, especially for users who are new to macros, to delete a macro and record it over again. With time and a little experience, you'll begin to get a feel for how your macros will run based on the actions you record.

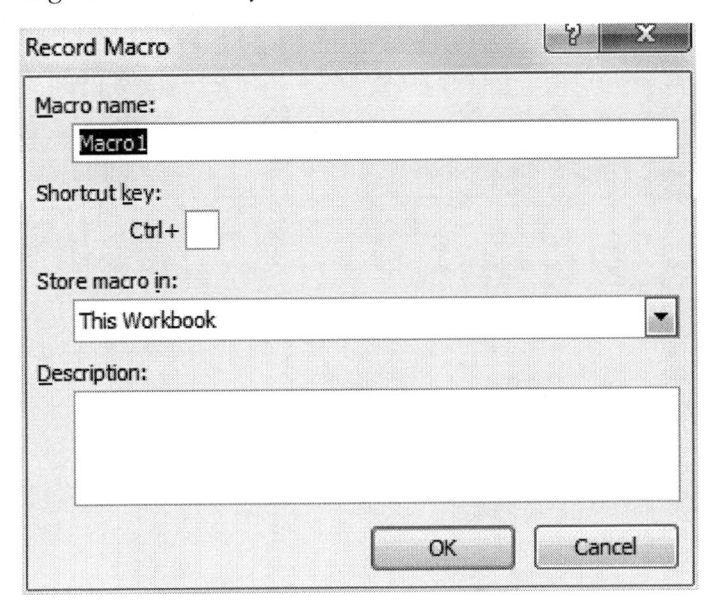

Figure 3-12: Use the Record Macro dialog box to begin the process of recording a macro.

The Use Relative References Command

When you record macros, you can record nearly any action that accomplishes a task in Excel, such as selecting a cell, a range, or a command; or entering data in a cell. As such, you can record the process of adding data and formulas to cells. This means absolute and relative cell references become extremely important. Just as a simple example, let's say you record the process of entering the following data and formula into an Excel worksheet.

If you use absolute references when you record the macro, when you run the macro, it will always enter the values and the formula in the range **A1:A6**. If you use relative references, it will place the values and the formula in six consecutive cells within the same column starting at the currently selected cell.

To control whether Excel records the macro by using relative or absolute references, toggle the **Use Relative References** command on or off. You can even toggle it on and off during the same recording so you can use a mix of absolute and relative references within the same macro. You can access the **Use Relative References** command in the **Code** group on the **Developer** tab.

The Macro Dialog Box

You will use the **Macro** dialog box to manage and run your macros. From the **Macro** dialog box, you can view all available macros, run them, delete them, open them in the Visual Basic Editor to edit or debug them, and configure keyboard shortcuts. You can access the **Macro** dialog box by selecting **Developer→Code→Macros**.

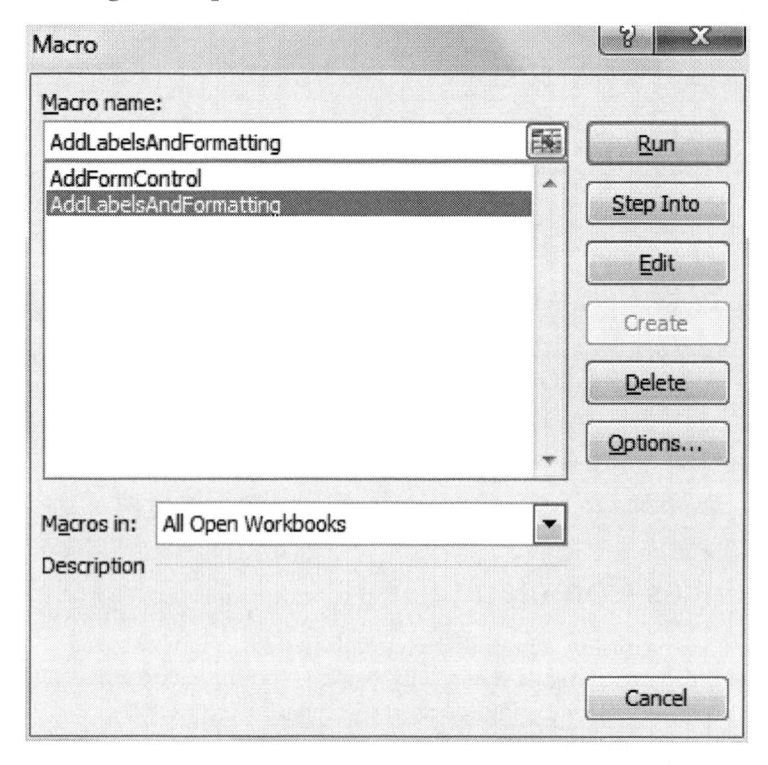

Figure 3-13: Use the Macro dialog box to manage your macros.

The following table describes the functions of the various elements of the **Macro** dialog box.

Macro Dialog Box Element	Function
Run button	Executes the currently selected macro.
Step Into button	Opens the selected macro's code in the VB Editor for the purpose of debugging the code. Once the macro is open in the VB Editor, you can press the **F8** key to step through the macro one instruction at a time. In this way, you can watch the macro run on the worksheet and view the code associated with the action. At each step, the VB Editor highlights the corresponding code.
Edit button	Opens the selected macro's code in the VB Editor so you can edit it.
Delete button	Deletes the selected macro.
Options button	Opens the **Macro Options** dialog box. From here, you can assign or change the macro's keyboard shortcut, or add or edit its description.
Macros in drop-down menu	Selects which macros Excel displays in the **Macro** dialog box.

Macro Names

All macros must have a name. And, like other named items in Excel, you must follow a particular convention when naming your macros. Macro names:

- Must begin with a letter.
- Must contain only letters, numbers, and underscores (_).
- Cannot contain any spaces.
- Should not be the same as cell references, as this may result in errors.

If you name a macro **Auto_Open**, Excel will automatically run the macro when you open the workbook that contains it.

The Personal Workbook

Although you can save macros in individual workbooks, when you do, you can use the macros only in the workbooks they're saved in. But you may also wish to create macros for use in other workbooks. In such cases, you can save the macro in a hidden workbook called the *personal workbook*. The first time you save a macro to your personal workbook, Excel automatically creates the workbook and names it PERSONAL.XLSB. This workbook automatically opens every time you open Excel on your computer once Excel creates it, which is why you can use macros saved here in any other macro-enabled workbook on your computer.

As the personal workbook is a hidden workbook, you will not be able to see it when you open Excel. If you wish to edit or delete a macro that you have saved to your personal workbook, you must first unhide the PERSONAL.XLSB workbook and then edit or delete the macro. You can then re-hide your personal workbook if you don't wish to view it every time you open Excel. After saving a new macro to the personal workbook, Excel will prompt you to save the personal workbook the next time you close Excel. You must save the personal workbook for the new macro to be available in other workbooks.

Figure 3-14: You must unhide the personal workbook to delete or edit macros that are saved there.

> Access the Checklist tile on your LogicalCHOICE course screen for reference information and job aids on How to Work with Macros.

ACTIVITY 3-4
Creating a Macro

Before You Begin
The my_author_master_roster.xlsx workbook file is open.

Scenario
You realize the workbook's users will need to look up more that just the authors' total income, so you want to add more form controls to the **Author_Dashboard** worksheet. Because the process is a bit cumbersome, you decide to create a macro that will add a new form control with a simple keyboard shortcut.

1. On the **Author_Dashboard** worksheet, select cell **A6**.

2. Select **Developer→Code→Use Relative References**.

   > **Note:** Ensure that the **Use Relative References** command is highlighted in orange, indicating it is active.

3. Begin recording the macro.
   a) Select **Developer→Code→Record Macro**.
   b) In the **Record Macro** dialog box, in the **Macro name** field, type *AddFormControl*
   c) In the **Shortcut key** section, place the insertion point in the field to the right of the **Ctrl+** text.
   d) Press **Shift+C**.

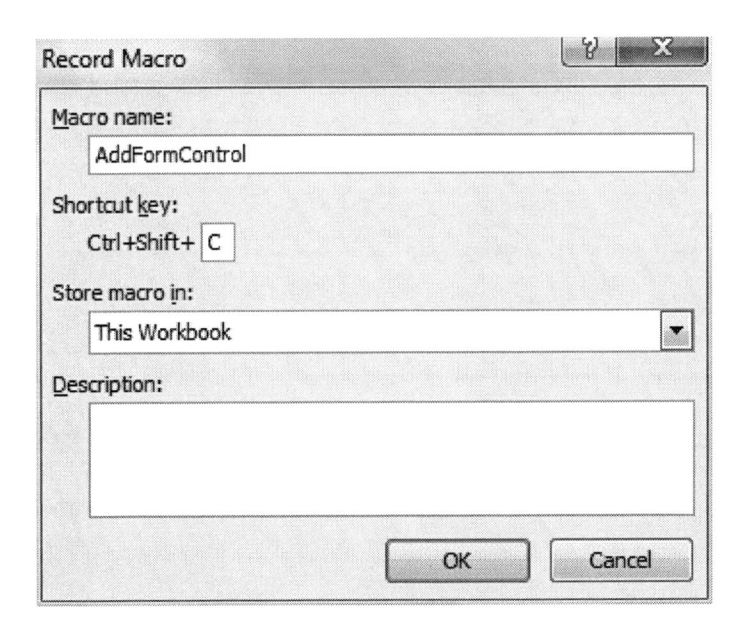

   e) From the **Store macro in** drop-down menu, ensure that **This Workbook** is selected.
   f) In the **Description** field, type *Enters a combo box and text labels at the selected cell.*
   g) Select **OK**.

4. Now that recording is active, record the macro steps.

a) Ensure that cell **A6** is still selected and type *Look Up Author Income*
b) Press **Enter** twice and type *AuthorID*
c) Press **Enter**, type *Income* and press **Ctrl+Enter**.
d) Select cell **B8**.
e) Select **Developer→Controls→Insert→Combo Box (Form Control)**.
f) Draw the form control on top of cell **B8**.
g) With the form control still selected, select **Developer→Controls→Properties**.
h) In the **Format Control** dialog box, ensure that the **Control** tab is selected.
i) In the **Input range** field, type *AuthorID*
j) In the **Cell link** field, type *B8*
k) Change the value in the **Drop down lines** field to *10* and select **OK**.
l) Select cell **C8**.
m) Select **Developer→Code→Stop Recording**.

5. Save the workbook as a macro-enabled workbook.
   a) Select **File→Save As**.
   b) From the **Save as type** drop-down menu, select **Excel Macro-Enabled Workbook (*.xlsm)** and select **Save**.

6. Select cell **A11** and press **Ctrl+Shift+C** to test the macro to ensure it works as expected.

   Note: Although it may, at first, appear that Excel did not add the combo box to the worksheet, this is not the case. You will discover in the next step what happened.

7. Right-click the combo box in cell **B8**, and then left-click and drag it to cell **B13**.

   Note: You will have to select the worksheet outside of the drop-down menu to close it before dragging the combo box.

8. Deselect the combo box and select an author ID from its drop-down menu.

9. Save the workbook.

ACTIVITY 3-5
Editing a Macro

Before You Begin
The my_author_master_roster.xlsm workbook file is open.

Scenario
Your macro is almost working as expected, but there are a few adjustments you need to make. Specifically, you want the macro to enter default, placeholder label text because the various dashboard controls will be used to determine a variety of information (not just author income) and you want the macro to enter all new combo boxes relative tp the new labels and for each combo box to be independent of the others. You decide to edit the macro's VBA code to make the corrections.

1. Select the range **A6:B14** and press **Delete**.

2. Right-click and delete the combo boxes in cells **B8** and **B13**. If necessary, delete any remaining values.

3. Open the **AddFormControl** macro in the Visual Basic Editor.
   a) Select **Developer→Code→Macros**.
   b) In the **Macro** dialog box, in the **Macro name** list, ensure that **AddFormControl** is selected and then select **Edit**.
   c) Verify that the macro opened in the Visual Basic Editor.

4. In the **my_author_master_roster.xlsx - Module1 (Code)** window, revise the text the macro inserts into cells.
   a) Below the **Keyboard Shortcut: Ctrl+Shift+C** text, change the second line of code to:
   ```
   ActiveCell.FormulaR1C1 = "Look Up <desired value>"
   ```
   > **Note:** The text you are replacing in the code here is part of the text the macro will enter in cells when run. The new text is simple placeholder text. In a real-world situation, this would cue a workbook user to change the text labels the macro creates based on what information the combo box is meant to look up.

   b) Change the seventh line of code to:
   ```
   Selection.FormulaR1C1 = "<desired value>"
   ```

5. Revise the macro code so Excel places the combo box in the desired location relative to the text the macro adds to the worksheet.
   a) Locate the following line of code (line 9):
   ```
   ActiveSheet.DropDowns.Add(115.5, 104.25, 48, 15.75).Select
   ```
   > **Note:** The values you see in this line of code may vary slightly from what you see in the book. This is because you manually drew the form control when recording the macro. It's likely that most people will have slightly different values here.

   b) Change the code to:
   ```
   ActiveSheet.DropDowns.Add ActiveCell.Left, ActiveCell.Top, ActiveCell.Width, ActiveCell.Height
   ```

6. Revise the macro code so Excel doesn't link the combo boxes to the same cell.
   a) Locate the following line of code (line 10):
   ```
   With Selection
   ```
   b) Change the code to:
   ```
   With ActiveSheet.DropDowns(ActiveSheet.DropDowns.Count)
   ```
   c) Locate the following line of code (line 12):
   ```
   .LinkedCell = "B8"
   ```
   d) Change the code to:
   ```
   .LinkedCell = ActiveCell.Offset(0, 0).Address
   ```

7. Press **Ctrl+S** to save the changes to the macro code and then close the Visual Basic Editor.

   ```
   Sub AddFormControl()
   '
   ' AddFormControl Macro
   ' Enters a combo box and text labels at the selected cell.
   '
   ' Keyboard Shortcut: Ctrl+Shift+C
   '
       Selection.NumberFormat = "General"
       ActiveCell.FormulaR1C1 = "Look Up <desired value>"
       ActiveCell.Offset(2, 0).Range("A1").Select
       Selection.NumberFormat = "General"
       ActiveCell.FormulaR1C1 = "AuthorID"
       ActiveCell.Offset(1, 0).Range("A1").Select
       Selection.FormulaR1C1 = "<desired value>"
       ActiveCell.Offset(-1, 1).Range("A1").Select
       ActiveSheet.DropDowns.Add ActiveCell.Left, ActiveCell.Top, ActiveCell.Width, ActiveCell.Height
       With ActiveSheet.DropDowns(ActiveSheet.DropDowns.Count)
           .ListFillRange = "AuthorID"
           .LinkedCell = ActiveCell.Offset(0, 0).Address
           .DropDownLines = 10
           .Display3DShading = False
   ```

8. Run the macro to ensure it behaves as expected.
   a) Select cell **A6** and then press **Ctrl+Shift+C**.

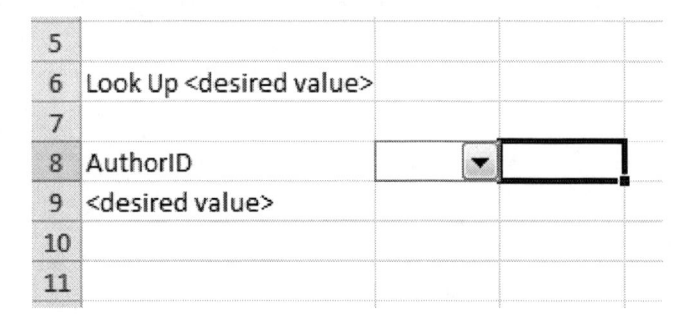

	A	B		
5				
6	Look Up <desired value>			
7				
8	AuthorID	▼		
9	<desired value>			
10				
11				

   b) Select cell **A11** and then run the macro.
   c) Select the down arrow in the combo box located in front of cell **B13** and then select any author ID.

d) Ensure the combo box located in front of cell **B8** remains empty.

5		
6	Look Up <desired value>	
7		
8	AuthorID	▼
9	<desired value>	
10		
11	Look Up <desired value>	
12		
13	AuthorID	1006 ▼
14	<desired value>	

9. Select the range **A11:B14**, press **Delete**, and then delete the combo box in front of cell **B13**.

10. Save and close the workbook.

Summary

In this lesson, you automated workbook functionality to save time and effort, and to maintain the data integrity of your workbooks. Even the most well-designed and complex workbooks are useless if you can't trust the data they contain and if users simply can't or don't want to use them. By taking advantage of Excel's automation functionality, you'll be able to relax knowing the analysis you generate from your workbooks provides sound organizational intelligence. Your workbook users just may thank you for making it easy for them to provide you with the information you need.

What, if anything, surprised you about the level of automation Excel is capable of?

Can you think of a past task that automation would have made easier, saving you time and effort?

> **Note:** Check your LogicalCHOICE Course screen for opportunities to interact with your classmates, peers, and the larger LogicalCHOICE online community about the topics covered in this course or other topics you are interested in. From the Course screen you can also access available resources for a more continuous learning experience.

4 Applying Conditional Logic

Lesson Time: 1 hour, 10 minutes

Lesson Objectives

In this lesson, you will apply conditional logic. You will:

- Use Lookup functions.
- Combine functions.
- Use logical and lookup functions to apply conditional formatting.

Lesson Introduction

Excel's formulas and functions provide you with a robust set of options for performing complex calculations on the data in your workbooks. But on their own, they may not always perform the precise calculations you need them to. For example, you may need a function to reference a value from another dataset based on some particular criteria. How do you tell the function how to look that up? Or perhaps you need one of your arguments to be the result of another formula or function. Although you could always enter that formula or function in another cell and then simply include a reference to that cell as an argument in the original function, this could quickly take up a lot of real estate on your worksheet, which isn't always desirable.

Excel provides you with a number of options for dealing with these and many other situations. But doing so requires an understanding of a new set of Excel functions, Lookup functions, and a deeper understanding of function syntax. By investing the time it takes to elevate your understanding of how these functions work and how they work together, you'll begin to develop the ability to create incredibly complex functions and formulas that can perform any number of calculations. In short, you'll begin to understand how to, essentially, program Excel to perform tasks there are no built-in functions to perform.

TOPIC A

Use Lookup Functions

So, you've collected a massive amount of data about your operations, upon which you can perform an amazing variety of analysis. But what if you want quick access to just a particular bit of data? In some cases, you may be able to search for it. But suppose you don't know what the value is. For example, what if you need to find out who employee 1287's manager is or in which region he or she works? If you don't know the answer you're looking for, you don't know what search criteria to enter. Or perhaps you need to enter the total number of units sold for a particular product into a formula. Although you could search for the product and look up the value yourself, you wouldn't want to do this for multiple products over and over.

Fortunately, Excel 2010 enables you to look up such values, even in massive datasets, with relative ease. By using a set of functions known as Lookup functions, you'll be able to look up or include in a formula any one particular entry in any dataset. This level of functionality can quickly give you a detailed view of how any one individual value contributes to the overall operation of your organization. This can help you make clear, informed decisions that affect large-scale operations based on just a single chunk of data.

Lookup Functions

In Excel, Lookup functions do exactly what you'd think they would: They look up some value. Specifically, Lookup functions search through a particular dataset to return a particular value based on some criteria. Take a look at this simple example of how you might use a Lookup function.

	A	B	C	D	E
1	Employee ID	Dept.	Region	Manager	Salary
2	1001	ENG	NE	Jones, M	$85,000.00
3	1002	PDV	S	Allie, S	$65,000.00
4	1003	SLS	W	Phillips, T	Comm
5	1004	ENG	S	Martinez, V	$76,000.00
6	1005	TRS	NE	Chan, A	$43,000.00
7	1006	PDV	NE	Shinto, K	$58,000.00
8	1007	SLS	S	Oriz, V	Comm
9	1008	SLS	W	Martin, C	Comm
10	1009	MGT	NE	Tallis, D	$87,000.00
11	1010	ITS	S	Toner, R	$72,000.00
12					
13	Employee ID	1004			
14	Salary	$76,000.00			

In this example, the Lookup function is looking up employee 1004's salary. A lookup function can identify the range **A2:E11**, search down column **A** until it finds **1004**, and then look across the row to the **Salary** column to return the result $76,000. Lookup functions can perform other tasks as well. For example, they can look across a row to find the lookup value, and then count down rows to return another value. They can return a value in the equivalent location as another value in separate ranges. Or, they can return a value's place in a range.

The particular Lookup function in the given example, which is in cell **B14**, references cell **B13**. So, for any employee ID a user enters, the function will return the salary. And, to add another level of functionality, you could add a data validation drop-down list in cell **B13** to create a dashboard tool that looks up the salary for any selected ID. Now, take this one step further and assume cell **B14** is an argument in another function that performs some calculation based on the returned salary, say the employee's bonus for the year. It's easy to see how quickly a simple Lookup function can add complexity and functionality that produces valuable results.

As is the case with all Excel functions, the key to leveraging Lookup functions is understanding function syntax. Let's take a look at the syntax for some of the most commonly used Lookup functions.

The VLOOKUP Function

Syntax: =VLOOKUP(lookup_value, table_array, col_index_num, [range_lookup])

Description: You can use the VLOOKUP function to search down the first column of a dataset to find a specified value and then return any value in any column in the row that contains the specified value. Here is a description of the function's arguments.

VLOOKUP Function Argument	Description
lookup_value	This is the value the function will search for in the first column of the specified dataset. The **lookup_value** argument can either be a hard-coded value or a reference to the value in another cell.
table_array	This argument specifies the dataset the VLOOKUP function searches. This argument can be a range reference, a defined name, or an array constant.
col_index_num	This argument is a positive whole number that specifies the column number from the dataset that the function will return a value from. If you enter 3, the function returns the value in the third column that is in the same row as the lookup value. If you enter a 4, it returns the value from the fourth column of the same row. Note that if you enter 1 for this argument, the function will return the lookup value itself as that is the value in the first column of the specified dataset.
[range_lookup]	This is an optional argument that determines whether the function looks for an exact match of the lookup value or an approximate equivalent. If you enter the value FALSE for this argument, the function will look for only exact matches. If you omit this argument or enter a value of TRUE, the function will look for either an exact match or an approximate match. An approximate match is the largest value that is less than the value of the lookup value. If the **[range-lookup]** argument is FALSE, the values in the first column (the one containing the lookup value) do not need to be sorted. In all other cases, they must be sorted in ascending order.

Note: When the lookup value in the first column is a text label, it's a best practice to enter the **[range_lookup]** argument as FALSE. This will only return a value based on an exact match. And, if you hard code the **lookup_value** argument, as opposed to using a cell reference, you must enclose the text string in double quotation marks (" ").

Note: Like with most logical values, you can simply enter 1 for TRUE or 0 for FALSE in the **[range_lookup]** argument.

Examples: For the following examples, refer to this simple dataset.

	A	B	C	D	E
1	Employee ID	Dept.	Region	Manager	Salary
2	1001	ENG	NE	Jones, M	$85,000.00
3	1002	PDV	S	Allie, S	$65,000.00
4	1003	SLS	W	Phillips, T	Comm
5	1004	ENG	S	Martinez, V	$76,000.00
6	1005	TRS	NE	Chan, A	$43,000.00
7	1006	PDV	NE	Shinto, K	$58,000.00
8	1007	SLS	S	Oriz, V	Comm
9	1008	SLS	W	Martin, C	Comm
10	1009	MGT	NE	Tallis, D	$87,000.00
11	1010	ITS	S	Toner, R	$72,000.00

To Return This Value	Enter This Function
$43,000.00	=VLOOKUP(1005, A2:E11,5)
S	=VLOOKUP(1002, A2:E11,3)
Toner, R	=VLOOKUP(1010, Employee_ID,4)
	This example assumes the dataset has been assigned the defined name Employee_ID.

The HLOOKUP Function

Syntax: =HLOOKUP(lookup_value, table_array, row_index_num, [range_lookup])

> **Note:** You will likely find yourself using the VLOOKUP function far more often than the HLOOKUP function, as most datasets are configured with individual records in rows.

Description: You can use the HLOOKUP function to search across the first row of a dataset to find a specified value, and then return any value in any row in the column that contains the specified value. Here is a description of the function's arguments.

HLOOKUP Function Argument	Description
lookup_value	This is the value the function will search for in the first row of the specified dataset. The **lookup_value** argument can either be a hard-coded value or a reference to the value in another cell.
table_array	This argument specifies the dataset the HLOOKUP function searches. This argument can be a range reference, a defined name, or an array constant.
row_index_num	This argument is a positive whole number that specifies the row number from the dataset that the function will return a value from. If you enter 3, the function returns the value in the third row that is in the same column as the lookup value. If you enter a 4, it returns the value from the fourth row of the same column. Note that if you enter 1 for this argument, the function will return the lookup value itself, as that is the value in the first row of the specified dataset.

HLOOKUP Function Argument	Description
[range_lookup]	This is an optional argument that determines whether the function looks for an exact match of the lookup value or an approximate equivalent. If you enter the value FALSE for this argument, the function will look for only exact matches. If you omit this argument or enter a value of TRUE, the function will look for either an exact match or an approximate match. An approximate match is the largest value that is less than the value of the lookup value. If the **[range_lookup]** argument is FALSE, the values in the first row (the one containing the lookup value) do not need to be sorted. In all other cases, they must be sorted in ascending order.

Note: When the lookup value in the first row is a text label, it's a best practice to enter the **[range_lookup]** argument as FALSE. This will only return a value based on an exact match. And if you hard code the **lookup_value** argument, as opposed to using a cell reference, you must enclose the text string in double quotation marks (" ").

Note: As with most logical values, you can simply enter 1 for TRUE or 0 for FALSE in the **[range_lookup]** argument.

Examples: The following examples refer to this simple dataset.

	A	B	C	D	E	F
1	Rep	Qtr 1	Qtr 2	Qtr 3	Qtr 4	Total
2	Smith, A	$4,513.00	$2,488.00	$2,191.00	$5,953.00	$15,145.00
3	Jones, T	$2,946.00	$2,324.00	$3,643.00	$3,588.00	$12,501.00
4	Rios, J	$1,526.00	$5,232.00	$6,163.00	$3,739.00	$16,660.00
5	Chan, P	$4,422.00	$2,620.00	$2,009.00	$3,941.00	$12,992.00
6	Parker, L	$1,763.00	$6,869.00	$6,940.00	$3,233.00	$18,805.00
7	Rossi, D	$2,663.00	$6,218.00	$4,602.00	$3,114.00	$16,597.00
8	Sanchez, M	$5,623.00	$3,787.00	$3,868.00	$6,017.00	$19,295.00
9	Torres, M	$6,589.00	$6,670.00	$6,075.00	$6,865.00	$26,199.00
10	Anderson, C	$5,455.00	$6,868.00	$6,725.00	$5,463.00	$24,511.00
11	Lamott, S	$5,535.00	$4,342.00	$3,623.00	$1,784.00	$15,284.00

To Return This Value	Enter This Function
$2,191.00	=HLOOKUP("Qtr 3", A1:F11, 2, FALSE)
Parker, L	=HLOOKUP("Smith, A", A2:F11, 5, 0)
$15,284.00	=HLOOKUP(15145, A2:F11, 10)

The MATCH Function

Syntax: =MATCH(lookup_value, lookup_array, [match_type])

Description: This function returns the numerical representation of a value's place within a single-row or a single-column range. For example, consider this list: blue, red, green, orange, yellow. If you enter this list in a range of cells and then ask the MATCH function to look up "orange," it will return the value 4 because "orange" is the fourth item in the list. This function is often used to return, for example, an item's row number for use as an argument in other Lookup functions. Here is a description of the function's arguments.

MATCH Function Argument	Description
lookup_value	This is the value the function will search for in the specified range. The **lookup_value** argument can be either a hard-coded value or a reference to a cell containing a value. If you are entering a text string for this argument, you must enclose the value in double quotation marks (" ").
lookup_array	This argument specifies the range the function will search. This must represent a single row or a single column of values that may have to be sorted in either ascending or descending order to avoid errors.
[match_type]	This argument determines whether the MATCH function looks for an exact match to the lookup value or an approximate match. This function has three possible values: –1, 0, and 1. • The value 1 tells the function to look for the largest value that is less than or equal to the lookup value. If you enter this value for the **[match_type]** argument, the values in the **lookup_array** argument must be sorted in ascending order. 1 is the default value for this argument, so it's the same as omitting the argument entirely. • The value 0 tells the function to look only for an exact match of the lookup value. In this case, the values do not need to be sorted in any particular order. • The value –1 tells the function to look for the smallest value that is greater than or equal to the lookup value. If you enter this value for the **[match_type]** argument, the values in the **lookup-array** argument must be sorted in descending order.

Examples: The following examples refer to this simple dataset.

	A	B	C	D	E	F
1	Rep	Qtr 1	Qtr 2	Qtr 3	Qtr 4	Total
2	Anderson, C	$1,526.00	$2,324.00	$6,725.00	$5,463.00	$16,038.00
3	Chan, P	$1,763.00	$2,488.00	$2,009.00	$3,941.00	$10,201.00
4	Jones, T	$2,663.00	$2,620.00	$3,643.00	$3,588.00	$12,514.00
5	Lamott, S	$2,946.00	$3,787.00	$3,623.00	$1,784.00	$12,140.00
6	Parker, L	$4,422.00	$4,342.00	$6,940.00	$3,233.00	$18,937.00
7	Rios, J	$4,513.00	$5,232.00	$6,163.00	$3,739.00	$19,647.00
8	Rossi, D	$5,455.00	$6,218.00	$4,602.00	$3,114.00	$19,389.00
9	Sanchez, M	$5,535.00	$6,670.00	$3,868.00	$6,017.00	$22,090.00
10	Smith, A	$5,623.00	$6,868.00	$2,191.00	$6,000.00	$20,682.00
11	Torres, M	$6,589.00	$6,869.00	$6,075.00	$6,865.00	$26,398.00

To Return This Value	Enter This Function
5	=MATCH("Parker, L", A2:A11, 0)
6	=MATCH("Rios, J", A2:A11, 0)

The INDEX Function

Syntax: =INDEX(array, row_number, [column_name])

> **Note:** The syntax presented here is for the array form of the INDEX function. There is also a less commonly used version of the INDEX function called the reference form. The reference form of this function returns a cell reference as opposed to a particular value. You can review the reference form's syntax in Excel Help or at Office.com.

Description: The INDEX function returns the value in a particular row and/or column of a given range of cells. If the specified range of cells contains both multiple rows and columns, you must specify both a row and a column for the function to search. In these cases, the INDEX function returns the value at the intersection of the specified row and column. If the specified range of cells represents a single row, you need only specify a column reference (all of the cells are in the same row). The opposite is true of a range that represents only a single column. Here is a description of the function's arguments.

INDEX Function Argument	Description
array	This argument specifies the dataset that the function will search.
row_number	This argument is a positive whole number that specifies the row number from the specified dataset the function will look in.
[column_name]	This argument is a positive whole number that specifies the column number from the specified dataset the function will look in.

> **Note:** Although the INDEX function's syntax indicates the **row_number** argument is required and the **[column_name]** argument is optional, this isn't necessarily true. When the dataset specified in the **array** argument contains multiple rows and multiple columns, both arguments are required. If the dataset is a single row, only the **[column_name]** argument is required. If the dataset is a single column, only the **row_number** argument is required.

Examples: The following examples refer to this simple dataset, which tracks the number of paid days off each employee takes per year.

	A	B	C	D	E	F
1	Employee	2008	2009	2010	2011	2012
2	Anderson, C	10	18	19	19	14
3	Chan, P	15	16	17	16	10
4	Jones, T	16	12	20	15	13
5	Lamott, S	16	20	18	20	12
6	Parker, L	13	11	11	18	10
7	Rios, J	18	11	14	20	20
8	Rossi, D	19	11	18	19	17
9	Sanchez, M	14	15	11	17	19
10	Smith, A	11	12	20	10	11
11	Torres, M	13	16	13	20	10

To Return This Value	Enter This Function
Rios, J	=INDEX(A1:A11, 7)
11	=INDEX(A1:F11,9,4)
20	=INDEX(A4:F4,4)

> **Note:** For information on how to use the MATCH and the INDEX function together to return cell entries, watch the LearnTO **Combine Excel's MATCH and INDEX Functions to Look Up Data** presentation from the **LearnTO** tile on the LogicalCHOICE Course screen.

> **Access the Checklist tile on your LogicalCHOICE course screen for reference information and job aids on How to Use Lookup Functions.**

ACTIVITY 4-1
Using Lookup Functions

Data File
C:\091020Data\Applying Conditional Logic\author_master_roster_04.xlsm

Before You Begin
Excel 2010 is open.

Scenario
You continue to develop your author master roster workbook. Now that the macro for adding form controls is working properly, you can begin adding INDEX functions so users can look up author information. Because the combo boxes you've already added return only an entry reference, you realize you'll also need to use other Lookup functions to give users all of the functionality they will need. Specifically, you wish to add functions that:

- Look up total income by author.
- Look up total number of books sold by author.
- Look up the average income per title by author.

You have already added some of the necessary labels and cell formatting to accommodate the new entries.

---

1. Open the **author_master_roster_04.xlsm** workbook and ensure that the **Authors** worksheet is selected.

2. Define a name for the entire dataset on the **Authors** worksheet.
   a) In the **Name Box**, type **A2:Q900** and then press **Enter**.

   > **Note:** The named range will include a number of empty rows to accommodate future entries. This includes the same number of rows as the existing named ranges for the columns.

   b) Select **Formulas→Defined Names→Define Name**.
   c) In the **New Name** dialog box, in the **Name** field, type *Author_Dataset*
   d) Ensure that the scope is set to **Workbook**.
   e) In the **Refers to** field, ensure that the reference is entered as **=Authors!$A$2:$Q$900**
   f) Select **OK**.

3. Enter an INDEX function so users can quickly look up the total income generated by any author.
   a) Select the **Author_Dashboard** worksheet.
   b) From the combo box in front of cell **B3**, select author ID **1005**.
   c) Select cell **B4** and enter the following function: *=INDEX(Author_Dataset,B3,14)*

   f_x =INDEX(Author_Dataset,B3, 14)

   d) Adjust the width of column **B** to accommodate the value and then left-align the text in all cells in column **B**.

> **Note:** This will re-hide the entry reference returned by the combo box.

    e) Verify that Excel returned **$4,227,628.85** as the total income for author **1005**.

    f) Select several other author IDs from the combo box and ensure that the INDEX function returns the correct results.

4. Enter an INDEX function so users can quickly look up the number of books an author has sold.
   a) On the **Author_Dashboard** worksheet, change the text in cell **A6** to *Look Up No. Books Sold*
   b) Change the text in cell **A9** to *No. Books Sold*
   c) Select author ID **1005** from the combo box in front of cell **B8**.
   d) Select cell **B9** and enter the following function: *=INDEX(Author_Dataset,B8,12)*
   e) Ensure that Excel returned **529,115** as the total number of books sold for author **1005**.

5. Enter a VLOOKUP function so users can quickly look up the average income per title for any author.
   a) Select cell **B14** and enter the following function: *=VLOOKUP(B13,Author_Dataset,15)*
   b) Select author ID **1005** from the drop-down list in cell **B13**.

   > **Note:** As the named range **AuthorID** was used to define the criteria for the data validation drop-down menu, there will be a number of empty cells at the bottom of the list. You may need to scroll up in the drop-down list to view the author IDs.

   c) Verify that Excel returns the value **$169,105.15** in cell **B14**.

6. Save the workbook to the **C:\091020Data\Applying Conditional Logic** folder as *my_author_master_roster_04.xlsm* and close the file.

TOPIC B

Combine Functions

Excel functions and formulas provide you with an incredible array of options for performing calculations on your worksheets. But, as you may have already noticed, they aren't always exactly what you need, and sometimes, they just aren't capable of performing the task you want them to. For example, you know how to use an IF function to produce two different results based on a logical test. But, what if you want to include more than one logical test? What if there are a dozen or more? Or, suppose you need to use the values returned by several different functions as arguments in another function.

These may at first seem like difficult challenges to overcome. You may think you need to use a variety of functions in a variety of cells, and then include references to the results in other formulas to pull this off. But that's not really the case. Excel 2010 has the capability to consider multiple functions or calculations simultaneously, and to do so within just a single cell. Once you begin to understand one simple concept, you'll be able to start cobbling together highly complex functions and formulas that can perform a sophisticated, powerful set of calculations based on a wide variety of criteria.

Nesting

The key to combining multiple calculations into a function in a single cell is *nesting*. Nesting is, simply, using a function as an argument within another function. Whatever value the nested function returns becomes the value the main function uses for the argument. This works much like including a reference to the value in a cell in a formula or function. Nesting enables you to craft highly complex functions that perform a wide variety of calculations or perform multiple logical tests in order to achieve a single result in a single cell.

Excel enables you to nest more than one function within the same larger function, and you can nest functions within nested functions. In fact, Excel 2010 supports up to 64 levels of nesting. A function nested within another function is referred to as a second-level function. A function nested within the nested function is called a third-level function, and so on.

=IF(A1>100,SUM(A1:A10),A1*10)

(Main function / Nested function)

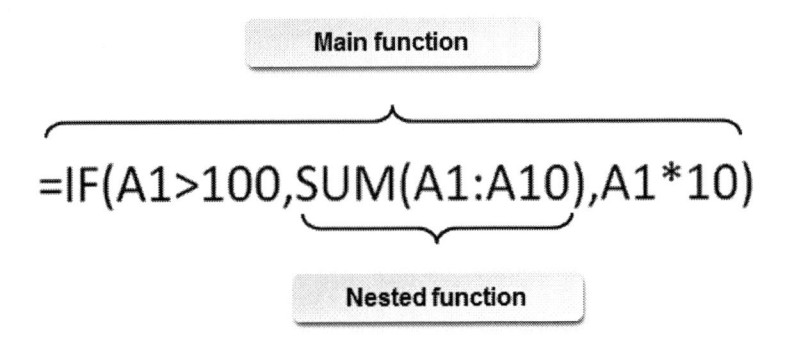

Figure 4-1: *Nesting enables you to use the value returned by one function as an argument in another function.*

Nested Function Syntax

As is the case with all other Excel functions, the key to understanding nested functions is understanding nested function syntax. Because the particular syntax of any one nested function depends on the particular syntax of the first-level function and all of the other functions you wish to nest, this section will mainly focus on presenting a couple of examples of nested functions and then breaking down the syntax into chunks to examine the specific calculation.

Before looking at a few examples, however, there are some important points to keep in mind regarding nested functions:

- Any function used as an argument must return a value of the same data type as the argument.
- You do not include the equal sign (=) before a nested function, but all remaining function syntax is the same as it usually is for the function. You still must include the equal sign before the first-level function.
- Each function, both the first-level function and all nested functions, must have a complete set of parentheses. These can become tricky to track, but they must all be present.

Now, let's take a look at two examples.

In this first example, the user is trying to determine if members of a group of sales reps qualify for a bonus. The bonus is based on meeting two criteria, having sales greater than $3,000 and having sold more than 2,000 units of product. It's easy to use an IF function to determine whether or not someone qualifies for a bonus based on a single criteria, but what about two criteria? For this, you'll need to nest an AND function within an IF function.

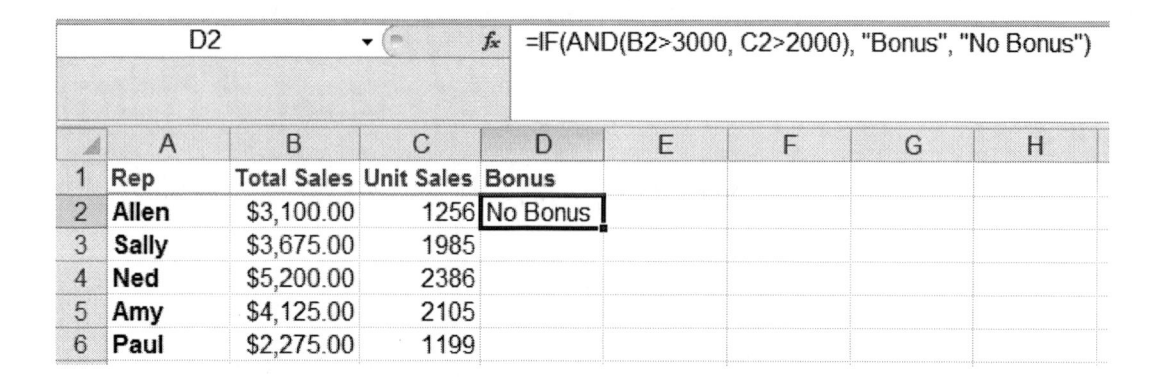

	D2		fx	=IF(AND(B2>3000, C2>2000), "Bonus", "No Bonus")

	A	B	C	D
1	Rep	Total Sales	Unit Sales	Bonus
2	Allen	$3,100.00	1256	No Bonus
3	Sally	$3,675.00	1985	
4	Ned	$5,200.00	2386	
5	Amy	$4,125.00	2105	
6	Paul	$2,275.00	1199	

Here, the AND function is being used as the **logical_test** argument in the IF function. So the logical test includes both conditions stipulated by the AND function. As Allen has met only one of the conditions set out in the AND function, the IF function returns a value of FALSE. Remember that the **logical_test** argument can be either a logical test or a logical value. As the argument evaluates to the logical value FALSE, the IF function returns the **value_if_false** value, which in this case is "No Bonus."

> **Note:** Note that the AND function contains a complete set of parentheses and is fully contained within the space between the IF function's opening parenthesis and the IF function's first comma. This makes sense, as the entire AND function is the IF function's first argument. The IF function ignores the comma within the AND function's parentheses as it is only looking for the value returned by the AND function.

In this second example, the user is calculating commission payments for a group of sales reps. But the particular commission rate depends on the sales volume generated by each rep. If the rep's sales are less than $2,000, he or she receives a 5-percent commission. If sales are between $2,000 and $4,999, the commission rate is 7 percent. If sales are $5,000 or more, the rep receives a 9-percent commission. If this were only a matter of two different rates, a simple IF function would suffice. But how do you add the second logical test? You nest one IF function within another.

	A	B	C	D	E	F	G	H
1	Rep	Sales	Commission	Total				
2	Allen	$2,500.00	$175.00	$2,675.00				
3	Sally	$3,675.00		$3,675.00				
4	Ned	$5,200.00		$5,200.00				
5	Amy	$4,125.00		$4,125.00				
6	Paul	$2,275.00		$2,275.00				

Cell C2: =IF(B2<2000, B2*0.05, IF(B2<5000, B2*0.07, B2*0.09))

Let's break down the function's syntax. If this had been a case of applying one of two commission rates, say either 5 or 7 percent, the function could have looked like this:

=IF(B2<2000, B2*0.05, B2*0.07)

But there is a third condition. Instead of telling Excel to multiply any value greater than $2,000 by a single value, you have to specify a second logical test. This second logical test, on its own, would typically look something like this:

=IF(B2<5000, B2*0.07, B2*0.09).

This function should be included as the third argument in the original function, without the leading equal sign, to get this:

=IF(B2<2000, B2*0.05, IF(B2<5000, B2*0.07, B2*0.09))

If you were to read this function aloud, it would sound something like, "If the value in cell B2 is less than 2,000, then multiply it by 5 percent; if the value is less than 5,000, multiply it by 7 percent; otherwise, multiply it by 9 percent." You do not need to include a logical argument for the value being greater than or equal to 5,000 as the first two logical arguments already include all values that don't match that description.

It is easy to see how nesting can quickly become highly complex. If you break the first-level function and all nested functions down into chunks and carefully think about what each function's syntax is asking Excel to do, you can read or write nearly any combination of nested functions.

Guidelines for Combining Functions

> **Note:** All of the Guidelines for this lesson are available as checklists from the **Checklist** tile on the LogicalCHOICE Course screen.

As long as you understand the syntax of all functions you wish to nest, you can combine up to seven levels of functions within a single first-level function. You must also carefully follow these guidelines:

- To nest a function within another, include the nested function as an argument in the first-level function. Subsequent, lower-level functions can be nested within the nested function(s).
- You must include the equal sign (=) for the first-level function.
- Do not include an equal sign for any of the nested functions. The rest of the syntax for all nested functions remains the same.
- All functions, nested or otherwise, must include a full set of parentheses.
- Higher-level functions ignore the commas within the parentheses of nested functions. Those commas separate only the arguments for the associated function.
- Any function used as an argument must return a value of the same data type as the argument.
- You can combine nested functions and other calculations within a single argument. For example, an argument that needs to be a numeric value can be made up of a function multiplied by a constant or by the value in a cell.
- You can include more than one nested function within a single argument.

ACTIVITY 4-2
Combining Functions

Data File
C:\091020Data\Applying Conditional Logic\author_master_roster_04a.xlsm

Before You Begin
Excel 2010 is open.

Scenario
You are pleased with the progress of your author dashboard, but there are some figures you'd like users to be able look up that require more complex functions. You realize you will need to use nested functions to achieve this functionality. One item of particular importance is a new author bonus initiative you started. As a one-time reward for authors whose work consistently generates significant income, Fuller and Ackerman (F&A) will pay authors their royalty rate times their average income per title. Because you already have a dashboard function that looks up income per title, you decide to link that result to the function that calculates the bonus royalty for all qualifying authors. The threshold F&A management has set for your bonus program is $500,000 in income per title.

Additionally, F&A would like to reward newer authors whose titles are generating more than $1,000,000 each. This additional bonus will be awarded to authors who meet this threshold and who have been with the company for four years or less. As the dashboard is beginning to grow, you have started formatting some of the cells to make the worksheet easier to read. You have also already added and formatted some of the necessary text labels for the bonus information.

---

1. Open the **author_master_roster_04a.xlsm** workbook file and ensure that the **Author_Dashboard** worksheet tab is selected.

2. Enter the following function in cell **B15** to look up an author's number of years under contract: *=VLOOKUP(B13,Author_Dataset,3)*

3. Enter a nested function in cell **D13** that returns the appropriate bonus for the author selected in cell **B13**.
   a) Select cell **D13** and enter the following function: *=IF(B14>500000, ,0)*

   > fx   =IF(B14>500000, ,0)

   b) To enter a nested VLOOKUP function as the second argument to perform the bonus calculation for eligible authors, between the two commas, type *B14*VLOOKUP(B13,Author_Dataset,16)*

   > **Note:** Remember to not type the equal sign (=) for the nested function.

   c) Press **Ctrl+Enter**.

   > fx   =IF(B14>500000,B14*VLOOKUP(B13,Author_Dataset,16),0)

4. Test the function to verify that it works as expected.
   a) From the drop-down menu in cell **B13**, select author ID **1016**.

    b) Adjust the width of column **D**.
    c) Verify that Excel returned the value **$46,908.36** in cell **D13**.

5. Enter a nested function in cell **D14** that returns the appropriate additional bonus for the author selected in cell **B13**.
    a) Select cell **D14**.
    b) Type *=IF(AND(B14>1000000,B15<4),5000,0)* and press **Ctrl+Enter**.

    f_x | =IF(AND(B14>1000000,B15<4),5000,0)

6. Test the function to verify that it works as expected.
    a) From the drop-down menu in cell **B13**, select author ID **1129**.
    b) Verify that Excel returned the value **$5,000** in cell **D14**.
    c) If necessary, adjust the width of column **D** to accommodate all of the data.

7. Add a SUM function in cell **D15** to add the values in cells **D13** and **D14**.

8. Save the workbook to the **C:\091020Data\Applying Conditional Logic** folder as *my_author_master_roster_04a.xlsm* and then close the workbook.

TOPIC C

Use Formulas and Functions to Apply Conditional Formatting

Applying conditional formatting to worksheets is a convenient way to help users quickly make sense of the data in a particular column. But applying conditional formatting by using some of the more common methods can be limiting. Many users simply apply conditional formatting to the same range of cells they ask Excel to evaluate. But, what if you want Excel to examine and evaluate the data in one column, but then apply the specified conditional formatting to another column? Or, suppose you wish to format the cells in numerous columns based on criteria in a different column.

You might want to do this, for example, if you wish to highlight the names of employees who have achieved a certain goal or who have been with the company for some period of time. If you want to keep your data and formatting clean and intact, applying the conditional formatting in the name column would be a perfect way to quickly be able to tell who meets the criteria while keeping the data columns unchanged. Is this even possible? The answer is yes, but you have to combine your knowledge of conditional formatting with your knowledge of Excel functions to do so. Taking the time to grasp how this works will open a whole new world of possibilities when it comes to using visual cues to analyze data.

The Use a Formula to Determine Which Cells to Format Option

Typically, when you apply conditional formatting to a range of cells, say a particular column of data, you're asking Excel to evaluate the entries in that range and then apply the specified formatting to any cell that meets some specified criteria. Any of the basic, preconfigured conditional formatting rules and most of the rules available in the **New Formatting Rule** dialog box are well suited to performing this task. But applying formatting to cells based on the data entered in other cells will require the use of formulas or functions. This means you'll need to select the **Use a formula to determine which cells to format** option in the **New Formatting Rule** dialog box when you go to define the conditional formatting rule.

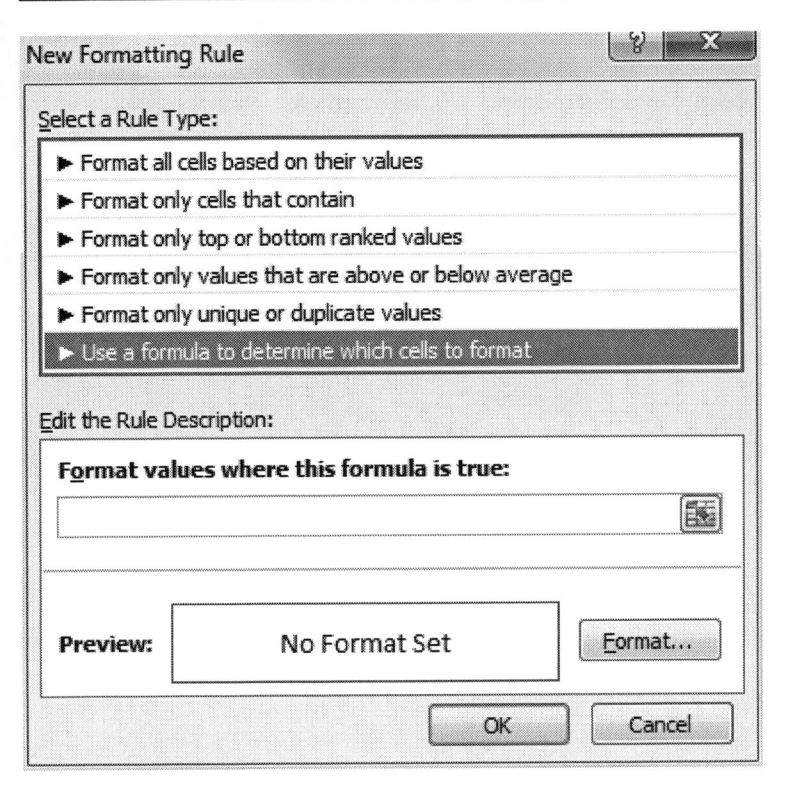

Figure 4-2: Excel enables you to define your own custom rules for the application of conditional formatting.

This option is, essentially, an IF function that Excel uses to determine which cells to apply formatting to. Excel treats any formula or function you enter in the **Format values where this formula is true** field like the **logical_test** argument in a standard IF function. The difference here is that the **value_if_true** argument is the application of the specified conditional formatting, whereas the **value_if_false** argument is not applying the specified formatting. To get a better idea of how this works, let's take a look at an extremely simple example, one in which Excel is asked to highlight the number of years an employee, in this case a sales rep, has been with a company if it has been more than 10 years.

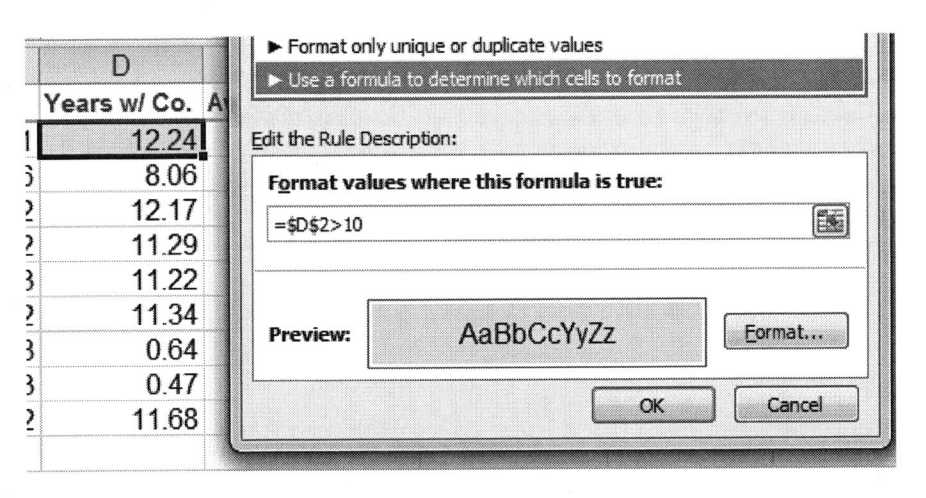

Note: As with entering formulas or functions in worksheet cells, you must add the equal sign (=) before the formula or function in the **Format values where this formula is true** field.

Here, a formula is used to apply formatting to the same cell Excel is evaluating. In this example, if you were to read aloud the "IF" function Excel is applying, it would sound something like "If the value in cell **D2** is greater than 10, then apply the formatting. Otherwise, don't apply the formatting." Obviously, this is a task Excel could easily perform by using one of the preconfigured **Highlight Cells Rules** from the **Conditional Formatting** drop-down menu. Now you want to use the value in cell **D2** to apply the formatting to the sales rep's name instead of the value itself. That would look something like this:

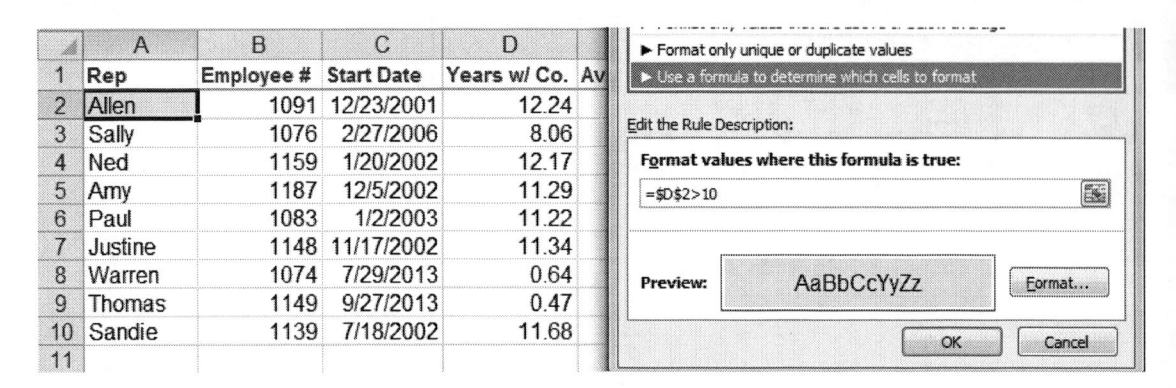

	A	B	C	D
1	Rep	Employee #	Start Date	Years w/ Co.
2	Allen	1091	12/23/2001	12.24
3	Sally	1076	2/27/2006	8.06
4	Ned	1159	1/20/2002	12.17
5	Amy	1187	12/5/2002	11.29
6	Paul	1083	1/2/2003	11.22
7	Justine	1148	11/17/2002	11.34
8	Warren	1074	7/29/2013	0.64
9	Thomas	1149	9/27/2013	0.47
10	Sandie	1139	7/18/2002	11.68

Format values where this formula is true:
=$D$2>10

The only difference between the first example and this example is that cell **A2** is highlighted, not cell **D2**, before creating the conditional formatting rule. So, although the formula is still looking to cell **D2** to perform the logical test, Excel is applying the conditional formatting to cell **A2**. This forms the basis for using formulas to apply conditional formatting to cells other than those Excel evaluates. In order to apply the same formatting across a much wider range of cells, you'll first need to consider how absolute and relative references come into play.

Note: Although the main focus of this topic is on using formulas and functions to apply conditional formatting to multiple columns simultaneously and to cells other than the ones Excel evaluates, it is important to understand that you can also use formulas and functions to create custom formatting rules when the existing conditional formatting options don't suit your needs.

Cell References and Conditional Formatting

Excel provides you with several options for applying a conditional formatting rule to more than one cell, row, or column at a time. You can select the entire range to which you wish to apply the formatting before defining the rule, or you can use the **Format Painter** or the **Paste Special** options to copy and paste the formatting to other cells once you've already defined the rule. But there is an extremely important consideration to keep in mind when doing this: Whether you select the entire range first or you copy the formatting later, Excel treats the operation as if you were dragging (or copying and pasting) the formatting to the new cells. This means that, as with reusing formulas and functions themselves, absolute and relative cell references become extremely important once you begin to reuse conditional formatting rules. When you define your conditional formatting rule, you must think in these terms or you won't get the results you desire. Let's take a look at a few examples to see how this works.

In this first example, you are trying to apply the same conditional formatting you did for the employee who has been with a company for more than 10 years. You used the **Format Painter** to apply the conditional formatting rule to the remaining cells in the first column.

	A	B	C	D
1	Rep	Employee #	Start Date	Years w/ Co.
2	Allen	1091	12/23/2001	12.24
3	Sally	1076	2/27/2006	8.06
4	Ned	1159	1/20/2002	12.17
5	Amy	1187	12/5/2002	11.29
6	Paul	1083	1/2/2003	11.22
7	Justine	1148	11/17/2002	11.34
8	Warren	1074	7/29/2013	0.64
9	Thomas	1149	9/27/2013	0.47
10	Sandie	1139	7/18/2002	11.68

Format values where this formula is true:
=$D$2>10

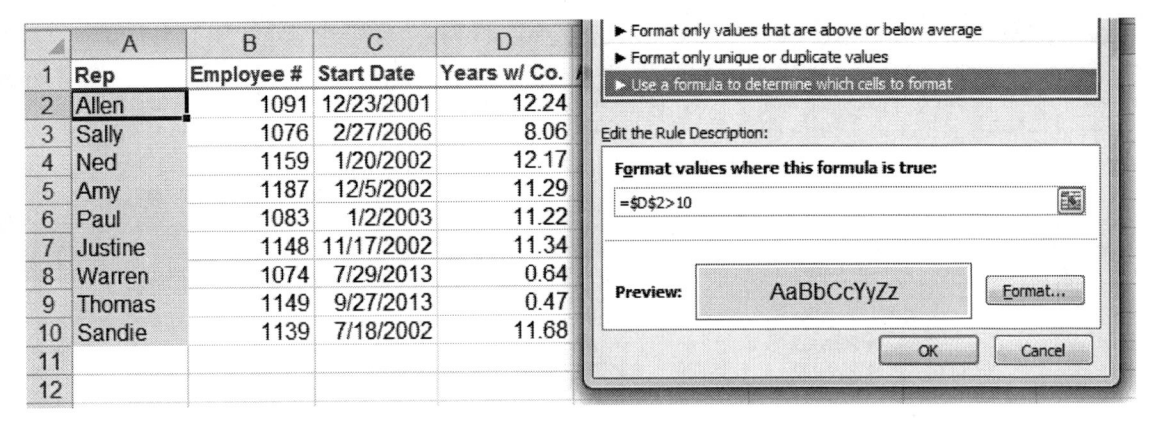

Clearly, there is an issue as reps who have been with the company fewer than 10 years are still highlighted. This is because the reference to cell **D2** in the formula is an absolute reference. Excel is looking to that cell for all of the cells in column **A** when applying the rule. To resolve this, simply change the reference to cell **D2** from an absolute reference to a relative reference.

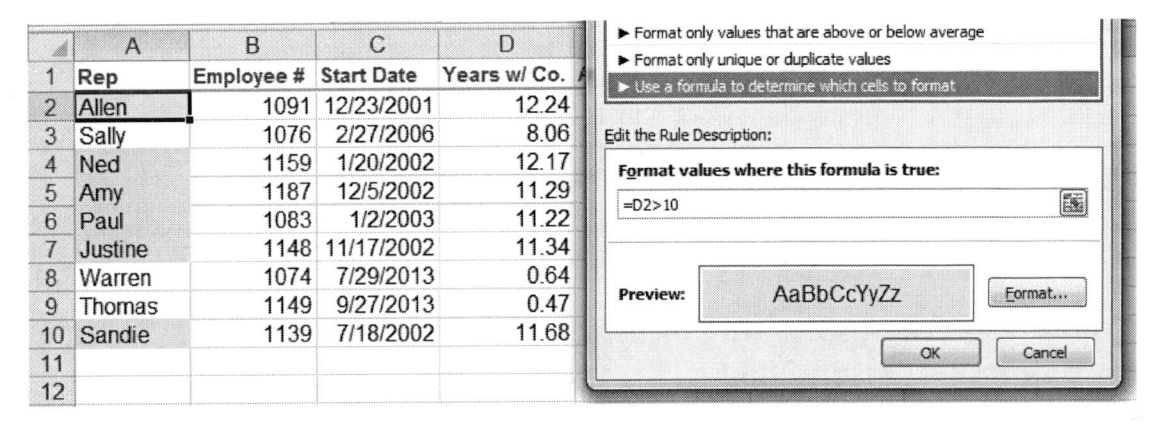

	A	B	C	D
1	Rep	Employee #	Start Date	Years w/ Co.
2	Allen	1091	12/23/2001	12.24
3	Sally	1076	2/27/2006	8.06
4	Ned	1159	1/20/2002	12.17
5	Amy	1187	12/5/2002	11.29
6	Paul	1083	1/2/2003	11.22
7	Justine	1148	11/17/2002	11.34
8	Warren	1074	7/29/2013	0.64
9	Thomas	1149	9/27/2013	0.47
10	Sandie	1139	7/18/2002	11.68

Format values where this formula is true:
=D2>10

Now the rule is behaving as you'd expect it to. Things get a bit more complex when you try to apply the same conditional formatting rule to more than one column at a time. Continuing with this example, let's say you now want to use the same rule to apply formatting to both the rep's name and his or her employee number based on the values in column **D**. If you simply copy the formatting to the second column without changing the formula, this would be the result.

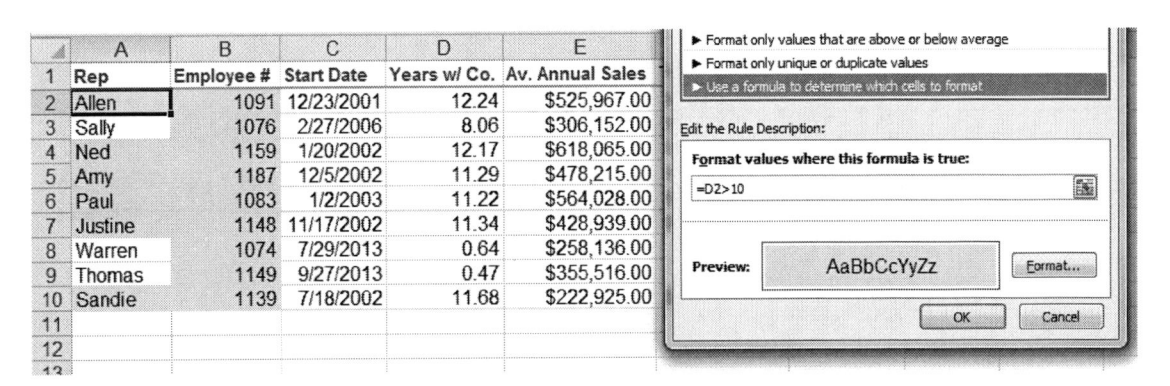

	A	B	C	D	E
1	Rep	Employee #	Start Date	Years w/ Co.	Av. Annual Sales
2	Allen	1091	12/23/2001	12.24	$525,967.00
3	Sally	1076	2/27/2006	8.06	$306,152.00
4	Ned	1159	1/20/2002	12.17	$618,065.00
5	Amy	1187	12/5/2002	11.29	$478,215.00
6	Paul	1083	1/2/2003	11.22	$564,028.00
7	Justine	1148	11/17/2002	11.34	$428,939.00
8	Warren	1074	7/29/2013	0.64	$258,136.00
9	Thomas	1149	9/27/2013	0.47	$355,516.00
10	Sandie	1139	7/18/2002	11.68	$222,925.00

Format values where this formula is true:
=D2>10

Although Excel applied the correct formatting in column **A**, it did not in column **B**. This is because both the column and the row are relative references for cell **D2** in the formula. Keep in min that regardless of how you apply the conditional formatting rule to the range, Excel treats it as if you entered it in cell **A2** and then dragged it down column **A** and then across to column **B**. For all of the cells in column **B**, Excel is looking to the values in column **E** and not column **D**. As all of those values are well above 10, Excel applied the formatting to all of the cells in column **B**. In this example, you want Excel to always look in column **D** to find the value to evaluate. We also want it to look for the values per sales rep, so the row will need to change. Because of this, you need to use a mixed reference that locks the column reference but allows the row reference to change. To get this example working the way you expect it to, the formula would look like this.

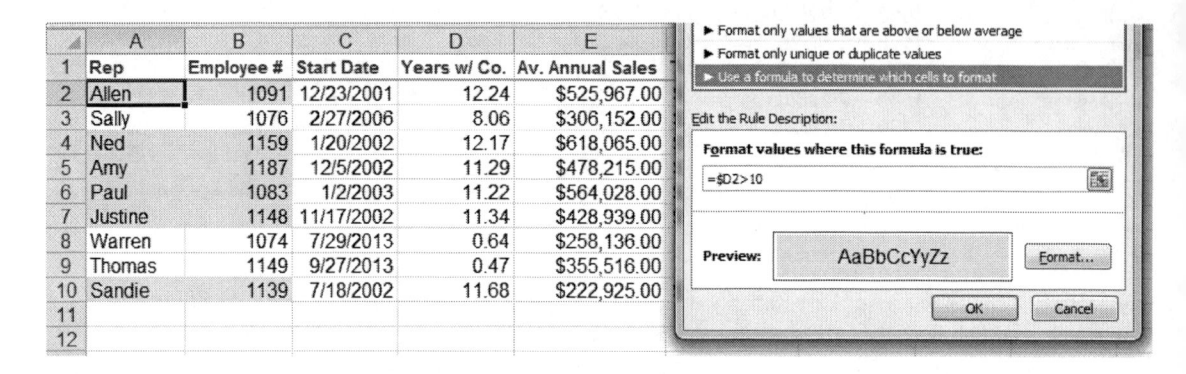

When using formulas or functions to apply conditional formatting across ranges of cells, always think in terms of dragging the formula or function from the first cell to all others, and then write you cell and range references accordingly.

Access the Checklist tile on your LogicalCHOICE course screen for reference information and job aids on How to Use Formulas and Functions to Apply Conditional Formatting.

Guidelines for Applying Conditional Formatting to Cells Based on Values in Other Cells

Although you can use formulas and functions to apply conditional formatting to wide ranges of data, when doing so based on data in other cells, you must keep absolute and relative references in mind. Excel treats all conditional formatting rules applied in this manner as if they were entered into a single cell and then dragged across the rest of the range. When applying conditional formatting to cells based on data stored in other cells:

- You must use a formula or a function to define the conditional formatting rule.
- You must enter the formula or function in the **Format values where this formula is true** field in the **New Formatting Rule** dialog box.
- The formula or function must begin with an equal sign (=).
- If you are applying the rule to a single cell, you can use either a relative or an absolute reference to the evaluated cell in the formula or function.
- If you are applying the rule to multiple cells in a single column and the rule will be evaluating the data in only a single cell, you must use an absolute reference to the evaluated cell in the formula or function.
- If you are applying the rule to multiple cells in a single column and the rule will be evaluating the associated data stored in multiple rows in another column, you must use a mixed reference that locks the column for the evaluated cells, but that is relative for rows in the formula or function.
- If you are applying the rule to a range that includes multiple rows and columns and the rule will be evaluating the associated data stored in a single cell, you must use an absolute reference for the evaluated cell in the formula or function.
- If you are applying the rule to a range that includes multiple rows and columns and the rule will be evaluating the associated data stored in multiple rows in another column, you must use a mixed reference that locks the column for the evaluated cells, but that is relative for rows in the formula or function.

ACTIVITY 4-3
Using Logical and Lookup Functions to Apply Conditional Formatting

Data File
C:\091020data\Applying Conditional Logic\author_master_roster_indexed.xlsm

Before You Begin
Excel 2010 is open.

Scenario
In addition to having users be able to quickly look up author information using the author dashboard, you want users to be able to know particular information about an author simply by viewing the **Authors** worksheet. As a majority of Fuller and Ackerman's authors are based in the United States, you want to know when U.S. authors reach the 500,000-books-sold threshold. You use that information to invite authors to an annual event celebrating the company's successes, so you want to highlight the author IDs for all authors who meet these conditions.

You have also instituted a new incentive program for authors based on the selling price of their books. For each price point, you have added a percentage increase to the authors' standard royalty rate. The higher the selling point for an author's books, the more his or her royalty rate increases. You have added an index reference on the worksheet you will use to perform the calculations. Though you want to reward authors whose books generate a lot of revenue, you also want to monitor the new incentive to get a sense of its impact. You decide to highlight the author information for all authors whose royalty rate is higher than 15 percent, whether by default or because of the royalty index.

---

1. Open the **author_master_roster_indexed.xlsm** workbook and ensure that the **Authors** worksheet is selected.

2. Apply conditional formatting to highlight author IDs for U.S.-based authors who have sold more than 500,000 books.
    a) Select cell **A2** and press **Ctrl+Shift+down arrow**.
    b) Select **Home→Styles→Conditional Formatting→New Rule**.
    c) In the **New Formatting Rule** dialog box, in the **Select a Rule Type** section, select **Use a formula to determine which cells to format**.
    d) In the **Edit the Rule Description** section, in the **Format values where this formula is true** field, enter the following formula: **=AND(J2=001,L2>=500000)**

    > **Note:** As you are applying this conditional formatting rule to a single column, you can use relative references in the formula.

    > **Caution:** When entering formulas in the **Format values where this formula is true** field, you must type cleanly. Trying to use the arrow keys to move the cursor will change the current cell or range selection, altering the formula you are entering. You can, however, use the mouse to move the insertion point.

    e) Select **Format**.
    f) In the **Format Cells** dialog box, ensure that the **Fill** tab is selected.

g) In the **Background Color** section, from the first column of the **Background Color** menu, select a light-gray color and then select **OK**.
h) In the **New Formatting Rule** dialog box, select **OK**.
i) Deselect the cells in column **A** to verify that Excel applied the formatting as expected.

3. Apply conditional formatting to the author information for all authors whose royalty rates are greater than 15 percent.
   a) Select the range **D2:J839** and select **Home→Styles→Conditional Formatting→New Rule**.
   b) Select **Use a formula to determine which cells to format**.
   c) In the **Format values where this formula is true** field, enter the following formula:
      =(VLOOKUP($M2,$S$2:$T$10,2)*$P2)>15%

   > **Note:** As you are applying this conditional formatting to cells in multiple columns, you must lock the column, but not the row, references for the author data in the formula.

   d) Select **Format** and then select **Fill Effects**.
   e) In the **Fill Effects** dialog box, select the **Color 2** down arrow and then select a light-red color from the gallery.
   f) Select **OK** and, in the **Format Cells** dialog box, select **OK** again.
   g) In the **New Formatting Rule** dialog box, select **OK**.

4. Examine the entry for author 1014 to verify the formatting works as expected.

   > **Note:** Author 1014's royalty rate is normally 9%. But, because her royalty index pushed her overall royalty rate over 15%, Excel applied the formatting.

5. Save the workbook to the **C:\091020Data\Applying Conditional Logic** folder as *my_author_master_roster_indexed.xlsm* and then close the workbook.

Summary

In this lesson, you used conditional logic and Excel functions to expand Excel's capabilities beyond the basic functionality of formatting rules and built-in functions. As you advance in your mastery of Excel, you can build upon this foundational knowledge to write highly complex formulas, using numerous functions, and define conditional formatting rules that can give you an incredibly deep understanding of the details stored in your data.

How will incorporating lookup functions into your workbooks affect your ability to analyze organizational data?

What are some challenges you anticipate in getting up to speed with nesting functions?

> **Note:** Check your LogicalCHOICE Course screen for opportunities to interact with your classmates, peers, and the larger LogicalCHOICE online community about the topics covered in this course or other topics you are interested in. From the Course screen you can also access available resources for a more continuous learning experience.

5 | Auditing Worksheets

Lesson Time: 45 minutes

Lesson Objectives

In this lesson, you will audit worksheets. You will:

- Trace cells.
- Search for invalid data and formulas with errors.
- Watch and evaluate formulas.

Lesson Introduction

Let's face it, everybody makes mistakes. And, as you likely collaborate with a number of other people on nearly all of your projects, you may have noticed that mistakes made by multiple individuals can add up quickly. This is especially true if you develop very large workbooks that contain large, complex formulas with multiple nested functions, references to other worksheets, and links to other workbooks. And, as your workbooks become larger and more complex, searching for the cause of errors or unexpected results and troubleshooting your formulas and functions can become a nightmare.

Excel 2010 provides you with a robust set of tools to help you audit your workbook content to find, troubleshoot, and correct a number of different errors. Developing the skills you need to perform these audits can save you tremendous amounts of time, effort, and frustration when errors arise and will give you the peace of mind that comes with knowing you can trust your data and analysis.

TOPIC A

Trace Cells

As users can introduce errors nearly anywhere within a workbook, making tracking down errors an important first step in resolving them. Additionally, errors aren't always obvious. Sometimes your only clue that a workbook contains an error at all is that some of the data on your worksheets doesn't seem to fit with surrounding figures. In these cases, you'll want to identify precisely which cells are feeding the erroneous data. That way, you can systematically check the data, formulas, or functions in only the cells that affect the erroneous result. But reading over the content in numerous cells to track which other cells feed into them can be a painstaking and error-prone process.

Excel provides you with a clear, graphical method for determining precisely how the cells in your workbooks connect to one another: cell tracing. Taking advantage of this type of functionality will give you an instant snapshot of the relationships that exist in your workbooks. This means you won't have to painstakingly examine large, complex workbooks to isolate issues affecting your data and analysis.

Precedent and Dependent Cells

There are two basic types of relationship cells can have to one another: One cell can feed data into another cell, or it can be fed data by another cell. Cells that feed data into other cells are known as *precedent cells*. These cells precede other cells in a chain of relationships. A common example of precedent cells is a group of cells containing raw data that a function in some other cell adds together, as in the case of adding up a sales rep's quarterly sales to find his or her annual total. The cells that contain the raw quarterly sales figures are precedent cells that feed the function adding those figures up to return the annual total.

Cells that contain a formula or function that is fed by data in other cells are known as *dependent cells*. These cells depend on the data in other cells to perform some calculation. Continuing with the aforementioned example, the cell containing the function that adds up the quarterly sales figures is a dependent cell. Cells can be, and often are, both precedent and dependent cells simultaneously.

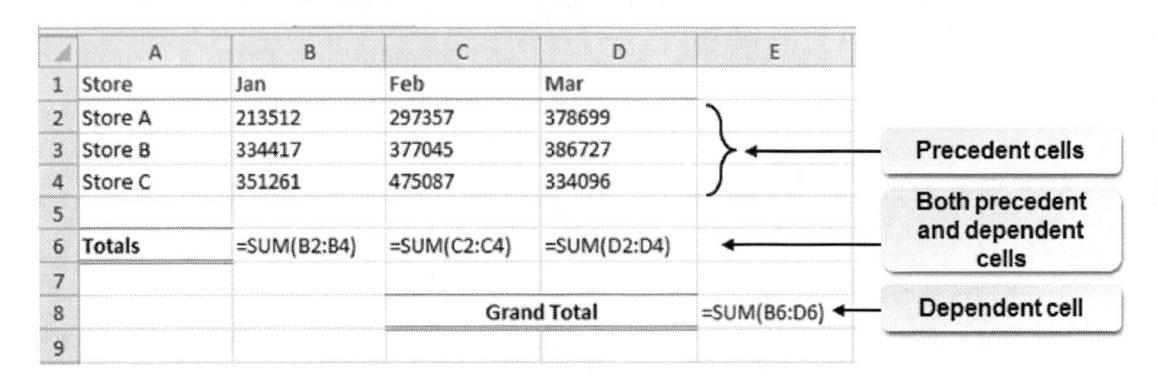

	A	B	C	D	E
1	Store	Jan	Feb	Mar	
2	Store A	213512	297357	378699	
3	Store B	334417	377045	386727	← Precedent cells
4	Store C	351261	475087	334096	
5					
6	Totals	=SUM(B2:B4)	=SUM(C2:C4)	=SUM(D2:D4)	← Both precedent and dependent cells
7					
8				Grand Total	=SUM(B6:D6) ← Dependent cell
9					

Figure 5-1: Precedent and dependent cells on an Excel worksheet.

> **Note:** This worksheet had formulas displayed instead of calculated values to demonstrate the concepts of precedent and dependent cells.

The Trace Precedents and Trace Dependents Commands

You can use the **Trace Precedents** and **Trace Dependents** commands to graphically view the relationships among worksheet and workbook cells. When you select a cell and then select either of these commands, Excel displays one or more arrows on the worksheet that illustrate which cells either feed into or are fed by the selected cell. Although you can display these arrows for more than one cell simultaneously, you have to execute the commands for each cell one at a time.

You can trace more than one level of cell connectivity at a time by using these commands. The first time you select one of these commands with a cell selected, Excel displays arrows that trace the cell to the other cells that most directly relate to it. If you select one of these commands for a cell a second time, it traces either the precedent or the dependent cells one more level to display the cells that are feeding or fed by them and so on. You can access the **Trace Precedents** and **Trace Dependents** commands in the **Formula Auditing** group on the **Formulas** tab.

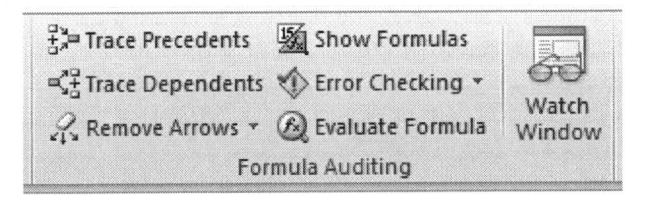

Figure 5-2: Use the Trace Precedents and Trace Dependents commands to view cell relationships.

Trace Arrows

The arrows that Excel displays when you execute either the **Trace Precedents** or the **Trace Dependents** command are called *trace arrows*. Trace arrows begin with a small dot, which indicates the precedent cell in th relationship, and end with an arrow, which indicates the dependent cell in the relationship. This is true regardless of which cell was traced.

Cells with more than one precedent or dependent cell will yield multiple trace arrows to show all first-level connections. There are three styles of trace arrows that each represent a different type of relationship: blue trace arrows, red trace arrows, and black, dashed-line trace arrows.

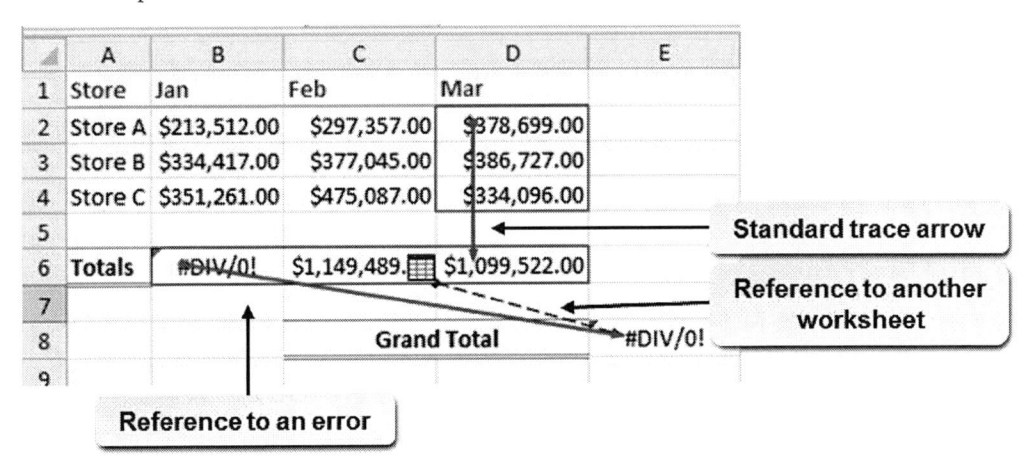

Figure 5-3: The various trace arrows not only display the direct relationships among cells, but they can also indicate links to other worksheets and workbooks, or formula errors.

The following table describes the three types of Excel trace arrows.

Trace Arrow Style	Traces
Blue arrow	Relationships of cells on the same worksheet.
Red arrow	Relationships of cells to other cells that contain formula or function errors.
Black, dashed-line arrow	Relationships of cells to other cells on different worksheets or in different workbooks.

> **Note:** Red trace arrows only indicate a relationship to a cell that contains an actual cell error, such as the #DIV/0! or #VALUE! errors. Excel will not display red trace arrows if the precedent or dependent cells contain invalid data due to data validation criteria, formulas or functions that are inconsistent with surrounding functions (or other errors that Excel flags by using the small, green triangle error indicator), or simply the wrong data.

The Go To Dialog Box and Trace Arrows

You can use the **Go To** dialog box to navigate to precedent or dependent cells to examine them and or correct errors in them. Excel displays the **Go To** dialog box when you double-click a trace arrow. This is the same **Go To** dialog box that you can access by selecting **Home→Editing→Find & Select→Go To** from the ribbon. The only difference in its functionality in relation to trace arrows is that the **Go To** dialog box displays a list of all of the precedent or dependent cells connected to the cell you're tracing, enabling you to quickly navigate to any of them.

Figure 5-4: The Go To dialog box provides you with quick access to precedent and dependent cells.

The Remove Arrows Options

Once you've identified the errors in your worksheet cells, you will likely want to remove trace arrows from view. Excel provides you with three different options for removing trace arrows, which you can access by selecting **Formulas→Formula Auditing→Remove Arrows down arrow**.

Remove Arrows Option	Removes
Remove Arrows	All trace arrows from the currently selected worksheet. This option will not remove trace arrows from other worksheets.
Remove Precedent Arrows	All trace arrows from the currently selected cell to its precedent cells. This option will not remove trace arrows to dependent cells.

Remove Arrows Option	Removes
Remove Dependent Arrows	All trace arrows from the currently selected cell to its dependent cells. This option will not remove trace arrows to precedent cells.

> Access the Checklist tile on your LogicalCHOICE course screen for reference information and job aids on **How to Trace Precedent and Dependent Cells.**

ACTIVITY 5-1
Tracing Precedent and Dependent Cells

Data File
C:\091020Data\Auditing Worksheets\book_sales_dashboard.xlsx

Before You Begin
Excel 2010 is open.

Scenario
You keep and maintain an Excel workbook that tracks all raw book sales for Fuller and Ackerman (F&A). The workbook also contains a number of dashboard-type sections that allow users to look up or view particular information based on a variety of criteria. Some users have noticed, however, that there seem to be a number of errors in the workbook. You suspect it is due to the increase in the number of people using it.

As you open the workbook to inspect it for errors, several discrepancies jump right out at you because of the values in some of the cells. You decide to use the **Trace Precedents** and **Trace Dependents** commands to determine what is causing these errors. While you also notice several other issues with the workbook, you decide to resolve the more obvious problems first.

1. Open the **book_sales_dashboard.xlsx** workbook file and ensure that the **Sales_Dashboard** worksheet is selected.

2. Trace cells to identify the issue in cell **C4**.
   a) Select cell **C4** and then select **Formulas→Formula Auditing→Trace Precedents**.
   b) As the connection to cell **A4** seems fine, double-click the black, dashed arrow between the worksheet icon and cell **C4**.
   c) In the **Go To** dialog box, in the **Go to** list, select the first item and then select **OK**.
   d) Verify that Excel navigated to and selected the cells in the **Market** column on the **Raw_Book_Sales** worksheet.
   e) As the function in cell **C4** on the **Sales_Dashboard** worksheet should be referring to the values in the **Market** column, and so is fine as is, switch back to the **Sales_Dashboard** worksheet and double-click the black, dashed arrow again.
   f) In the **Go To** dialog box, select the second item and select **OK**.
   g) Verify that Excel navigated to and selected the cells in the **Sell Price** column on the **Raw_Book_Sales** worksheet.
   h) As the function in cell **C4** should be referring to the values in the **Total Earnings to Date** column, navigate back to the **Sales_Dashboard** worksheet to correct the formula.
   i) If necessary, select cell **C4** and change the function to: *=SUMIF(Market,A4,Total_Earnings_to_Date)*

3. Trace cells to identify the issue in cell **C6**.
   a) Select cell **C6** and select **Formulas→Formula Auditing→Trace Precedents**.
   b) As the function in cell **C6** should be referring to the value in cell **A6**, not **A7**, correct the function to:
   =SUMIF(Market,A6,Total_Earnings_to_Date)

4. Select the **Titles_to_Watch** worksheet tab.

5. Trace cells to identify the issues in row **12**.

a) Verify the value in cell **B12** seems out of place compared to the other values in the **Total Copies Sold** column.

15,732,506
16,334,608
14,212,021
11,687,155
15,732,506
17,493,550
14,224,005
4,257,658

b) Select cell **B12**, and then select **Formulas→Formula Auditing→Trace Dependents**.
c) Verify that Excel traces the cell to cell **E12** and that the value in **E12** seems out of place compared to the other values in the **Total Revenue** column.

14,212,021	1,292,002	$11.99	$170,402,131.79
11,687,155	899,012	$15.99	$186,877,608.45
15,732,506	1,210,193	$12.99	$204,365,252.94
17,493,550	1,345,658	$12.99	$227,241,214.50
14,224,005	1,094,154	$15.99	$227,441,839.95
4,257,658	327,512	$15.99	$68,079,951.42

d) Select **Formulas→Formula Auditing→Remove Arrows**.
e) Select cell **E12** and select **Formulas→Formula Auditing→Trace Precedents**.
f) As the formula in cell **E12** should be referring to the values in cells **B12** and **D12**, select the **Trace Precedents** command again to trace those cells back to other cells.
g) As the price in cell **D12** seems correct, double-click the black, dashed line between the worksheet icon and cell **B12** to investigate what may be causing the issue in cell **B12**.

e1294	14,212,021	1,292,002	$11.99	$170,402,131.79
e1338	11,687,155	899,012	$15.99	$186,877,608.45
e1414	15,732,506	1,210,193	$12.99	$204,365,252.94
e1508	17,493,550	1,345,658	$12.99	$227,241,214.50
e1613	14,224,005	1,094,154	$15.99	$227,441,839.95
e1702	4,257,658	327,512	$15.99	$68,079,951.42

h) In the **Go To** dialog box, select the item in the **Go to** list and select **OK**.
i) Verify that Excel navigated to and selected the range **O1703:R1703**.
j) As this is not the entire range that contains all book sales for **BookTitle1702**, navigate back to the **Titles_to_Watch** worksheet to correct the function.
k) Select cell **B12**.

> **Note:** You will have to use keyboard navigation to select cell **B12** because of the trace arrows.

l) Change the function to: **=SUM(Raw_Book_Sales!F1703:R1703)**
m) Select **Formulas→Formula Auditing→Remove Arrows**.

n) Verify the figures in row **12** are more in line with the other values on the worksheet.

6	BookTitle1119	16,334,608	1,256,508	$15.99	$261,190,381.92
7	BookTitle1294	14,212,021	1,292,002	$11.99	$170,402,131.79
8	BookTitle1338	11,687,155	899,012	$15.99	$186,877,608.45
9	BookTitle1414	15,732,506	1,210,193	$12.99	$204,365,252.94
10	BookTitle1508	17,493,550	1,345,658	$12.99	$227,241,214.50
11	BookTitle1613	14,224,005	1,094,154	$15.99	$227,441,839.95
12	BookTitle1702	15,237,992	1,172,153	$15.99	$243,655,492.08
13					

6. Save the workbook to the **C:\091020Data\Auditing Worksheets** folder as *my_book_sales_dashboard.xlsx*

TOPIC B

Search for Invalid Data and Formulas with Errors

Although it's handy to be able to trace a cell to its precedent and dependent cells, you won't always immediately be able to recognize where an error exists within your worksheets. In these cases, you'll need a way to scan entire worksheets to locate particular types of errors out of all of the data, formulas, and functions they contain. Fortunately, Excel provides you with access to two useful features for doing so: error checking and invalid data circling. Taking advantage of these features means you won't have to know ahead of time which cells contain errors and you'll be able to scan even the largest worksheets for errors in just a few seconds.

Invalid Data

In Excel, *invalid data* is any cell data that does not meet the criteria specified in data validation applied to the cell. Cells that you have not applied data validation criteria to cannot contain invalid data.

The Circle Invalid Data Command

You will use the **Circle Invalid Data** command to quickly identify cells on a worksheet that contain invalid data. When you execute this command, Excel scans the currently selected worksheet for invalid data and temporarily displays a red circle or oval around any cells containing invalid data. These circles disappear after a short period of time and when you save the workbook, so you may have to re-display them if it takes some length of time to identify and correct all instances of invalid data. You can access this command by selecting **Data→Data Tools→Data Validation down arrow→Circle Invalid Data**.

C	D	E
Feb	Mar	
$297,357.00	$378,699.00	
$377,045.00	$386,727.00	
$475,087.00	$334,096.00	
$1,149,489.00	$1,099,522.00	
Grand Total		$3,148,201.00

Figure 5-5: Circled instances of invalid data on an Excel worksheet.

The Error Checking Command

You are already familiar with the two basic kinds of errors that can occur within Excel worksheets. The relatively minor errors, such as an inconsistent formula, that may return a valid value from a function but Excel still flags as something you want to check, and major errors, such as the #DIV/0! error, that do not return a valid value from a function. Excel flags the former with a small green triangle in the corner of the cell, whereas the latter returns an error value in the cells themselves. On smaller worksheets, these errors are relatively easy to spot. But on very large worksheets, you might have to scroll through many rows and columns of data to locate them. Excel provides you with a single command that enables you to scan entire worksheets to locate and identify all of the errors they contain with ease: the **Error Checking** command.

If Excel finds errors on a worksheet, it displays the **Error Checking** dialog box. From here you can browse through all errors on the worksheet, search for Help resources about the errors, and manage how you would like to resolve the errors. You can check a worksheet for errors by selecting **Formulas→Formula Auditing→Error Checking**.

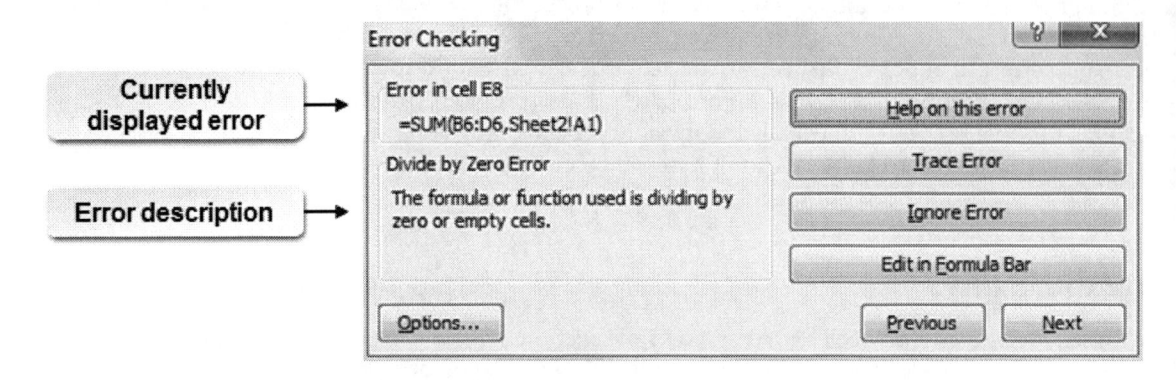

Figure 5-6: The Error Checking dialog box.

The following table describes the various elements of the **Error Checking** dialog box.

Error Checking Dialog Box Element	Description
Currently displayed error	Identifies the location of and displays the contents of the currently displayed error.
Error description	Displays a descriptions of the currently displayed error.
Options button	Opens the **Excel Options** dialog box with the **Formulas** tab selected. From there, you can configure Excel's error checking options.
Help on this error button	Opens the **Excel Help** window with search results for Help resources about the currently displayed error showing.
Show Calculation Steps button	Opens the **Evaluate Formula** dialog box, which you can use to determine what part of a formula or function is causing an error.
Ignore Error button	Leaves the cell content associated with the currently displayed error as it is.
Edit in Formula Bar button	Opens the formula or function causing the currently displayed error in the **Formula Bar** for editing.
Previous button	Displays the previous worksheet error in the **Error Checking** dialog box.
Next button	Displays the next worksheet error in the **Error Checking** dialog box.

Error Types

It is one thing to be able to locate and identify which cells contain errors; it is something else entirely to know how to resolve errors once you've identified them. There are seven major types of errors that will return an error value in worksheet cells instead of flagging the issue with a green error icon. The following table identifies and describes these seven error values, and identifies common solutions to them.

Error Value	Excel Returns This Error When	Resolution(s)
#NULL!	You use an intersection operator (which is a blank space between range references) with two ranges that don't actually intersect.	Either replace the intersection operator with the intended operator or correct the range references to two ranges that intersect.
#DIV/0!	A formula or a function is trying to divide some value by zero. This can also be caused when a formula or function is trying to divide by the value in a blank cell.	Replace the value zero with the correct numerical value, correct the cell reference to a populated cell, or correct the formula or function that is returning the zero that Excel is trying to divide by.
#VALUE!	When a formula or function is referencing an incorrect data type. For example, if a function is asking Excel to multiply a numerical value by a text label.	Correct the data entry causing the error to the correct data type, or correct a formula or function so that it returns the correct data type.
#REF!	A formula or a function contains an invalid reference. This typically occurs when you delete a row or column containing cells a formula or function is referencing.	Restore the deleted cells or update the references in the formula or function.
#NAME?	It does not recognize text that you include in a formula or function. Common causes of this are misspelling a defined name, misspelling the name of a function or a nested function, excluding quotation marks around text that requires them, and omitting the range operator (:) in a range in a function.	Correct the spelling of the defined name or function, using the Paste Name dialog box instead of typing defined names, adding quotation marks around text in function arguments, and adding the range operator to range references that are missing one.
#NUM!	An argument in a function that should be a numeric value is some other data type. This error can also be caused by a calculation that returns a numeric value that is too small or too large for Excel to express.	Revise the function or the data feeding the function to ensure that all arguments are of the correct data type, or revise the formula or function to return a numeric value that Excel can express.
#N/A	A function or a formula cannot access a required value. Common causes of this error include an invalid **lookup_value** argument in Lookup functions, trying to use Lookup functions to search an unsorted dataset, using array functions with different sized arrays, and omitting required arguments from functions.	Ensure that the **lookup_value** argument in a Lookup function is valid, sort the dataset you are searching with a lookup function, ensure that all arrays in array formulas are the same size, and ensure that all functions include all required argument.

Access the Checklist tile on your LogicalCHOICE course screen for reference information and job aids on **How to Search for Invalid Data and Formulas with Errors**.

ACTIVITY 5-2
Searching for Invalid Data and Formulas with Errors

Before You Begin
The my_book_sales_dashboard.xlsx workbook file is open.

Scenario
Now that you have corrected the more obvious errors in the workbook, you decide to check for other, potentially more subtle, issues. As you know you applied data validation to some of the workbooks' columns, you decide to scan the workbook for invalid data. Also, you noticed some formula errors on one of the worksheets, so you decide to scan the workbook for other errors as well.

1. Select the **Sales_Dashboard** worksheet, and then select cell **A1** to scan the worksheet for formula errors from the beginning.

2. Scan the worksheet for formula errors.
   a) Select **Formulas→Formula Auditing→Error Checking**.
   b) In the **Error Checking** dialog box, verify that Excel flagged the formula in cell **F19** as containing a divide by zero error.
   c) Select **Next** and verify that Excel flagged the function in cell **F25** as containing an invalid name error.
   d) Select **Next** and, in the **Microsoft Excel** dialog box, select **OK**.

3. Scan the **Titles_to_Watch** and the **Raw_Book_Sales** worksheets for formula errors.

4. Scan the workbook for invalid data.
   a) Select the **Titles_to_Watch** worksheet and select **Data→Data Tools→Data Validation down arrow→Circle Invalid Data**.
   b) Verify that Excel circled cell **D3**.
   c) Select the **Raw_Book_Sales** worksheet, select cell **A1**, and scan the worksheet for invalid data.
   d) Verify that Excel circled cell **P6**, and then scroll down the worksheet to verify that Excel circled several other cells for containing invalid data.

5. Navigate back to the top of the **Raw_Book_Sales** worksheet and save the workbook.

TOPIC C

Watch and Evaluate Formulas

When you develop and work with workbooks that contain large numbers of complex functions or that have a number of interconnected cells, it becomes tricky to fully troubleshoot and resolve all problems. For example, if the errors in a function are being caused by multiple cells throughout the workbook, it can become tedious to find the offending cells, resolve the issues in them, and then navigate back to the function to check to see if the change reflected there. Or, you may encounter errors in highly complex functions with numerous levels of nesting and multiple other functions as argument. In such complicated functions, it may not be immediately clear precisely what is causing the issue. It could be an error in entering a function or its arguments, an error in a precedent cell for any argument in any of the nested functions, or any number of other issues. At first glance, it could be nearly impossible to determine what part of the function is truly the problem.

Although you could painstakingly scour your worksheets to determine if the changes you're making reflect in all connected cells or break down complex functions to determine precisely where an issue is coming from, you likely don't have that kind of time, and who would really want to do this anyway? Fortunately, Excel provides you with a couple of powerful tools that can help you watch formulas and their results and to break down complex functions argument-by-argument to home in on the issue. It's easy to see how this type of automated help can save you a ton of time, numerous headaches, and a lot of effort.

The Watch Window

Once you've found the cells containing the errors that you need to resolve, you want to be sure the changes you are making are actually taking effect in the dependent cells fed by the errors. In many cases, this will be easy to do, as the cells may all be near each other on the same worksheet. What if the related cells are on opposite sides of a massive worksheet or are on different worksheets or in different workbooks entirely? Or, perhaps, you're correcting an error in a cell that is affecting formulas and functions in a number of different places. In these cases, you'll want a way to be able to watch the effects of correcting errors take place in the dependent cells regardless of where they are in a workbook. To do this, you can use the *Watch Window*.

The **Watch Window** is a floating pane that you can either move around the screen or dock within the Excel user interface above the **Formula Bar**. You can add any cells you want to watch to the **Watch Window**. For each cell you add to it, the **Watch Window** displays the cell's location, its displayed value, and, if it contains one, the formula or function entered into it. As you update the values or other formulas and functions in the precedent cells for cells in the **Watch Window**, the cell's information updates in real time. This ensures you don't have to navigate through or across workbooks to see the effects of updating information or correcting errors. You can access the **Watch Window** by selecting **Formulas→Formula Auditing→Watch Window**.

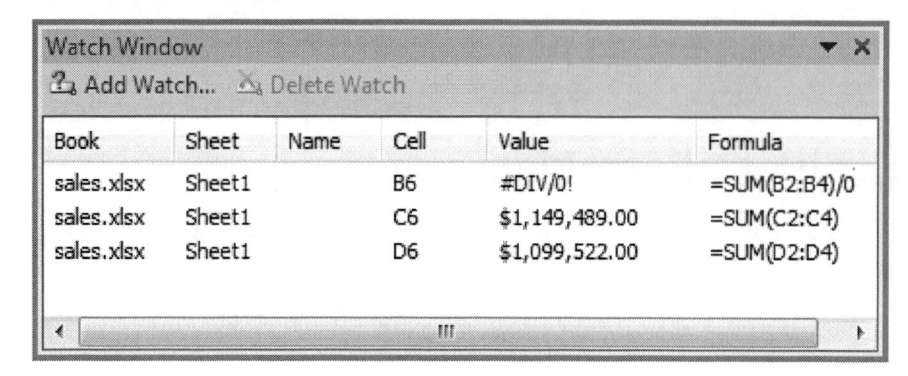

Book	Sheet	Name	Cell	Value	Formula
sales.xlsx	Sheet1		B6	#DIV/0!	=SUM(B2:B4)/0
sales.xlsx	Sheet1		C6	$1,149,489.00	=SUM(C2:C4)
sales.xlsx	Sheet1		D6	$1,099,522.00	=SUM(D2:D4)

Figure 5-7: Use the Watch Window to instantly see updates to cells when you make changes to their precedent cells.

Formula Evaluation

When you need to correct errors in large, complex formulas or functions, it's helpful to break them down into their component parts (function arguments or elements of formula expressions) to examine each chunk by itself. This process is known as *formula evaluation*. Performing this type of task manually can be a painstaking, time-intensive process, but you don't have to do this manually. Excel 2010's Evaluate Formula feature can do this for you. When you evaluate a formula in Excel, Excel breaks the formula or function down into its component parts, runs the calculation on each part one at a time, and displays the result of that calculation to you in relation to the rest of the larger formula. This enables you to watch how Excel evaluates the formula to determine precisely where an error is taking place.

The Evaluate Formula feature evaluates the formula in the same order that Excel does when performing the calculation. In other words, it follows the order of operations just as Excel does when you first enter the formula. You can access the Evaluate Formula feature by selecting **Formulas→Formula Auditing→Evaluate Formula**.

The Evaluate Formula Dialog Box

When you run the Evaluate Formula feature on a formula or function, Excel opens it in the **Evaluate Formula** dialog box. When Excel first opens the **Evaluate Formula** dialog box, it displays the selected formula or function exactly as it is entered into the cell, and it underlines the first element of the formula or function that Excel would evaluate according to the order of operations. When you evaluate that element of the formula or function, Excel runs the calculation and changes the argument or calculation to the result of that argument or calculation. Excel then underlines the next element of the function or formula that it would normally evaluate. You can then ask Excel to perform that calculation, which will, in turn, display the result of it inline with its place in the larger formula. You can continue this process until you have evaluated the entire formula or function.

Excel also provides you with the option to step in to the currently evaluated formula element to view information about where it's coming from. When you step in to an element of a formula or function, Excel opens a new text field in the **Evaluate Formula** dialog box. This field displays the nature of that particular formula or function element. If that element is a hard-coded numeric value, it appears simply as the value. If the element is the result of a formula or function, the field displays the formula or function that produced the result. If that element is a cell reference, then the field displays the location of that reference, and so on.

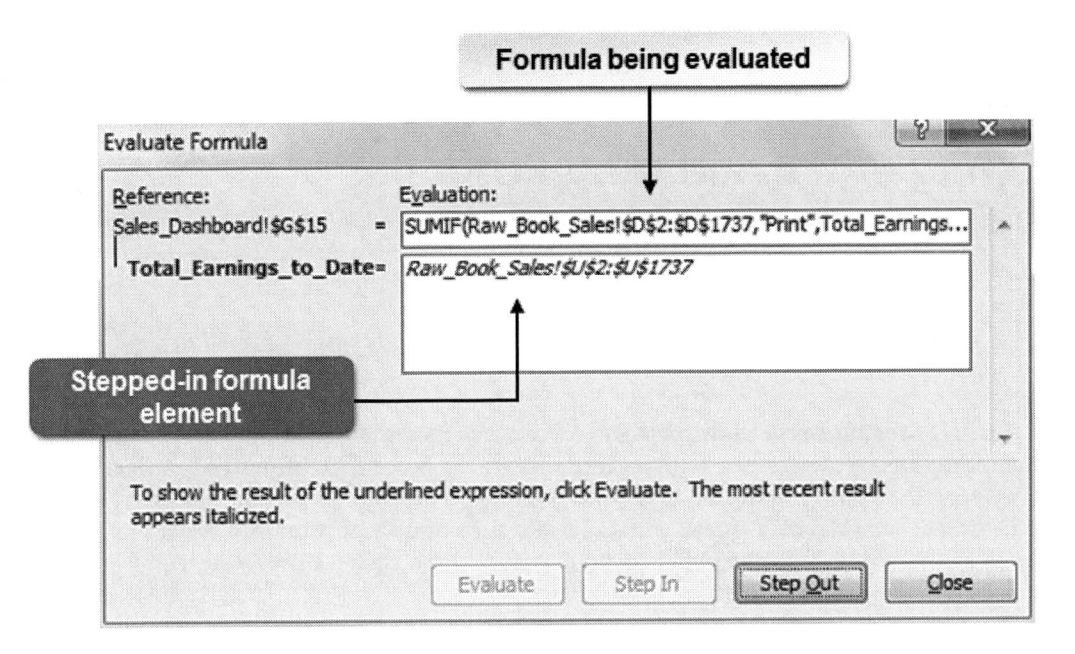

Figure 5-8: Use the Evaluate Formula dialog box to break complex formulas and functions down into component parts to examine how Excel is returning the result.

Access the Checklist tile on your LogicalCHOICE course screen for reference information and job aids on How to Watch and Evaluate Formulas.

ACTIVITY 5-3
Watching and Evaluating Formulas

Before You Begin
The my_book_sales_dashboard.xlsx workbook file is open.

Scenario
Now that you have identified several formula and invalid data issues in the workbook, you are ready to make the corrections. As the issues with the formulas on the **Sales_Dashboard** worksheet aren't immediately apparent to you, you decide to use the **Evaluate Formula** dialog box to identify the issues. And, as there is invalid data spread across a wide range of cells on various worksheets, you decide that using the **Watch Window** will help you verify that the changes you make to the invalid data are reflected in the formulas referring to that data.

---

1. Evaluate the formula in cell **F19** on the **Sales_Dashboard** worksheet.
    a) Select the **Sales_Dashboard** worksheet and select cell **F19**.

    > **Note:** Ensure that you can view the cells in the **Sales by Year** dashboard section, especially cell **C27**, during this step.

    b) Select **Formulas→Formula Auditing→Evaluate Formula**.
    c) In the **Evaluate Formula** dialog box, in the **Evaluation** section, ensure Excel displays the formula from cell **F19** and that **$C$27** is underlined.

    ```
    Evaluation:
    $C$27/COUNTIF(C28,"<>")
    ```

    d) Select **Evaluate** to evaluate the cell reference.
    e) Verify that the cell reference **$C$27** evaluates to the value stored in that cell.

    ```
    Evaluation:
    15972312649.23/COUNTIF(C28,"<>")
    ```

    f) Select **Evaluate** again to evaluate the COUNTIF function contained in the formula.
    g) Verify that Excel evaluated the COUNTIF function to return a value of zero.

    ```
    Evaluation:
    15972312649.23/0
    ```

    h) Select **Evaluate** again to verify that the zero in the formula's denominator (bottom value) is causing the error, and then select **Close**.

2. Revise the COUNTIF function in the formula to correct the error.
    a) With cell **F19** still selected, press **F2** to put the cell in edit mode.

b) In the COUNTIF function, change the cell reference **C28** to the range reference *A14:A26* and press **Ctrl+Enter**.

> f_x =$C$27/COUNTIF(A14:A26,"<>")

3. Evaluate the function in cell **F25**.
   a) Select cell **F25**, and then select **Formulas→Formula Auditing→Evaluate Formula**.
   b) Select the **Evaluate** button four times to ensure that Excel evaluates the AVERAGEIF function in the IF function's first argument to a numerical value.

   > Evaluation:
   > IF(*2139400.40285714*>SUM,"Yes","Negotiate")

   c) With the text "SUM" underlined in the **Evaluation** window, select **Evaluate** again.
   d) Verify that Excel flagged the **SUM** text as the cause of the #NAME? error.

   > Evaluation:
   > IF(*2139400.40285714*> *#NAME?*,"Yes","Negotiate")

   e) Select **Close**.

4. Correct the function.
   a) With cell **F25** still selected, press **F2**.
   b) Change the text **SUM** to the value *4000000* and press **Ctrl+Enter**.

   > f_x =IF(AVERAGEIF(Author,F24,Total_Earnings_to_Date)>4000000,"Yes","Negotiate")

   c) Select several author IDs from the drop-down menu in cell **F24** to ensure that the function works as expected.

5. Add the first function you want to watch to the **Watch Window**.
   a) Select **Formulas→Formula Auditing→Watch Window**.

b) If Excel displays the **Watch Window** as a free-floating window, drag it toward the top of the **Formula Bar** until Excel pins the **Watch Window** horizontally across the user interface above the **Formula Bar**.

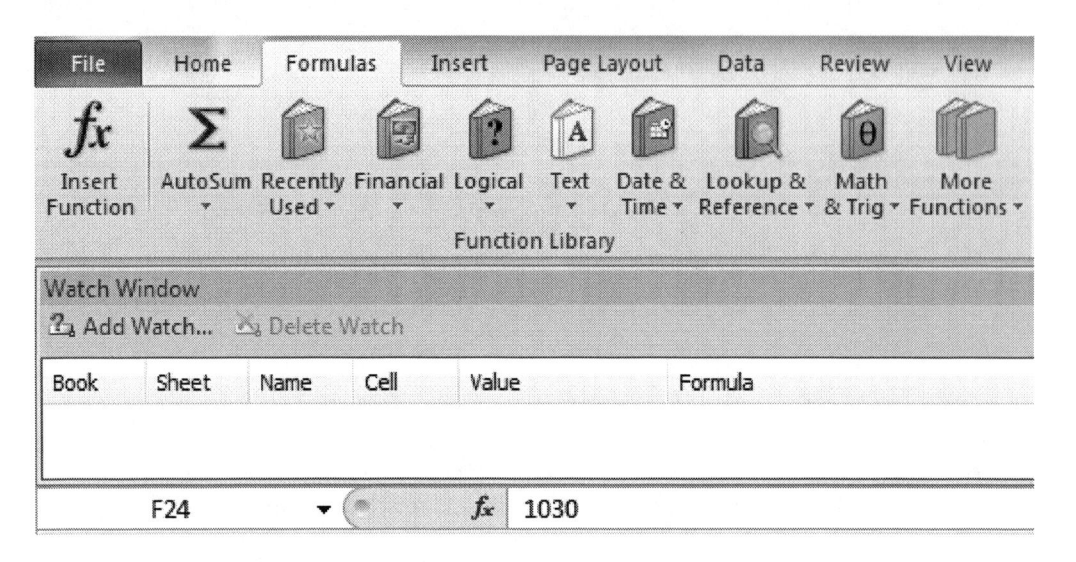

c) Select the **Titles_to_Watch** worksheet, and then select **Data→Data Tools→Data Validation** down arrow→**Circle Invalid Data**.

> **Note:** Excel automatically clears invalid data circles when you save a workbook. Here, you are merely re-displaying the one for this worksheet. Additionally, the circles may disappear occasionally over time. When that happens, you can simply select the **Circle Invalid Data** command again to turn them back on.

d) Select cell **D3** and then, in the **Watch Window**, select **Add Watch**.
e) In the **Add Watch** dialog box, select **Add** and then verify that Excel displays the function from cell **D3** in the **Watch Window**.

6. Add the second function you want to watch to the **Watch Window**.
   a) Select the **Raw_Book_Sales** worksheet and select **Data→Data Tools→Data Validation** down arrow→**Circle Invalid Data**.
   b) Select cell **X4**, and then select **Add Watch**.

   > **Note:** Here, you are adding cell **X4** to the **Watch Window** because the function in cell **X4** is being fed by the data in the **Total Earnings to Date** column. The figures in that column are being fed by some of the cells that contain invalid data.

   c) In the **Add Watch** dialog box, select **Add**.

7. Correct the instances of invalid data and use the **Watch Window** to verify the changes.
   a) Ensure that you can view both cell **P6** and cell **X4**.
   b) From the drop-down menu in cell **X3**, select author ID **1024**.
   c) Change the value in cell **P6** from a negative value to a positive value, and verify that Excel updates the value returned by the function in cell **X4**.
   d) Select author ID **1067** in cell **X3**, and then navigate to and select cell **R32**.

e) Change the value in cell **R32** to a positive value and, while pressing **Ctrl+Enter**, use the **Watch Window** to monitor the returned value for the function in cell **X4**.

Value	Formula
$10.99	=VLOOKUP(A3,Raw_Book_Sales!$B$2:$U$1737,19)
$91,746,046.12	=SUMIF(Author,X3,Total_Earnings_to_Date)

fx 445259

	N	O	P	Q	R	
	FY 2008	FY 2009	FY 2010	FY 2011	FY 2012	Total
	0	27813	50507	88325	152209	296293
.58	29979	39268	97719	26789	33093	
	0	0	0	0	0	445259
!05	74192	52156	25892	6377	4848	

f) In cell **X3**, select author ID **1027** and navigate to and select cell **P115**.
g) Change the values in cells **P115** and **Q115** from negative to positive and verify that the changes reflect in the **Watch Window**.
h) Navigate to and select cell **T960**.
i) Change the cell's value to *12.99* and, in the **Watch Window**, while pressing **Ctrl+Enter**, verify that Excel updates the value returned by the VLOOKUP function in cell **D3** on the **Titles_to_Watch** worksheet.

8. Select the **Titles_to_Watch** worksheet and verify that cell **D3** displays the value **$12.99**.

9. Close the **Watch Window** and save and close the workbook.

Summary

In this lesson, you audited worksheets to find, identify, and resolve a variety of errors and invalid data issues. As you begin or continue to develop complex workbooks with numerous links, references, and formulas and functions, the ability to quickly isolate and resolve issues will be of paramount importance. The more familiar you become with Excel's auditing features, the more quickly you'll be able to locate and fix problems. This means you'll be able to get back to the task of analyzing your data quickly, and you'll be able to trust that analysis.

Can you think of a time when using Excel's auditing and evaluation functionality would have come in handy?

What tasks do you think Excel's formula evaluation capabilities will help you with in your current role?

Note: Check your LogicalCHOICE Course screen for opportunities to interact with your classmates, peers, and the larger LogicalCHOICE online community about the topics covered in this course or other topics you are interested in. From the Course screen you can also access available resources for a more continuous learning experience.

6 | Using Automated Analysis Tools

Lesson Time: 1 hour, 15 minutes

Lesson Objectives

In this lesson, you will use automated analysis tools. You will:

- Determine potential outcomes by using data tables.
- Determine potential outcomes by using scenarios.
- Use the Goal Seek feature.
- Activate and use the Solver tool.
- Analyze data with Analysis ToolPak tools.

Lesson Introduction

By now, you're likely well acquainted with creating, building, and maintaining Excel workbooks, and you're performing all manner of data analysis. When you have all of the data you need and that data is in the correct format, there are practically limitless questions you can use Excel to answer. This is all fine and good when you have a specific question in mind and you're looking for one specific answer. But, what if you want to know how things will change if any number of variables, themselves, change? After all, you can never know for sure just how things will play out in the future. You could simply keep reentering your data with different values, or you could make numerous copies of your data or worksheets and update values as needed. But this all takes a lot of time and uses a lot of worksheet real estate to accomplish. And, you'll be saving ever larger workbook files in the process. In short, if you need to crunch your numbers with a variety of different values to anticipate a variety of possible scenarios, you'll want some sort of automated way to do so.

Excel contains a robust variety of functionality that is designed to help with such tasks. Becoming familiar with how these different features work and what they can do to help you analyze your data will open whole new worlds of possibilities in terms of data analysis. This can help you with planning, forecasting, scheduling, or any number of other tasks that require you to consider the very real possibility that any number of different outcomes is possible given the unpredictable nature of today's market.

TOPIC A

Determine Potential Outcomes by Using Data Tables

There are some things in business, as in life, that you just can't predict. It should come as no surprise then that this can makes things a bit tricky when it comes to analyzing your data in order to make predictions about the future. Even when you aren't looking to the future, you may simply need to know what an outcome will be if you change some input in some way. Although there are plenty of ways to do this manually, why would you want to? As you may have guessed by now, the good news is that you simply don't have to.

Excel 2010 includes several features that can help you answer the question, "What if?," for a variety of possibilities. What if my interest rate was 7.6 percent instead of 7.4 percent? What if only $3 million worth of product is sold instead of $3.2 million? What if the project is started in May instead of June? How will things change if these variables fluctuate? To get the answers to these questions, you just need to know how to ask Excel "What if?"

What-If Analysis

When you need to examine multiple possibilities while analyzing a particular dataset, you need to perform what is know in Excel as *what-if analysis*. What-if analysis enables you to perform calculations on the same formula or formulas with one or more variables included at a number of different values. For example, you could calculate your total payment for a car loan based on a variety of different interest rates, or if you put down a variety of different down payments, or both. This enables you to make the best decision possible for your situation based on all of the potential scenarios. Or, let's say you already have a particular outcome in mind: "I can spend a total of $18,000 for this car." How much of a loan can you afford at 5.8 percent interest? Excel can help you figure that out too.

Excel includes three different built-in what-if analysis tools: the Scenario Manager, the Goal Seek feature, and data tables. Each approaches the question "what if?" in a different way. You can access these features by selecting **Data→Data Tools→What-If Analysis**.

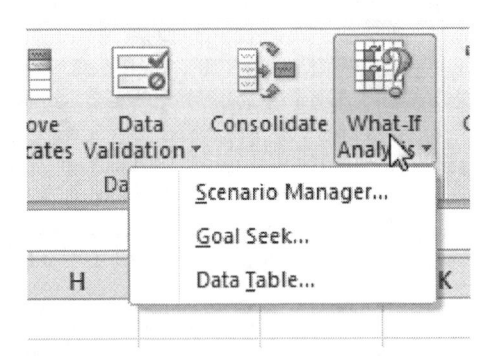

Figure 6-1: You can perform a variety of different analyses based on varying inputs by using Excel's what-if analysis tools.

Data Tables

The first type of what-if analysis tool we'll look at is *data tables*. Data tables enable you to view a variety of different outcomes for particular formulas or functions given a set of different values for either one or two variables. The main advantage of data tables is that they support any number of values for the variables you are calculating. The main disadvantage is that the more variables you test for, the more space data tables take up; this is because data tables display the results for all variables, or sets of variables, in tabular form.

Each individual data table references at least one formula. The column and/or row labels in a data table represent the values for the one or two variables you wish to calculate on. The variables you wish to change in the formulas or functions must be entered into their own cells, which are known as input cells, and must be included as a reference to the input cells in the formulas or functions. When you create the data table, Excel calculates the formula or function results for each variable or set of variables, and then displays the results for each in the data table. As with most other Excel functionality, when you change the other values feeding the formulas or functions, the results automatically update in the data table.

One-Variable Data Tables

Because you can create data tables that calculate formula results for either one or two variables, there are two general types of data tables: one-variable data tables and two-variable data tables. *One-variable data tables* replace the value in one cell with any number of values you choose, plug each of those values into the formulas or functions that reference the cell, and then display the results in the table next to the row or column label for each corresponding value. Because of the way you must set up data tables on your worksheets, one-variable data tables are the only kind that can replace values for more than one formula or function.

One-variable data tables can be oriented either horizontally or vertically. When they are oriented horizontally, meaning the values for the changing variable are in a single row and serving as column labels, the tables are said to be row-oriented. When data tables are oriented vertically, or with the variable values in a single column serving as row labels, they are said to be column oriented. This is an important distinction because it determines whether you need to enter the input cell reference into the **Row input cell** field or the **Column input cell** field in the **Data Table** dialog box when you create the data table.

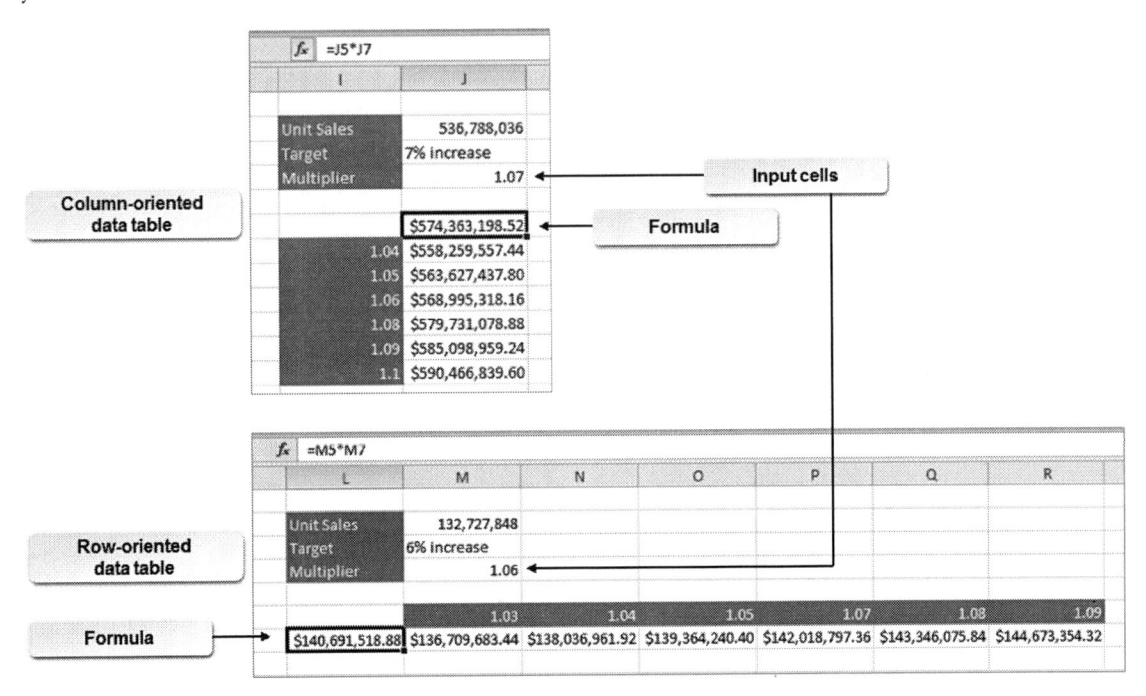

Figure 6-2: One-variable data tables can be column- or row-oriented and can replace a single variable with any number of values for multiple formulas or functions.

Two-Variable Data Tables

Two-variable data tables enable you to replace the values for two different variables in a formula or function. As with any data table, you can include as many variations for each variable as you would like. In contrast, with one-variable data tables, you can include only a single formula or function in a two-variable data table. With two-variable data tables, you need two input cells. The values for one of the input cells will be the column labels, and the values for the other input cell will be the row labels. The formula or function referenced by the data table must refer to both input cells.

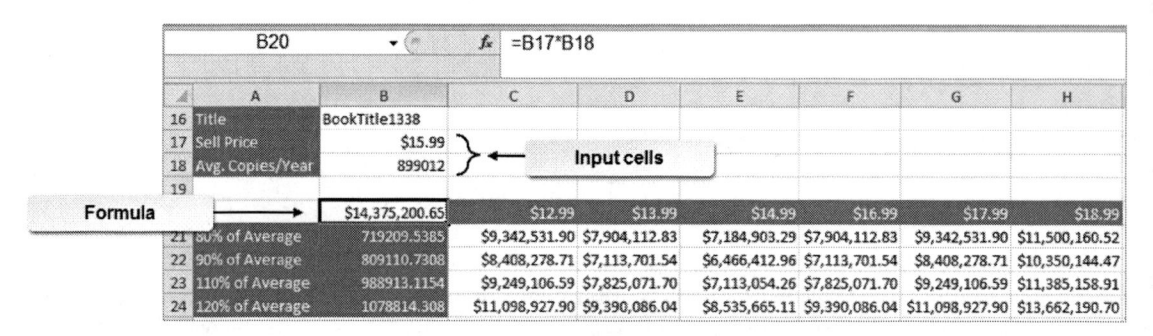

Figure 6-3: Two-variable data tables allow for more than one variable, but work only on a single formula or function.

The Data Table Dialog Box

You will use the **Data Table** dialog box to define the input cells for your data tables. Enter the cell reference for the input cell containing the value you want to replace with the values in data table column labels in the **Row input cell** field. This may, at first, seem counterintuitive, but remember that column labels all exist within the same row. The opposite is true for the values you have stored in a single column. They serve as row labels, so enter the cell reference for the input cell whose value you want to vary with these in the **Column input cell** field. There is no field to enter the formula or function you are calculating variables for; you will enter it when you create a data table.

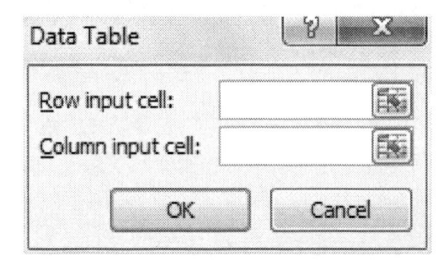

Figure 6-4: Use the Data Table dialog box to define your input cells.

> Access the Checklist tile on your **LogicalCHOICE** course screen for reference information and job aids on How to Create a Data Table.

ACTIVITY 6-1
Determining Potential Outcomes Using Data Tables

Data File
C:\091020Data\Using Automated Analysis Tools\book_sales_dashboard_06.xlsx

Before You Begin
Excel 2010 is open.

Scenario
You have decided to add some greater analysis capabilities to the workbook in which you track raw book sales. Specifically, you would like to start analyzing your data to determine future sales goals, optimum price points for titles, and category-specific scenarios to help Fuller and Ackerman (F&A) make informed business decisions moving forward. You will start by using data tables to determine potential genre-specific sales projections for the upcoming year based on how close you come to your sales targets. You will also analyze potential future revenue from F&A's top-selling titles based on a variety of sales potentials at a variety of price points. You have already added the labels, formatting, and some of the data you will need for this analysis, and you have named the dataset on the **Titles_to_Watch** worksheet **Top_Titles**.

---

1. Open the **book_sales_dashboard_06.xlsx** workbook file and ensure that the **Sales_Dashboard** worksheet is selected.

2. Use a one-variable data table to project unit sales in the fantasy genre based on several sales increase possibilities.

   a) Select cell **J9** and then enter the following formula: *=J5*J7*
   b) Select the range **I9:J15** and select **Data→Data Tools→What-If Analysis→Data Table**.
   c) In the **Data Table** dialog box, in the **Column input cell** field, enter *J7* and select **OK**.

Fantasy	
Unit Sales	536,788,036
Target	7% increase
Multiplier	1.07

	574,363,199
1.04	558,259,557
1.05	563,627,438
1.06	568,995,318
1.08	579,731,079
1.09	585,098,959
1.1	590,466,840

3. Repeat the analysis for the nonfiction genre.
   a) Enter the following formula in cell M9: *=M5*M7*
   b) Create a one-variable table in the range L9:M15.

Nonfiction	
Unit Sales	132,727,848
Target	6% increase
Multiplier	1.06
	140,691,519
1.03	136,709,683
1.04	138,036,962
1.05	139,364,240
1.07	142,018,797
1.08	143,346,076
1.09	144,673,354

4. Use a two-variable data table to perform a potential revenue analysis on the selected top-selling title at a variety of sales potentials and price points.
   a) Select the **Titles_to_Watch** worksheet tab.
   b) Select cell **B20** and enter the following formula: *=B17*B18*
   c) Enter the following formulas in the following cells so Excel automatically populates them with the desired unit sales variables for the data table:
      - B21: *=B18*.8*
      - B22: *=B18*.9*
      - B23: *=B18*1.1*
      - B24: *=B18*1.2*
   d) Select the range **B21:B24** and copy the cell contents to the clipboard, then paste the formulas back into the cells as values by selecting **Home→Clipboard→Paste drop-down arrow→Values**.
   e) Select the range **B20:H24** and select **Data→Data Tools→What-If Analysis→Data Table**.
   f) In the **Data Table** dialog box, in the **Row input cell** field, type *B17*
   g) In the **Column input cell** field, type *B18* and select **OK**.
   h) Adjust the column widths as necessary.

5. Save the workbook to the **C:\091020Data\Using Automated Analysis Tools** folder as *my_book_sales_dashboard_06.xlsx* and close the workbook.

TOPIC B

Determine Potential Outcomes by Using Scenarios

Data tables are a convenient way to perform what-if analysis when you need to account for only one or two variables. But what if you need to account for more than two variables? And although convenient, data tables take up a considerable amount of space on worksheets, especially if you include numerous values for the variables. Wouldn't it be nice to be able to perform the same type of analysis, for more than two variables, without making your worksheets unwieldy? This is what the next type of what-if analysis, scenarios, can do.

Scenarios

Scenarios are a type of what-if analysis that enable you to define multiple variables for multiple formulas or functions to determine a variety of outcomes. Unlike data tables, which create new datasets comprised of the various calculation results, scenarios change the displayed values of both the cells containing the variables, which are known as changing cells in scenarios, and the cells with the formulas or functions fed by the variables. As you display each scenario, Excel simply replaces the displayed values in place. Another key difference is that, when you create scenarios, Excel converts formulas or functions in changing cells to values, so you lose the original formulas and functions. For this reason, it is a good idea to make a copy of your dataset before creating scenarios for it, or to include a scenario that represents all of the original values.

You can create any number of scenarios you like for a particular dataset, but each scenario can contain only up to 32 changing values. Any formulas or functions that are fed by the changing cells will update when you display the various scenarios. In addition to displaying various scenarios on your worksheet, you can create a scenario report that creates a new worksheet that displays the inputs and any specified results of all scenarios.

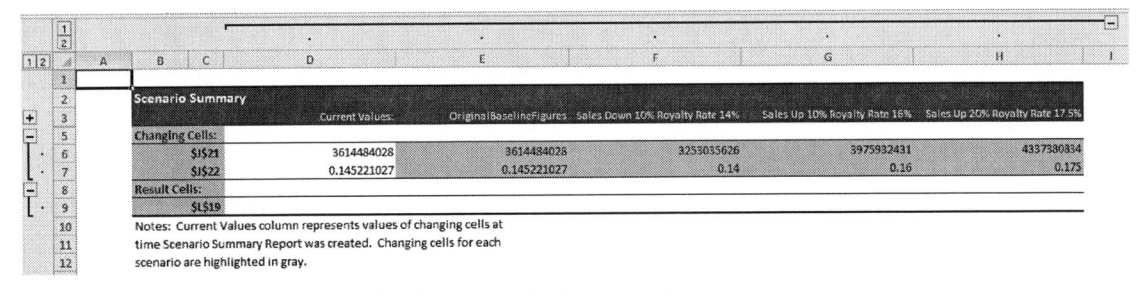

Figure 6-5: A scenario report displaying multiple scenarios.

The Scenario Manager Dialog Box

You will use the **Scenario Manager** dialog box to add scenarios to a worksheet, delete scenarios from a worksheet, edit existing scenarios, create scenario reports, or copy scenarios from other worksheets to the current worksheet. You can access the **Scenario Manager** dialog box by selecting **Data→Data Tools→What-If Analysis→Scenario Manager**.

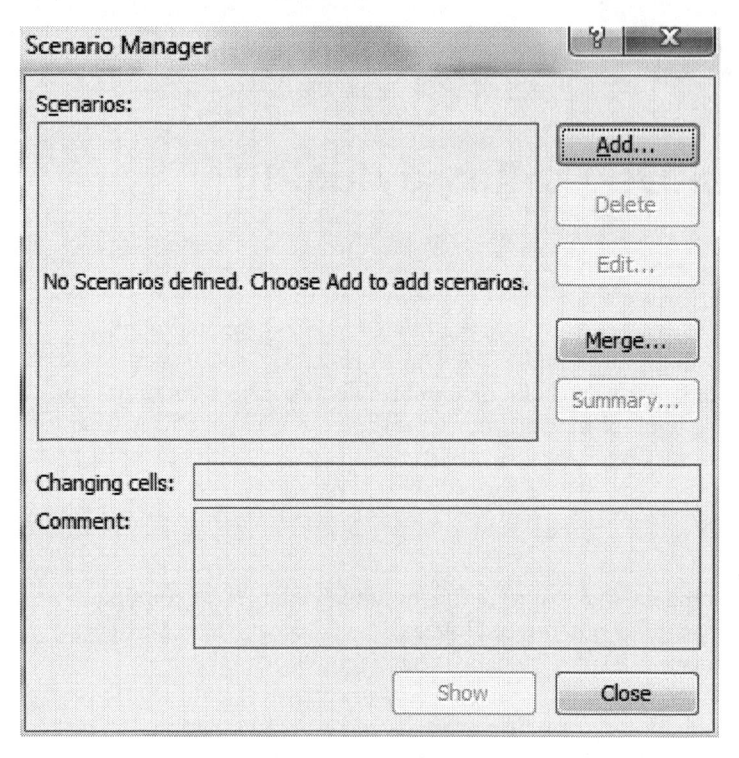

Figure 6-6: The Scenario Manager dialog box.

The following table describes the various elements of the **Scenario Manager** dialog box.

Scenario Manager Dialog Box Element	Description
Scenarios list	Displays all scenarios that have been added to the currently selected worksheet.
Changing cells field	Displays the changing cells for the currently selected scenario in the **Scenarios** list.
Comment field	Displays the ID of the user who created the currently selected scenario, the date the scenario was created, and any comments added by the user who created the scenario.
Add button	Opens the **Add Scenario** dialog box, which enables you to define and add a new scenario to the currently selected worksheet.
Delete button	Deletes the currently selected scenario.
Edit button	Opens the currently selected scenario in the **Edit Scenario** dialog box, which you can use to edit the scenario.
Merge button	Opens the **Merge Scenarios** dialog box, which enables you to merge scenarios from other worksheets and other open workbooks with the currently selected worksheet.
Summary button	Opens the **Scenario Summary** dialog box, which enables you to create a scenario summary report on a new worksheet.
Show button	Shows the results of the currently selected scenario on the currently selected worksheet.
Close button	Closes the **Scenario Manager** dialog box.

The Add Scenario Dialog Box

When you select the **Add** button in the **Scenario Manager** dialog box, Excel opens the **Add Scenario** dialog box. Here, you will define a name and the changing cells for the scenarios you wish to add to your worksheets. You can also set protection formatting options for individual scenarios as you define them.

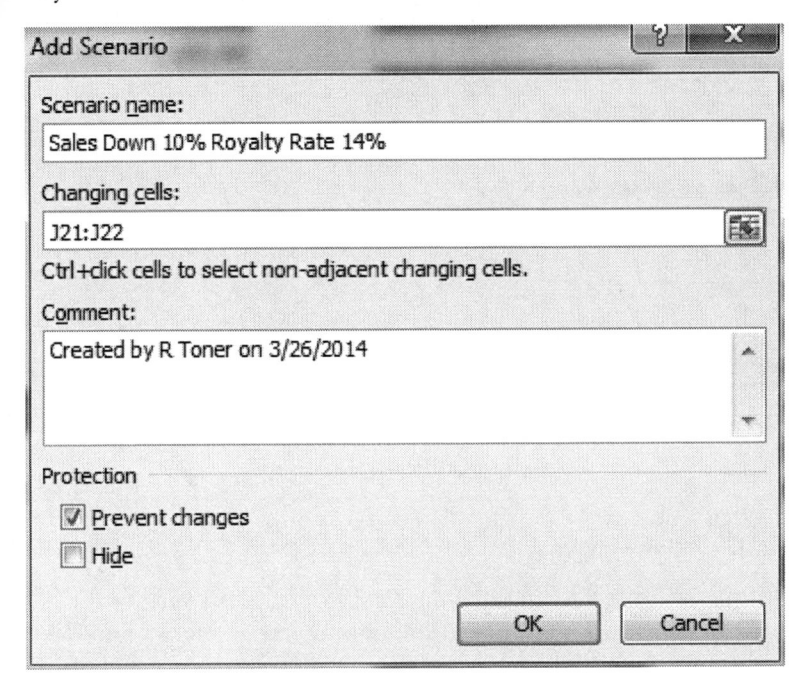

Figure 6-7: Use the Add Scenario dialog box to define new scenarios and apply protection formatting to them.

The following table describes the various elements of the **Add Scenario** dialog box.

Add Scenario Dialog Box Element	Use This To
Scenario name field	Define a name for the scenario.
Changing cells field	View or define the changing cells for the scenario. Whatever cell or range is selected when you create the scenario is displayed here by default.
Comment field	Add comments about the scenario to help other users understand what it's doing.
Prevent changes check box	Prevent other users from editing or showing the scenario. This functionality becomes active only if you also protect the worksheet, which is similar to how cell protection formatting works.
Hide check box	Hide the scenario from view in the **Scenario Manger** dialog box. This functionality becomes active only if you also protect the worksheet, which is similar to how cell protection formatting works.

The Scenario Values Dialog Box

Once you create a scenario, you will use the **Scenario Values** dialog box to define the values for its changing cells. The **Scenario Values** dialog box displays a text field for each of the changing cells you define for the scenario. You can populate these with either numeric values or with formulas. As with nearly all Excel formulas, you must first type an equal sign to use a formula to calculate the value for changing cells. Remember that Excel automatically converts formulas to values once you show a scenario on the worksheet.

Once you've defined the values for the changing cells in a scenario, you can either create further scenarios or return to the **Scenario Manager** dialog box. If you select the **Add** button in the **Scenario Values** dialog box, Excel displays the **Add Scenario** dialog box, enabling you to define further scenarios. If you select the **OK** button in the **Scenario Values** dialog box, Excel returns you to the **Scenario Manager** dialog box.

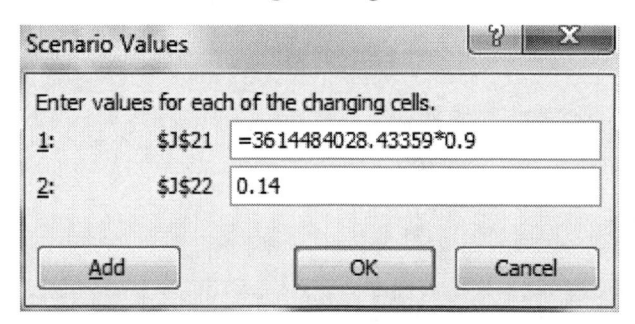

Figure 6-8: Use either hard-coded values or formulas to change the value in scenario changing cells.

The Scenario Command

While you can use the **Scenario Manager** dialog box to show the results of various scenarios on worksheets, Excel provides you with a much more convenient option for doing so: the **Scenario** command. Although it does not appear within the Excel user interface by default, you can add the **Scenario** command to either the **Quick Access Toolbar** or to a custom ribbon group. Selecting the **Scenario** command opens a drop-down menu that displays all defined scenarios for the currently selected worksheet. Selecting any of the scenarios from the drop-down menu will show the results of the scenario in the affected cells.

Figure 6-9: Use the Scenario command to quickly switch among scenarios for a worksheet.

Access the Checklist tile on your LogicalCHOICE course screen for reference information and job aids on How to Work with Scenarios.

ACTIVITY 6-2
Determining Potential Outcomes by Using Scenarios

Data File
C:\091020Data\Using Automated Analysis Tools\book_sales_dashboard_06a.xlsx

Before You Begin
Excel 2010 is open.

Scenario
You've just received a request for sales analysis that will be based on information sent to you by colleagues in the finance department. As authors' royalties are heavily influenced by how much their books generate in sales, the average royalty figure Fuller and Ackerman (F&A) pays its authors fluctuates based on which books sell more. When more high-cost books sell, sales and royalty percentages tend to rise. When more low-cost books sell, sales and royalty percentages either grow more slowly or decrease. The finance department has just sent you the estimated royalty percentages calculated for a variety of total sales scenarios based on an analysis of which books are likely to sell in the coming calendar year. F&A management would like to see estimated overall net sales based on the figures finance has provided you to compare them to the current average royalty rate and the baseline goal of a 7-percent annual sales increase; you have already included these figures in the workbook. You decide to use scenarios to perform the desired analysis as that will make it easier to present your findings to management. You also feel it will be beneficial to add the **Scenario** button to the **Quick Access Toolbar** so you can quickly switch among the various scenarios.

1. Open the **book_sales_dashboard_06a.xlsx** workbook file and ensure that the **Sales_Dashboard** worksheet is selected.

2. Enter the formulas for calculating the royalty payment and net sales.
    a) In cell J23, enter the following formula: *=J21*J22*
    b) In cell J24, enter the following formula: *=J21-J23*

3. Create a scenario that represents the data as it is currently entered into the worksheet.
    a) Select the range J21:J22.

    > **Note:** These will be the changing cells for the scenarios.

    b) Select **Data→Data Tools→What-If Analysis→Scenario Manager**.
    c) In the **Scenario Manager** dialog box, select **Add**.
    d) In the **Add Scenario** dialog box, in the **Scenario name** field, type *Original Baseline Figures*
    e) Ensure that the range J21:J22 appears in the **Changing cells** field and select **OK**.
    f) In the **Microsoft Excel** dialog box, select **OK**.

    > **Note:** Remember that the scenarios feature automatically converts formulas into figures. This is one of the reasons it's a good idea to create a scenario based on the original figures.

g) In the **Scenario Values** dialog box, ensure that the following figures appear.

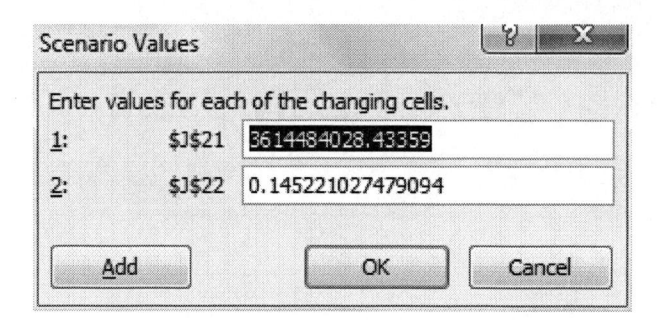

    Scenario Values dialog box showing $J$21 = 3614484028.43359 and $J$22 = 0.145221027479094

h) Select **Add**.

4. Add the first scenario based on the royalty rate and sales growth estimates from the finance department.
    a) In the **Scenario name** field, type *Sales Down 10% Royalty Rate 14%*
    b) Ensure that the range J21:J22 appears in the **Changing cells** field, and then select **OK**.
    c) In the **Microsoft Excel** dialog box, select **OK**.
    d) In the **Scenario Values** dialog box, change the displayed value for cell **$J:$21** to: *=3614484028.43359*0.9*

    > **Note:** This formula represents a 10-percent decrease in the original value. You only need to add the equal sign before the value and **0.9* after it. Do not delete the existing value and then retype the entire formula. Follow this process for each of the scenarios.

    e) Change the displayed vale for cell **$J$22** to: *0.14*

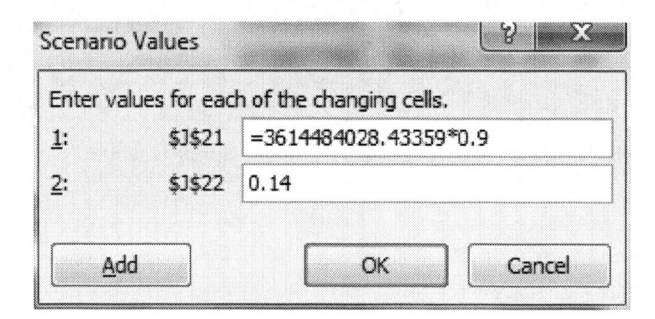

    *Scenario Values dialog box showing $J$21 = =3614484028.43359*0.9 and $J$22 = 0.14*

    f) Select **Add** to add the next scenario.
    g) In the **Microsoft Excel** dialog box, select **OK** to acknowledge that Excel will convert the formula to a value.

5. Add the next scenario based on the figures from the finance department.
    a) In the **Scenario name** field, type *Sales Up 10% Royalty Rate 16%* and ensure that J21:J22 still appears in the **Changing cells** field.
    b) Select **OK** twice.
    c) Enter the following values for the changing cells:
        - $J$21: *=3614484028.43359*1.1*
        - $J$22: *0.16*
    d) Select **Add** and then select **OK**.

6. Add a final scenario with sales up by 20 percent and a royalty rate of 17.5 percent.

Scenario Values dialog box:
- 1: $J$21 =3614484028.43359*1.2
- 2: $J$22 0.175

> **Note:** The value for the changing cell $J$22 should be multiplied by *0.175* for this scenario. Once you have entered the values for the last scenario, in the **Scenario Values** dialog box, select **OK** and *not* **Add**.

7. View the results of your scenario analysis.
   a) In the **Scenario Manager** dialog box, in the **Scenarios** list, select **Sales Down 10% Royalty Rate 14%**, and then select **Show**.
   b) Verify that the values in the range J21:J24 are updated when you show the scenario.
   c) Review the remaining two scenarios and close the **Scenario Manager** dialog box.

8. Add the **Scenario** button to the **Quick Access Toolbar** so you don't have to open the **Scenario Manager** dialog box to view your scenarios.
   a) Select the **Customize Quick Access Toolbar** button, and then select **More Commands**.
   b) In the **Excel Options** dialog box, ensure that the **Quick Access Toolbar** tab is selected.
   c) In the **Choose commands from** drop-down menu, select **All Commands**.
   d) In the commands list, scroll down, select **Scenario**, select **Add**, and then select **OK**.

9. Use the **Scenario** button to view your scenarios.
   a) From the **Quick Access Toolbar**, select the **Scenario** button and then select the desired scenario.
   b) View the remaining scenarios.

10. Save the workbook to the C:\091020Data\Using Automated Analysis Tools folder as *my_book_sales_dashboard_06a.xlsx* and close the workbook.

TOPIC C

Use the Goal Seek Feature

Excel provides you with a number of options for determining potential outcomes based on varying inputs. Suppose you already know the outcome you desire? For example, if you need to borrow money to buy a piece of equipment for your business and you know the total amount you wish to pay back and how long you want to pay on the loan. How do you determine the interest rate you can afford? How would you go about determining which input will result in the desired outcome? Trial and error seems a time-consuming, hit-or-miss proposition.

In addition to the what-if analysis tools that enable you to crunch numbers to arrive at a solution, you can also do the reverse: Determine the value of a specific input to arrive at a predetermined outcome. Taking advantage of this functionality means you can avoid manually re-entering values until you achieve the desired result or coming up with complex formulas to perform the calculation for you.

The Goal Seek Feature

The Goal Seek feature is a type of what-if analysis that enables you to calculate the value of one input in order to arrive at a specific outcome. This is the opposite of how data tables and scenarios work. You can use the Goal Seek feature to determine the value of a specific input for any formula or function as long as that input can be expressed as a value within a single cell; the Goal Seek feature is capable of calculating for only a single value.

When you run the Goal Seek feature, you must define the set cell, which is the cell that contains the formula or function you want to arrive at the desired value, the value you want for the final outcome, and the changing cell. Excel will calculate the correct value for the changing cell to arrive at the desired value in the set cell. The set cell must contain a formula or a function and the changing cell must contain a numeric value; it cannot contain a formula or a function.

The Goal Seek Dialog Box

You will use the **Goal Seek** dialog box to define the set cell, the desired outcome value, and the changing cell for your goal. You can access the **Goal Seek** dialog box by selecting **Data→Data Tools→What-If Analysis→Goal Seek**.

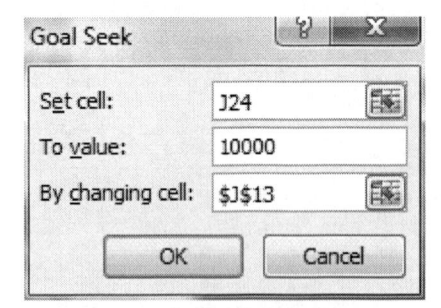

Figure 6-10: Use the Goal Seek dialog box to define the conditions for your goal.

Iterative Calculations

The Goal Seek feature is just one of a number of Excel features and functionality that relies on *iterative calculations*. During an iterative calculation, Excel rapidly changes the value of an input or several inputs by a particular increment until it arrives at some specific condition or desired outcome. In the case of using the Goal Seek feature, Excel will continue to replace the value in the changing cell and then recalculate the formula or function result, until the desired value is achieved. This is, essentially, the same as a user employing a trial-and-error method for calculating the variable input to achieve the desired goal. The benefit, of course, is that Excel does all the work for you.

Iterative Calculation Options

In many cases, iterative calculation functionality is baked into Excel's features or tools. The Goal Seek feature is just one example of this. But, there may be times you wish to develop your own formulas or functions to perform iterative calculations for you. In order to do this, however, you need to enable iterative calculations and set the desired iterative calculation options. By default, this functionality is disabled because, for most users, it could represent a common type of error: a *circular reference*. A circular reference is simply when a formula or function refers back, either directly or indirectly, to the cell that contains the formula or function. Here's a simple example.

	A	B	C	D	E
1	5				
2	10				
3	20				
4	0				

Cell A4 contains formula =SUM(A1:A4)

In this example, the formula in cell **A4** is referring to itself; the SUM function is trying to add the values in the range **A1:A3** to the value in cell **A4**. The problem is that the function, itself, is in cell **A4**. Initially, there is no value in cell **A4**. When Excel goes to add the sum of **A1:A3** to the value in cell **A4**, there is no value to add. Excel recognizes that this is a circular reference and will actually display an error message alerting you to it. If you simply select **OK** to allow the formula anyway, Excel returns the value 0.

But, let's consider what Excel would do if it were able to handle this type of calculation. On the first pass, the function would add the first three values, totaling 35, add that to the value of zero in cell **A4**, and then return the value 35 in cell **A4**. But now that the value in cell **A4** is 35, the SUM function would have to return a value of 70 (35 + 35). If it were to run the calculation again, the result would be 105, and so on. As the value changes each time the calculation is run, Excel would have to work forever to calculate some final result as the returned figure kept getting higher and higher, increasing toward infinity. Clearly, Excel could never perform the calculation to completion. This is why this type of calculation is disabled by default.

But, there are times you may wish to have Excel perform an iterative calculation on a worksheet for you. Take this simple mathematical formula as an example: X=1/sin(X). Because, in this case, X is a function of itself and you don't, at first, know the value of X, you would have to estimate an initial value, run the calculation, and then check to see if X truly does equal the inverse of its own sine. If it didn't, you would have to supply a different value for X, see if the values on each side of the equal sign got closer or further apart in value, and then, perhaps, run the calculation again, making adjustments for the value of X accordingly. We would continue this process until the values on each side of the equal sign either exactly matched each other, or got close enough for the necessary level of precision. To do this manually would be both painstaking and time consuming.

In this case, you would want to enable iterative calculations, feed the output of the formula back into itself as the value for X, and then have Excel run the calculation for you until the values on each side were equal or simply close enough to your preferred precision level. As this type of calculation, however, often has no precise answer, rather a series of closer and closer solutions that approach, but never arrive at, the correct answer, you have to set a limit on either the number of times Excel should run the calculation or the level of precision at which it should stop. These are your two iterative calculation options in Excel. You can enable iterative calculations and set these options in the **Excel Options** dialog box.

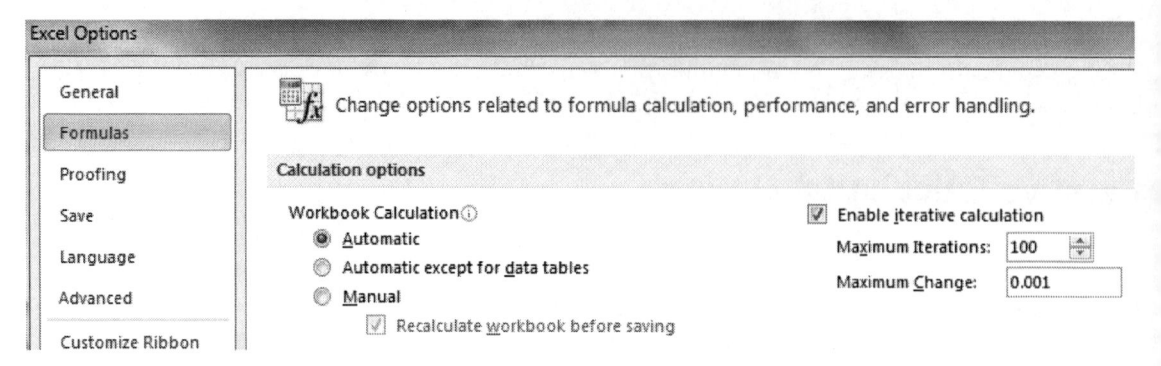

Figure 6-11: You can access the iterative calculation options on the Formula tab of the Excel Options dialog box.

The following table describes the iterative calculation options in Excel.

Calculation Option Element	Use This To
Enable iterative calculation check box	Enable or disable iterative calculations for Excel. This is a system-wide setting and will apply to any workbook you open on the same computer.
Maximum Iterations spin box	Set the maximum number of times Excel can perform iterative calculations.
Maximum Change field	Set the smallest acceptable amount of change from one iteration to the next before Excel stops iterating the calculation.

> Access the Checklist tile on your LogicalCHOICE course screen for reference information and job aids on **How to Use the Goal Seek Feature and Set Iterative Calculation Options.**

ACTIVITY 6-3
Using the Goal Seek Feature

Data File
C:\091020Data\Using Automated Analysis Tools\book_sales_dashboard_06b.xlsx

Scenario
Fuller and Ackerman leaders are interested in targeting company growth in the Latin American (LA) market. They are putting a lot of resources on the ground to increase sales there as it has traditionally had the slowest growth. In order to determine precisely how much to invest in a marketing and sales presence in the LA market, they would like to have a growth target in mind for the region. Specifically, they have asked you to determine how much growth the LA market would need to achieve to reach the company's stretch goal of hitting a total sales figure of $490 million. As growth is slowing in the remaining markets, company analysts are predicting only 3 percent growth in each of them. You decide that using the Goal Seek feature to identify the specific sales target for the LA market will be the best way to start. You can then use a simple calculation to provide company leaders with a sales increase percentage target.

---

1. Open the **book_sales_dashboard_06b.xlsx** workbook file and ensure that the **Sales_Dashboard** worksheet is selected.

2. Calculate a 3-percent sales growth for all markets except for the LA market.
    a) Select cell **C32** and enter the following formula: *=B32*1.03*
    b) Copy and paste the formula from cell **C32** into cells **C33** and **C35**.
    c) Enter a value of *0* (zero) in cell **C34**.

3. Use the Goal Seek feature to calculate the total sales needed in the LA market to achieve $490 million in total sales.
    a) Select cell **C36** and then select **Data→Data Tools→What-If Analysis→Goal Seek**.
    b) In the **Goal Seek** dialog box, verify that the **Set cell** field displays **C36**.
    c) In the **To value** field, enter *490,000,000*
    d) In the **By changing cell** field, enter **C34**.
    e) Select **OK**.
    f) In the **Goal Seek Status** dialog box, select **OK**.

4. Use a simple calculation to determine the percentage sales increase for the LA market represented by the value in cell **C34**.
    a) Select cell **C38**.

b) Enter the following formula: *=(C34-B34)/B34*

31	Market	FY 2012	FY 2013
32	APAC	$123,886,421.00	$127,603,013.63
33	EMEA	$93,754,216.00	$96,566,842.48
34	LA	$99,520,867.00	$122,506,624.45
35	NA	$139,149,048.00	$143,323,519.44
36			$490,000,000.00
37			
38		LA % Inc. Target	23.10%
39			

5. Save the workbook to the **C:\091020Data\Using Automated Analysis Tools** folder as *my_book_sales_dashboard_06b.xlsx* and close the workbook.

TOPIC D

Activate and Use the Solver Tool

The ability to determine some specific input for a calculation based on knowing the desired outcome is a handy capability that allows you run multiple calculations to arrive at the desired result without having to manually crunch the numbers yourself. Excel's Goal Seek feature, however, has one major limitation: It can solve only for a single value for a single variable. Suppose you need to plan the production schedule for a large operation to maximize sales based on a variety of constraints, such as the total number of labor hours available, the minimum or maximum number of particular products that need to be made, the amount of time it takes to produce each of the different products, and the amount of time and money the facility can dedicate to each product? Clearly, this is a set of conditions that what-if analysis won't be able to consider.

Excel 2010 includes a powerful tool than enables you to determine ideal values for multiple inputs to arrive at a solution for some formula or function based on a variety of constraints. Putting this kind of capability in your hands means you can plan for almost limitless constraints and still maximize your profits, improve efficiency, and utilize resources in the best way possible.

The Solver Tool

The Solver tool is an Excel add-in that comes loaded with Excel 2010 but is not activated by default. Once you activate the Solver tool, you can use it to optimize some set of conditions to determine the best possible outcome. The Solver tool works by examining and performing calculations on the three main components of an Excel optimization model: the target cell, the changing cells, and the constraints. Much like what-if analysis tools, the target cell is the cell containing the primary formula or function you're concerned with, and the changing cells are the cells whose values can change to arrive at the ideal solution. Additionally, you can set a number of *constraints*, or conditions that limit what the values in the changing cells can be. You would set constraints, for example, if you have only so many labor hours available to complete a project or there are only so many of some item in inventory. Clearly, an optimal solution could not use more labor than you have available or require you to sell more product than you have on hand.

The Solver tool can solve for the optimal solution based on three different criteria: maximizing some value, minimizing some value, or attaining a specific value. You would optimally seek a maximum value, for example, if you were solving for a way to maximize sales. You would want to find the minimum optimal solution if you were looking at costs. If you have some set value you must attain, say the total number of available hours of production time for a facility over the course of a year, you could set that specific value, and then optimize the inputs (for example, how much of each product to produce) to attain it based on other constraints. When using the Solver tool, changing cells can contain either values, or formulas or functions.

Figure 6-12: The Solver command appears in the Analysis group on the Data tab once you've activated it.

The Solver Parameters Dialog Box

You will use the **Solver Parameters** dialog box to set the criteria for your optimization calculation. Here, you will define the target cell and the changing cells, view and access your constraints, select a solving method, and set whether the Solver is solving for a minimum, maximum, or specific outcome. You can access the **Solver Parameters** dialog box by selecting **Data→Analysis→Solver**.

> **Note:** The **Analysis** group does not appear on the **Data** ribbon tab until you activate the Solver or other add-ins.

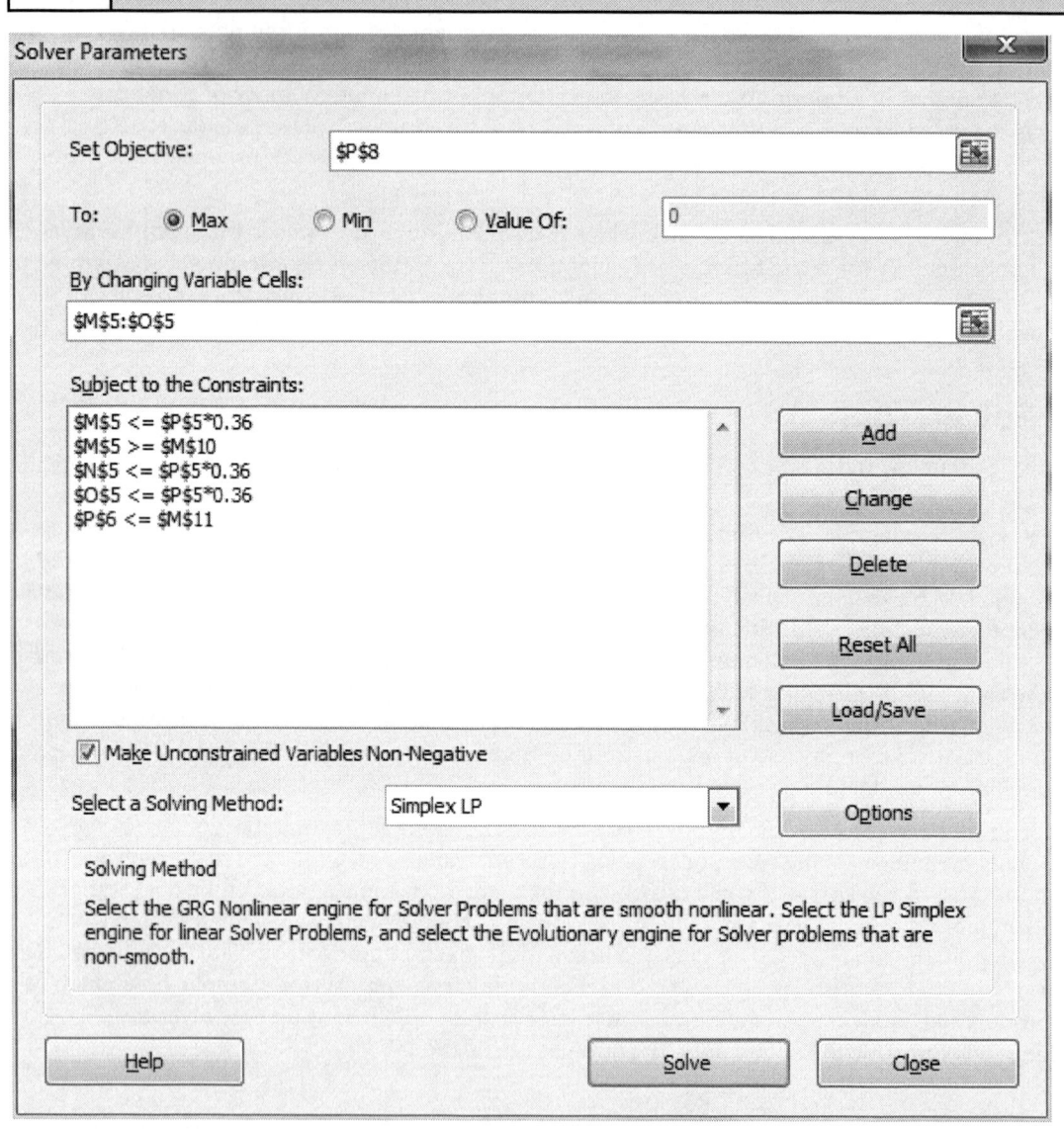

Figure 6-13: Use the Solver Parameters dialog box to define the conditions and constraints for optimizing your solution.

The following table describes the various elements of the **Solver Parameters** dialog box.

Solver Parameters Dialog Box Element	Use This To
Set Objective field	Set the target cell for the optimization.

Solver Parameters Dialog Box Element	Use This To
To section	Select whether you wish to solve to optimally minimize or maximize some value, or to attain some particular target value. If you select the **Value Of** radio button, you must also enter the desired final value for the formula or function in the target cell.
By Changing Variable Cells field	Define the changing cells for the optimization.
Subject to the Constraints list	View the currently defined constraints or to select constraints for editing or deletion.
Add button	Open the **Add Constraint** dialog box, which you will use to define new constraints.
Change button	Open the **Change Constraint** dialog box, which you will use to edit the selected constraint. The **Change Constraint** dialog box differs from the **Add Constraint** dialog box in name only. Otherwise, the two are identical.
Delete button	Delete the currently selected constraint.
Reset All button	Reset all fields and selections in the **Solver Parameters** dialog box. This command deletes the target cell, all changing cells, and all constraints currently configured.
Load/Save button	Load previous optimization models or save the current one. You would use this feature, for example, if you wanted to save multiple solutions for the same problem by using a variety of different constraints.
Make Unconstrained Variables Non-Negative check box	Ensure that all changing cell values that you have not subject to specific constraints return a value of greater than zero in the final solution.
Select a Solving Method drop-down menu	Select which method Excel uses to optimize the solution. The method you select will depend on the type of formula or function you have in the target cell.
Options button	Open the **Options** dialog box, which you can use to configure precise solution calculation options.
Solve button	Run the Solver tool.

Solving Methods

The Solver tool provides you with three main options for determining how it optimizes the changing cells while looking for a solution: GRG Nonlinear, Simplex LP, and Evolutionary. You should select the option that best fits the formula or function entered in the target cell. A complete understanding of these different algorithms is beyond the scope of this course, but the following table describes these options at a high level.

Note: For more information on these solving methods, visit **www.solver.com**.

Solving Method	Use This Method To
LP Simplex	Find optimization solutions involving linear mathematical relationships and equations. Linear equations involve variables that are proportionately related to each other. For example, if a car travels at a consistent rate of speed and you graph the distance it travels against the time that has passed, the resulting graph would display a straight line increasing in value for both speed and time. There is a linear relationship between speed and time.
GRG Nonlinear	Find optimization solutions involving smooth, nonlinear mathematical relationships and equations. Following on the previous example, if the car were to accelerate at a constant rate while you measure the distance it travels over time, the resulting graph would display a curved, upward-sloping line that has a smooth curvature. There is a smooth, nonlinear relationship between the time passed and the distance traveled when the car accelerates at a constant rate.
Evolutionary	Find optimization solutions involving complex, non-smooth, nonlinear mathematical relationships and equations, or for functions, such as IF and VLOOKUP, that are nonlinear and not smooth nonlinear. This method uses genetic algorithms to identify solutions.

The Add Constraint Dialog Box

You will use the **Add Constraint** dialog box to define any necessary constraints for the changing cells in your solutions. From here, you can select from among six different constraint options and, when appropriate, define the criteria by which they are enforced. For example, if you select the less than or equal to option, you must also specify a value for comparison. You can define multiple constraints before returning to the **Solver Parameters** dialog box. To do so, select the **Add** button to define additional constraints. If you select **OK** or **Cancel** from the **Add Constraint** dialog box, Excel returns you to the **Solver Parameters** dialog box.

Figure 6-14: Use the Add Constraint dialog box to define the constraints for changing cells.

The following table describes each of the constraint options you can select from the drop-down menu in the **Add Constraint** dialog box.

Constraint Option	Description
Less than or equal to	Constrains the value in the changing cell to a value that is less than or equal to the value you specify.
Equal to	Constrains the value in the changing cell to a value that is equal to the value you specify.
Greater than or equal to	Constrains the value in the changing cell to a value that is greater than or equal to the value you specify.

Constraint Option	Description
Int	Requires the value in the changing cell to be an integer.
Bin	Ensures the value in the changing cell is either a one or a zero. Use this option for yes/no type decisions.
Dif	Ensures the values in a range of changing cells are all different.

The Solver Results Dialog Box

When you run the Solver tool, Excel tries to identify an optimal solution to the problem that adheres to the given constraints for the changing cells. Whether Excel finds a solution or not, it displays the **Solver Results** dialog box after running the Solver tool. From here, you can identify whether or not Excel found a solution given the defined constraints and solving method, decide whether or not to accept the solution, and run a variety of reports to more closely examine the solution results. You can also decide to return to the **Solver Parameters** dialog box to refine your problem further, and ask for another solution.

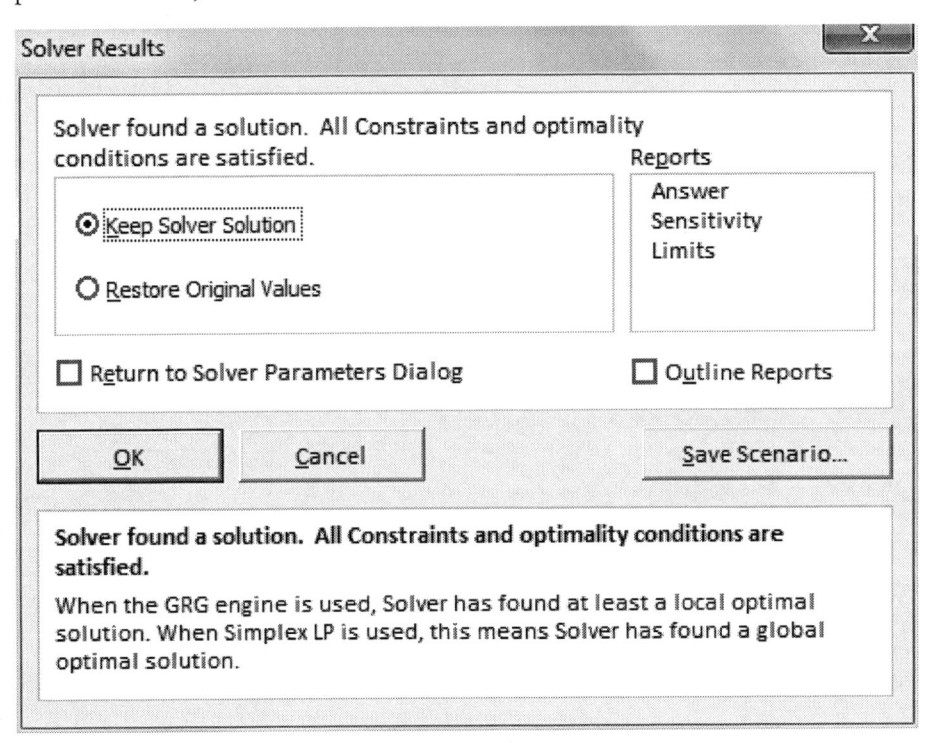

Figure 6-15: The Solver Results dialog box.

Access the Checklist tile on your LogicalCHOICE course screen for reference information and job aids on How to Activate and Use the Solver Tool.

ACTIVITY 6-4
Activating and Using the Solver Tool

Data File
C:\091020Data\Using Automated Analysis Tools\book_sales_dashboard_solver.xlsx

Before You Begin
Excel 2010 is open.

Scenario
You have received a request from the production manager at the print shop and bindery that produces the top-selling titles at Fuller and Ackerman (F&A). She would like to plan preliminary production levels for the titles at each of the price points for the coming year. The production manager needs some estimates on how many titles the facility will need to produce based on previous sales, projected sales increases, pre-orders, and the total number of production hours she has available for the titles.

The production facility produces titles at the various price points at different rates, depending on the page count and cover type. F&A has already received pre-orders nearing 6,000,000 copies for titles at the $11.99 price point, and the facility has 2,600 hours available to produce the top-selling titles. Additionally, you would like a fairly even distribution of title production, so you have asked that titles at any one price point make up no more than 36 percent of overall unit production. With so many variables to keep track of, you decide the best way to provide the production manager with production estimates is to activate and use the Solver tool to determine optimal production levels for books at each selling price. Of course, you would also like to ensure production levels drive the greatest possible sales totals. You have already set up your sales dashboard workbook with some of the preliminary production estimates based on an across-the-board 7 percent sales increase. You have also entered values for your constraints.

1. Activate the Solver tool.
    a) Select **File→Options**.
    b) In the **Excel Options** dialog box, select the **Add-Ins** tab.
    c) At the bottom of the **Add-ins** section, ensure that **Excel Add-ins** is selected in the **Manage** drop-down menu.
    d) Select **Go**.
    e) In the **Add-Ins** dialog box, check the **Solver Add-in** check box and select **OK**.
    f) Ensure that the **Solver** command appears in the **Analysis** group on the ribbon's **Data** tab.

2. Open the **book_sales_dashboard_solver.xlsx** workbook file and select the **Titles_to_Watch** worksheet tab.

3. Begin configuring the Solver tool to calculate production levels for titles at the various price points that optimize total sales.
    a) Select cell **P8** and then select **Data→Analysis→Solver**.
    b) In the **Solver Parameters** dialog box, select the **Collapse Dialog** button in the **Set Objective** field, select cell **P8**, and press **Enter**.
    c) In the **To** section, ensure that the **Max** radio button is selected.
    d) In the **By Changing Variable Cells** field, enter the range **$M$5:$O$5**.

4. Configure a constraint to ensure the facility produces at least 6,000,000 copies of the titles that sell for $11.99.
   a) In the **Subject to the Constraints** section, select **Add**.
   b) In the **Add Constraint** dialog box, in the **Cell Reference** field, enter *$M$5*
   c) In the drop-down menu, select **>=**.
   d) In the **Constraint** field, enter *=$M$10*

5. Configure a constraint to ensure that production efforts don't exceed 2,600 hours.
   a) Select **Add**.
   b) In the **Cell Reference** field, enter *$P$6*
   c) Ensure that **<=** is selected in the drop-down menu.
   d) In the **Constraint** field, enter *=$M$11*

6. Configure the constraints to ensure that no price point makes up more than 36 percent of overall production.
   a) Select **Add** and, in the **Cell Reference** field, enter *$M$5*
   b) From the drop-down menu, ensure that **<=** is selected.
   c) In the **Constraint** field, enter the following formula: *=$P$5*0.36* and then select **Add**.
   d) Enter the same constraint for cell **N5** and select **Add**.
   e) Enter the same constraint for cell **O5** and select **OK** to return to the **Solver Parameters** dialog box.

   ```
   Subject to the Constraints:
   $M$5 <= $P$5*0.36
   $M$5 >= $M$10
   $N$5 <= $P$5*0.36
   $O$5 <= $P$5*0.36
   $P$6 <= $M$11
   ```

7. Ensure that the **Make Unconstrained Variables Non-Negative** check box is checked.

8. From the **Select a Solving Method** drop-down menu, select **Simplex LP** and then select **Solve**.

9. In the **Solver Results** dialog box, ensure that the **Keep Solver Solution** radio button is selected and then select **OK**.

10. If necessary, adjust column widths to accommodate the new values.

11. Save the workbook to the **C:\091020Data\Using Automated Analysis Tools** folder as *my_book_sales_dashboard_solver.xlsx* and close the file.

TOPIC E

Analyze Data with Analysis ToolPak Tools

Excel provides you with many useful statistical functions to assist you with data analysis but these functions do have their limitations. Often, when using statistical functions, you can perform only a single operation at a time or analyze a very specific subset of data at once. However, you may find yourself with the need to perform a more in-depth statistical analysis of an entire dataset. Perhaps you'd like to view the mean, the median, and the mode for a particular set of values along with the standard deviation for the same. This is a handy set of figures for teachers analyzing large sets of grades or sales managers trying to get a better understanding of how their teams are performing as a whole. Or perhaps you'd like a bit of insight into how seemingly random sets of variables relate to each other. Is there some correlation between or among them? Do some variables tend to rise or fall in tandem while others operate independently of each other? Clearly, this type of analysis would either be difficult and time consuming, or practically impossible by using functions alone.

When it comes to performing large-scale statistical analysis, you'll likely want access to a set of tools that is capable of performing these types of tasks for you. By activating and becoming familiar with the Analysis ToolPak, a highly robust set of various analysis tools, you'll be giving yourself the ability to obtain a detailed statistical analysis of your data and you'll save yourself the time and effort it would take to organize your data, and then set up and run a variety of different, complex calculations.

The Analysis ToolPak

The Analysis ToolPak is a suite of statistical analysis tools that comes bundled with Excel 2010. Like the Solver tool, the Analysis ToolPak is an add-in that is not active by default. When you activate the Analysis ToolPak, Excel displays the **Data Analysis** command in the **Analysis** group on the **Data** ribbon tab. This command provides you with access to all of the various tools included with the Analysis ToolPak. The tools included in the suite use the existing data in your worksheets and the parameters you define to return a variety of statistical analyses in tabular or chart form automatically.

The Data Analysis Dialog Box

When you select the **Data Analysis** command, Excel opens the **Data Analysis** dialog box. You will use this dialog box to select the particular data analysis tool you wish to use. Each of the tools included in the Analysis ToolPak opens in its own unique dialog box that contains the parameters and options you can or must set for each tool.

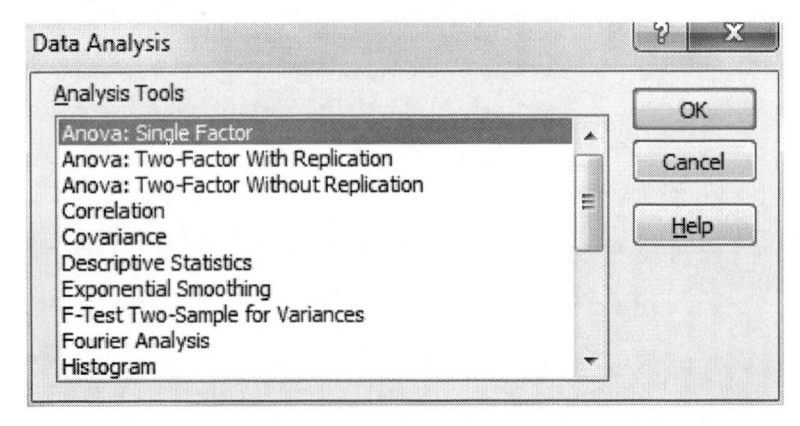

Figure 6-16: Use the Data Analysis dialog box to select the desired data analysis tool.

Analysis ToolPak Tools

The Analysis ToolPak comes loaded with 19 different tools you can use to perform a wide variety of statistical analyses. While an in-depth examination of each of these is well beyond the scope of this course, the following table describes each of them at a high level.

Analysis ToolPak Tool	Description
Anova: Single Factor	Analyzes data variance for two or more samples.
Anova: Two-Factor With Replication	Analyzes data variance for two or more samples that fall into two different categories. This analysis can examine variance when compared to the entire population or when considered strictly within one of the categories.
Anova: Two-Factor Without Replication	Analyzes data variance for two or more samples that fall into two different categories. This analysis examines each sample/category pair only in relation to the entire population.
Correlation	Generates a correlation matrix that examines a variety of measurement variables for a number of different subjects.
Covariance	Generates a correlation matrix that examines a variety of measurement variables for a number of different subjects. This analysis differs from the correlation analysis only in the scale used in the output figures. Correlation analysis scales the returned vales to fall with in the range -1 to 1; covariance does not.
Descriptive Statistics	Generates a report of univariate statistics for the dataset.
Exponential Smoothing	Uses a particular type of averaging to forecast future performance based on previous performance.
F-Test Two-Sample for Variances	Uses the F-test to compare the population variances for two samples.
Fourier Analysis	Performs Fast Fourier Transform (FFT) data transformations and their inverses.
Histogram	Generates a distribution of values for particular bins, or ranges, of values.
Moving Average	Forecasts the value for a variable based on its values for the previous X number of periods. For each new period, the number of past periods remains the same, meaning it moves as time progresses toward subsequent periods.
Random Number Generation	Fills in ranges of data based on particular distributions of existing data.
Rank and Percentile	Generates a table that identifies the position and percentile ranking of the values in a dataset.
Regression	Uses the least squares method to perform linear regression analysis on a dataset.
Sampling	Generates random or directed samples of data from the values that exist within a particular dataset.
t-Test: Paired Two Sample for Means	Performs a Student's t-Test on two different sets of observations to determine if both populations have equal population means.

Analysis ToolPak Tool	Description
t-Test: Two-Sample Assuming Equal Variances	Performs the same Student's t-Test, but under the assumption that the data from both observations come from populations with the same variances.
t-Test: Two-Sample Assuming Unequal Variances	Performs the same Student's t-Test, but under the assumption that the data from both observations come from populations with differing variances.
z-Test: Two Sample for Means	Performs a z-Test on two samples for means with known variances.

Note: For information about combining the functionality of this add-in suite and Excel's default capabilities, watch the LearnTO **Build a Histogram in Analysis ToolPak** presentation from the **LearnTO** tile on the LogicalCHOICE Course screen.

Access the Checklist tile on your LogicalCHOICE course screen for reference information and job aids on How to Activate and Use Analysis ToolPak Tools.

ACTIVITY 6-5
Analyzing Data with Analysis ToolPak Tools

Data File
C:\091020Data\Using Automated Analysis Tools\book_sales_dashboard_toolpak.xlsx

Before You Begin
Excel 2010 is open.

Scenario
Fuller and Ackerman (F&A) senior managers would like a statistical breakdown of all book sales to date. As you maintain the sales data on all F&A titles, they have asked you to provide a statistical breakdown of unit sales and total earnings for all of the titles currently in print. As this is a complex series of calculations, you decide to activate the Analysis ToolPak and use one of its tools to perform the analysis for you.

---

1. Activate the Analysis ToolPak.
   a) Select **File→Options**.
   b) In the **Excel Options** dialog box, select the **Add-Ins** tab.
   c) From the bottom of the **Add-ins** section, in the **Manage** drop-down menu, ensure **Excel Add-ins** is selected, and select **Go**.
   d) In the **Add-Ins** dialog box, check the **Analysis ToolPak** check box and select **OK**.

2. Open the **book_sales_dashboard_toolpak.xlsx** workbook file and select the **Raw_Book_Sales** worksheet tab.

3. Scroll to the right so the range **W2:AA6** is visible.

4. Perform the unit sales statistical analysis.
   a) Select **Data→Analysis→Data Analysis**.
   b) In the **Data Analysis** dialog box, select **Descriptive Statistics**, and select **OK**.
   c) In the **Descriptive Statistics** dialog box, if necessary, place the insertion point in the **Input Range** field and press **F3** to open the **Paste Name** dialog box.
   d) In the **Paste Name** dialog box, select **Total_Units_to_Date** and then select **OK**.
   e) Select the **Output Range** radio button and enter *$W$7* in the **Output Range** field.
   f) Check the **Summary statistics** check box and select **OK**.

5. Perform the same analysis on the data in the **Total Earnings to Date** column, setting the output range to cell **$Z$7**.

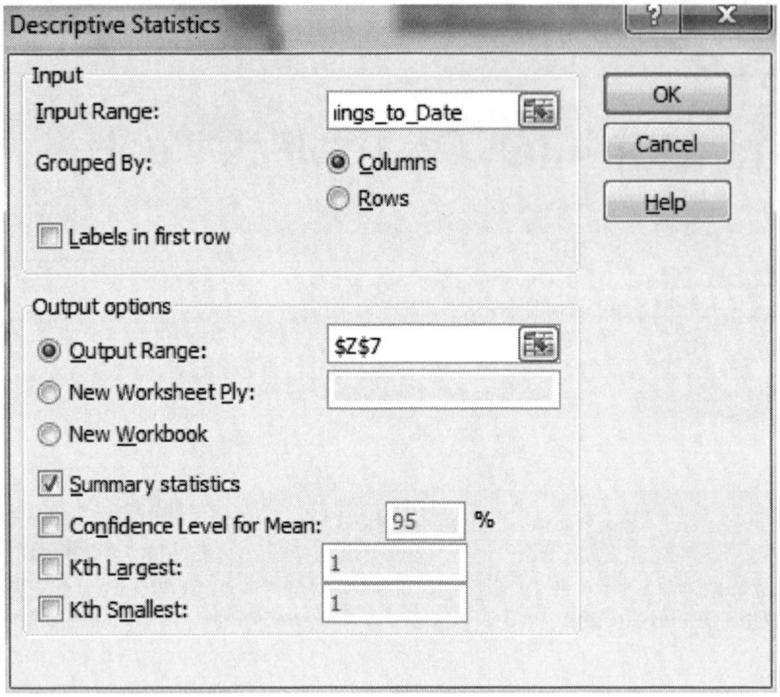

6. Adjust the column widths as necessary.
7. Save the workbook to the **C:\091020Data\Using Automated Analysis Tools** folder as ***my_book_sales_dashboard_toolpak.xlsx*** and close the workbook.

Summary

In this lesson, you used a variety of Excel's automated data analysis tools to gain insight into raw workbook data. Excel's built-in analysis capabilities can save you incredible amounts of time and effort. By using these tools, you can avoid repetitious entry of data with different variable values to determine specific outcomes and perform complex data analysis in a few simple steps. You can also account for a great variety of variable values and given constraints to determine the ideal steps to take in any number of different situations.

How will you be able to use what-if analysis right away when you return to your daily tasks?

What immediate benefit do you see automated analysis techniques having for you and your organization?

> **Note:** Check your LogicalCHOICE Course screen for opportunities to interact with your classmates, peers, and the larger LogicalCHOICE online community about the topics covered in this course or other topics you are interested in. From the Course screen you can also access available resources for a more continuous learning experience.

7 Presenting Your Data Visually

Lesson Time: 30 minutes

Lesson Objectives

In this lesson, you will present your data visually. You will:

- Use advanced chart features.
- Create sparklines.

Lesson Introduction

Often, images can tell a story or provide insight in an instantaneous fashion that isn't always possible with words and numbers. When presenting complex relationships among various bits of data to large groups of people, you may often find it easier to display a chart or a graph instead of asking the audience to pour over massive amounts of data to see your point. Data and relationships can be complex and Excel's basic charts aren't always sufficient for displaying such complexity. For example, you may wish to display a variety of relationships within a single chart, or you may want to graphically display how values relate to each other for massive datasets with far too many entries to reasonably display on a chart.

In these cases, you'll need to go beyond creating simple pie or column charts to get the right message across. Fortunately, Excel's capabilities for graphically presenting data go well beyond the use of these simple chart types. Investing a bit of time now to fully understand what these capabilities are and what they can do will give you the ability to make visual sense of your complex data for nearly any type of presentation or delivery situation.

TOPIC A

Use Advanced Chart Features

Have you ever needed to graphically display two widely different sets of data simultaneously? For example, you may wish to show how unit sales correlate to overall sales totals within the same chart. It's likely that the figures for total sales are much higher than they are for the number of units sold; after all, many, if not most, items cost far more than a dollar these days. Putting both figures on the same chart would likely make at least one of the data series difficult to read. Or suppose you want to display future projections for you datasets on the same chart you display the data itself. Without the future data, how can you create chart elements that visually convey the information you wish to share? What if you have to create a lot of these charts? Does all of this mean a lot of extra data entry, calculation, and formatting?

Excel 2010 includes a wide range of advanced charting features that enable you to display widely varying sets of data together, include forecasting trends on your charts, and reuse highly stylized or formatted charts again and again. It almost goes without saying that this level of functionality means you can quickly make at impact on nearly any presentation without having to put a lot of time and effort into doing so.

Dual-Axis Charts

A dual-axis chart is, simply, a chart that displays two sets of information on the same chart. This can be in the form of a dual-Y-axis chart, which displays two data series simultaneously, or a dual-X-axis chart, which displays two categories simultaneously. By far, dual-Y-axis charts are used far more frequently than dual-X-axis charts. But dual-X-axis charts can be useful for particular types of charts, such as bubble charts or XY (scatter) charts. Excel supports dual-axis charts only for 2-D chart types; they do not work with 3-D chart types. You can create a chart with a secondary X axis only if it already has a secondary Y axis.

The main advantage to dual-axis charts is the ability to not only display two different sets of data simultaneously, but also to format the different sets of data independently of each other. This means you can make the two, for example, data series easily visually distinguishable from each other and display within the same amount of space using different scales. For example, you can simultaneously display unit sales figures, which may range in the thousands, with total sales figures, which could range in the billions of dollars for expensive equipment. Clearly the data that is expressed in billions of units would be far easier to see within the same Y axis scale than the data with figures in the thousands. In fact, those figures may not even be visible with such a drastic difference in scale.

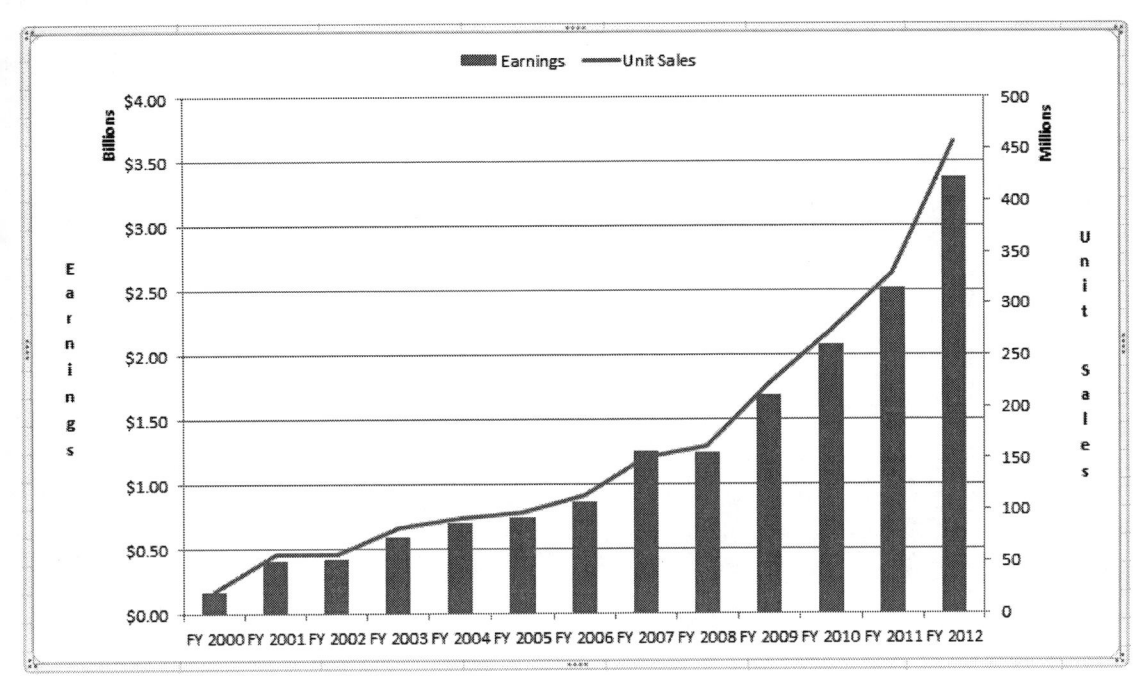

Figure 7-1: Dual-axis chart enable you to simultaneously display and independently format various sets of data within the same space.

> Access the Checklist tile on your LogicalCHOICE course screen for reference information and job aids on How to Create a Dual-Axis Chart.

Forecasting

In addition to creating secondary axes to display various data series or categories simultaneously, Excel includes a chart feature that can help you forecast trends in your data. *Forecasting* is the process of using the trends that exist within past data to predict future outcomes. By its nature, forecasting can never be entirely accurate, as one can never precisely predict all possible future outcomes. As a general rule, the more you forecast out into the future, the less accurate your forecasts become.

Trendlines

In Excel, trendlines are chart elements that can graphically represent both the current trends that exist within your data and past or future forecasts of those trends. You can add trendlines to any of the following non-stacked, 2-D chart types: column, line, bar, area, stock, XY (scatter), and bubble. You can name and format trendlines to make them easier to view on charts or to adhere to organizational branding standards. To access the options for adding trendlines to your charts, from the **Chart Tools** contextual tab, select **Layout→Analysis→Trendline**.

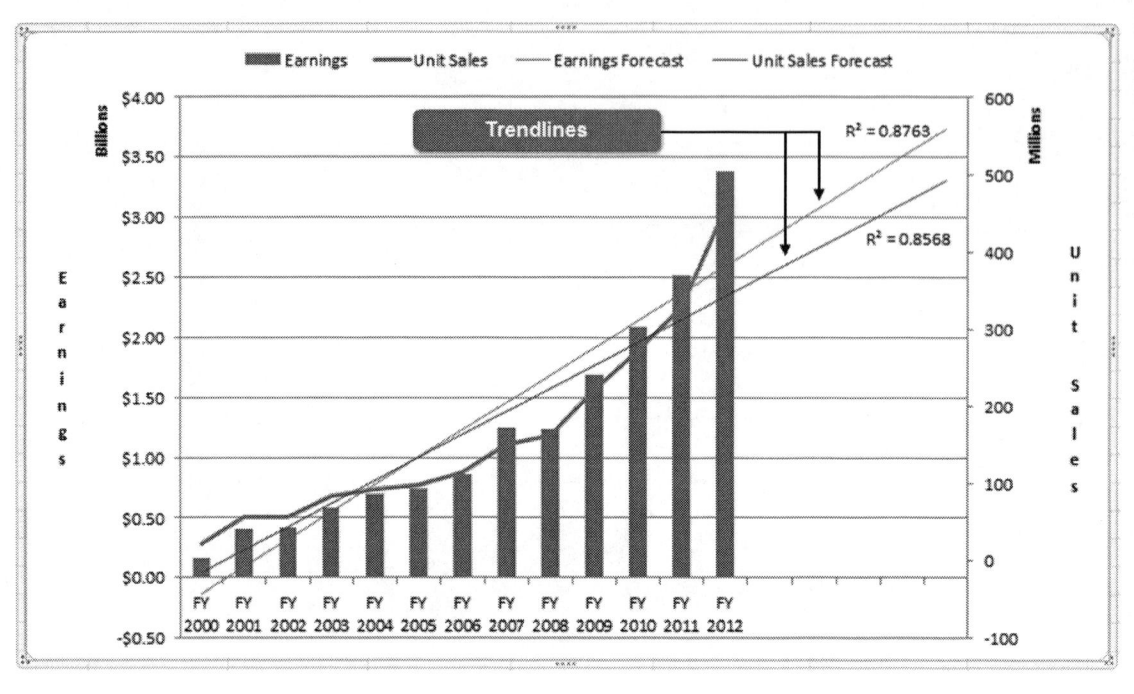

Figure 7-2: Trendlines on an Excel chart.

Trendline Types

You can use different types of trendlines to display and forecast data trends depending on the type of data you wish to analyze. Excel provides you with six options for adding trendlines to your charts.

Trendline Type	Use This to Display or Forecast Data That
Linear	Is linear in nature. When you graph linear relationships, the resulting graph is a straight line that represents a trend that holds steady, or that increases or decreases by a steady rate.
Logarithmic	Has a rapidly increasing or decreasing rate of change that eventually levels out.
Polynomial	Fluctuates over time.
Power	Increases in rate of change at a steady rate over time.
Exponential	Increases in rate of change at an ever-faster rate over time.
Moving average	Fluctuates randomly over time. Use this type of trendline to smooth out random patterns of values to give viewers a sense of the overall average change in values over time.

The Format Trendline Dialog Box

You will use the **Format Trendline** dialog box to apply formatting and effects to your chart trendlines and to change the type of trendlines in your charts. You can access the **Format Trendline** dialog box by selecting a trendline from the **Current Selection** drop-down menu and, from the **Chart Tools** contextual tab, selecting either **Layout→Current Selection→Format Selection** or **Format→Current Selection→Format Selection**.

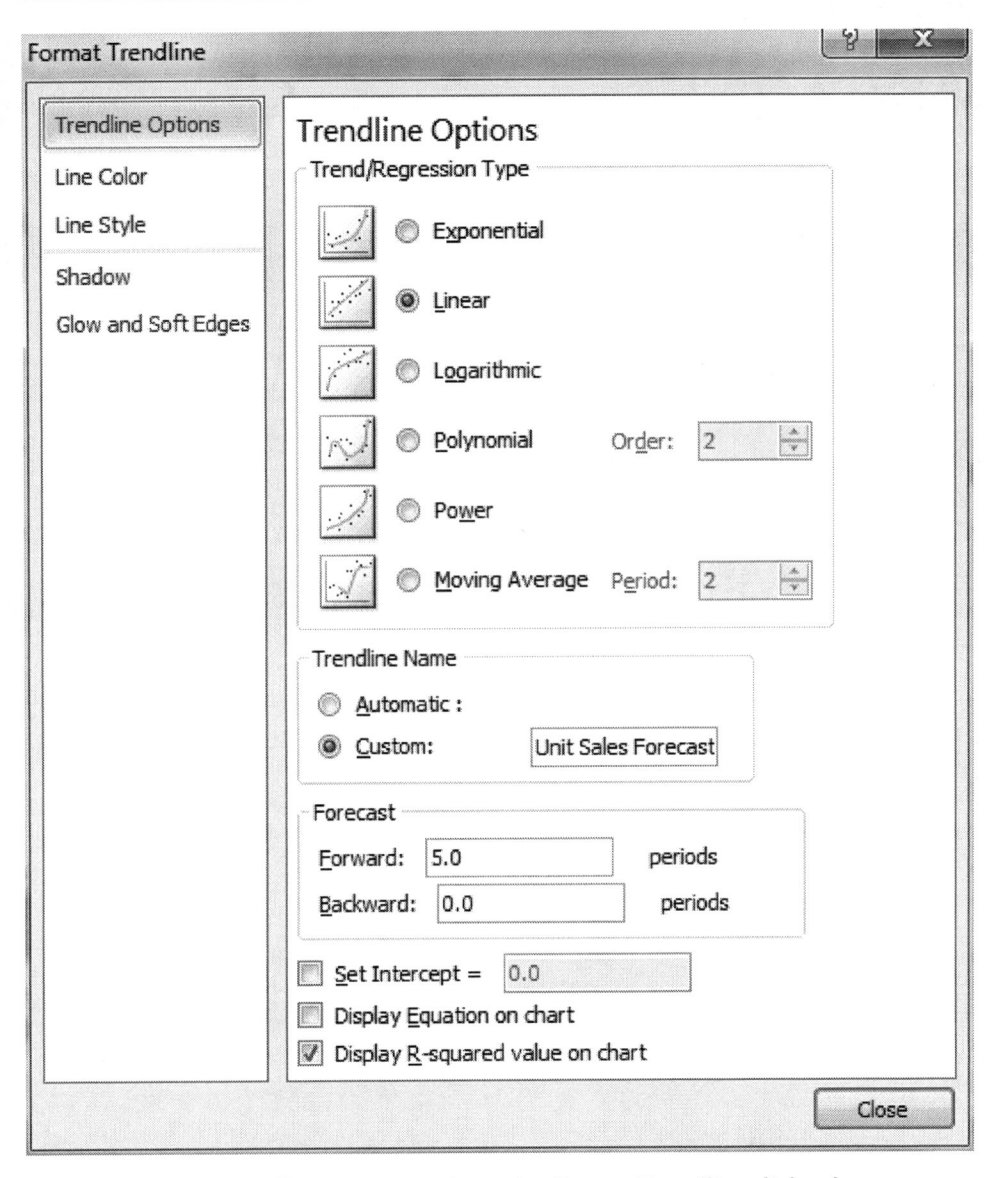

Figure 7-3: The Trendline Options tab on the Format Trendline dialog box.

The following table identifies the commands and options you can access from the various tabs on the **Format Trendline** dialog box.

Format Trendline Dialog Box Tab	Contains Commands For
Trendline Options	Changing a trendline from one type to another, naming a trendline, and forecasting a trendline out into the future or back into the past.
Line Color	Applying solid and gradient color formatting to a trendline.
Line Style	Changing a trendline's width, style, or end type; and adding arrows to the trendline.
Shadow	Applying drop-shadow formatting to a trendline.
Glow and Soft Edges	Applying effect formatting to a trendline.

Access the Checklist tile on your LogicalCHOICE course screen for reference information and job aids on How to Work with Trendlines.

ACTIVITY 7-1
Creating a Dual-Axis Chart and Forecasting with Trendlines

Data File
C:\091020Data\Presenting Your Data Visually\book_sales_dashboard_07.xlsx

Before You Begin
Excel 2010 is open.

Scenario
You're putting some finishing touches on the book sales dashboard you've been working on. You know senior leaders will ask you to present information from the workbook at several important events. You decide to add sales projections based on past sales that extend out five years. You feel this information will be best displayed visually, so you decide to add a chart with both unit sales and total earnings information, and then add trendlines to forecast for both sets of information. As the unit sales and total earning information are measured in vastly different value scales, you realize you'll need to add a second vertical axis to the chart to accommodate both data series. You have already added the labels and data you will need for the chart to a new worksheet named **Sales_Trends**.

The final result of the chart will look like this:

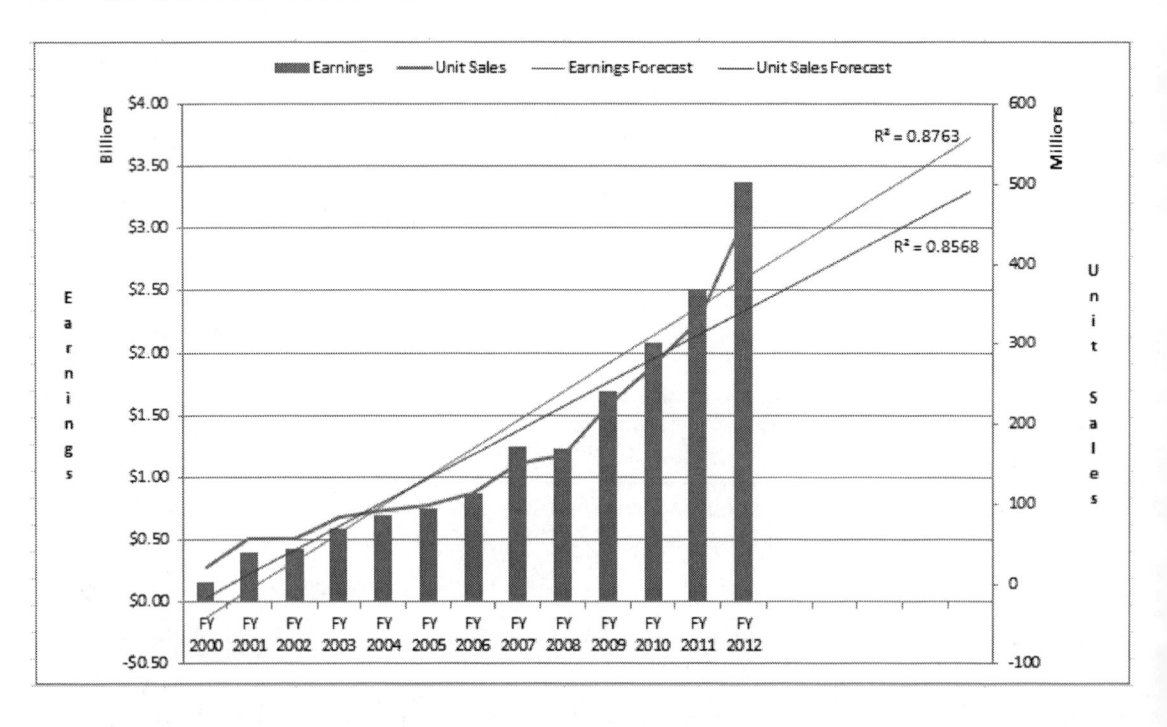

1. Open the **book_sales_dashboard_07.xlsx** workbook and select the **Sales_Trends** worksheet.

2. Add a column chart based on the dataset.

a) Select the range **A1:N3** and then select **Insert→Charts→Column→Clustered Column**.

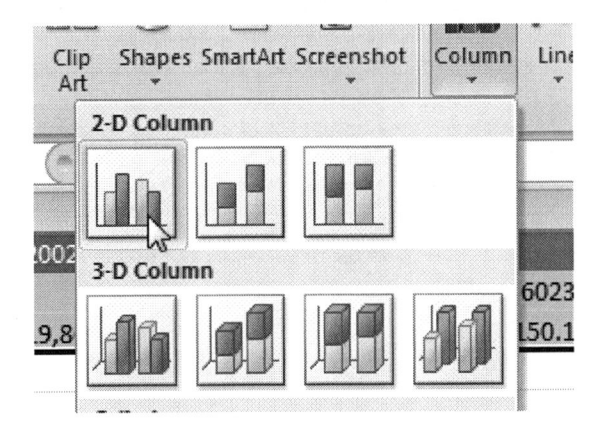

> Note: 3-D charts do not support multiple axes.

b) Position and size the chart so it roughly covers the range **C5:J28**.

> Note: The precise size of the chart isn't important. Just make sure to place the chart below the table and make it large enough to easily view and work with.

3. Create a second Y axis for the **Unit Sales** data series.
    a) Ensure that the chart is still selected and, on the **Chart Tools** contextual tab, select the **Layout** tab.
    b) From the **Chart Elements** drop-down menu in the **Current Selection** group, select **Series "Unit Sales."**
    c) Select **Layout→Current Selection→Format Selection**.
    d) In the **Format Data Series** dialog box, ensure that the **Series Options** tab is selected.
    e) In the **Plot Series On** section, select the **Secondary Axis** radio button, and then select **Close**.

4. Change the chart type for the **Unit Sales** data series.
    a) With the **Unit Sales** data series still selected, from the **Chart Tools** contextual tab, select **Design→Type→Change Chart Type**.
    b) In the **Change Chart Type** dialog box, in the left navigation pane, select **Line**.
    c) In the **Line** section, select the **Line** chart type.

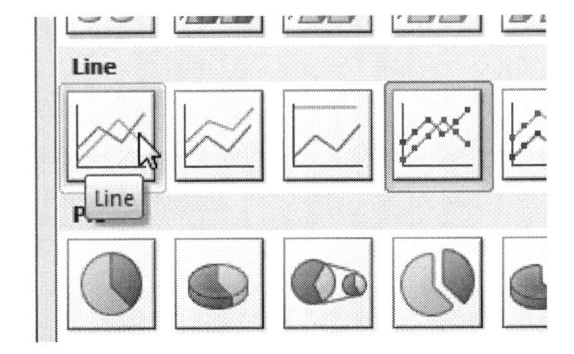

    d) Select **OK**.

5. Move the chart legend and format the Y axes.
    a) On the **Chart Tools** contextual tab, select **Layout→Labels→Legend→Show Legend at Top**.
    b) From the **Current Selection** drop-down menu, select **Vertical (Value) Axis**, and then select **Format Selection**.
    c) In the **Format Axis** dialog box, ensure that the **Axis Options** tab is selected.

d) From the **Display units** drop-down menu, select **Billions**.
e) Ensure that Excel automatically checked the **Show display units label on chart** check box and select **Close**.
f) From the **Current Selection** drop-down menu, select **Secondary Vertical (Value) Axis**, and then select **Format Selection**.
g) From the **Display units** drop-down menu, select **Millions**, ensure that Excel automatically checked the **Show display units label on chart** check box, and select **Close**.

6. Add titles for the primary and secondary vertical axes.
   a) From the **Chart Tools** contextual tab, select **Layout→Labels→Axis Titles→Primary Vertical Axis Title→Vertical Title**.
   b) Type *Earnings* and then press **Enter**.
   c) Add a vertical axis title to the secondary vertical axis, type *Unit Sales* and then press **Enter**.

7. Add a trendline to forecast total earnings for five years.
   a) From the **Current Selection** drop-down menu, select **Series "Earnings."**
   b) From the **Chart Tools** contextual tab, select **Layout→Analysis→Trendline→Linear Trendline**.
   c) From the **Current Selection** drop-down menu, select **Series "Earnings" Trendline 1**, and then select **Format Selection**.
   d) In the **Format Trendline** dialog box, from the **Trendline Options** tab, in the **Trendline Name** section, select the **Custom** radio button.
   e) In the **Custom** field, type *Earnings Forecast*
   f) In the **Forecast** section, in the **Forward** field, enter *5.0*
   g) Check the **Display R-squared value on chart** check box.
   h) Select the **Line Color** tab and then select the **Solid line** radio button.
   i) From the **Color** drop-down menu, in the top row of the **Theme Colors** section, select **Red, Accent 2**.
   j) Select **Close**.

8. Add a trendline to forecast unit sales for five years.
   a) From the **Current Selection** drop-down menu, select **Series "Unit Sales,"** and then select **Layout→Analysis→Trendline→Linear Trendline**.
   b) From the **Current Selection** drop-down menu, select **Series "Unit Sales" Trendline 1**, and then select **Format Selection**.
   c) Name the trendline *Unit Sales Forecast*
   d) Configure the trendline to forecast forward five years, and to display the R-squared value on the chart.
   e) Format the line with the **Dark Blue, Text 2** color and close the **Format Trendline** dialog box.

9. Drag the displayed R-squared value for the **Unit Sales Forecast** trendline below the **Unit Sales Forecast** trendline.

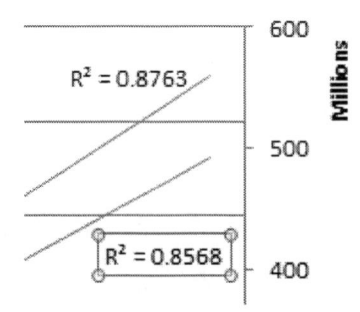

10. Save the file to the **C:\091020Data\Presenting Your Data Visually** folder as *my_book_sales_dashboard_07.xlxs*

Chart Templates

Working with advanced charting features can require quite a bit of chart formatting and modification. It's likely you'll need to reuse at least some of your charts for multiple purposes, projects, or periods. You could benefit from the ability to save all of the formatting and modification work that went into creating your charts for use in future workbooks. This can be especially helpful if you've painstakingly formatted chart elements to adhere to organizational branding guidelines and will frequently need to create charts that follow those guidelines. Fortunately, Excel provides you with the ability to save charts as chart templates that you can apply to other datasets in the same workbook or to datasets in other workbooks.

Like other Excel templates, a chart template is a type of file that stores a chart type and all of the associated formatting you've applied to it. The file extension for Excel 2010 chart templates is .crtx. Excel stores chart templates in a sub-folder in the Microsoft **Templates** folder named **Charts**. Once saved, you can access chart templates from the **Templates** tab in either the **Insert Chart** dialog box or the **Change Chart Type** dialog box, just as you can any other chart type. This is true only if you save your chart templates in the **Charts** folder. Do not save chart templates in any other folder if you wish to access them from the dialog boxes.

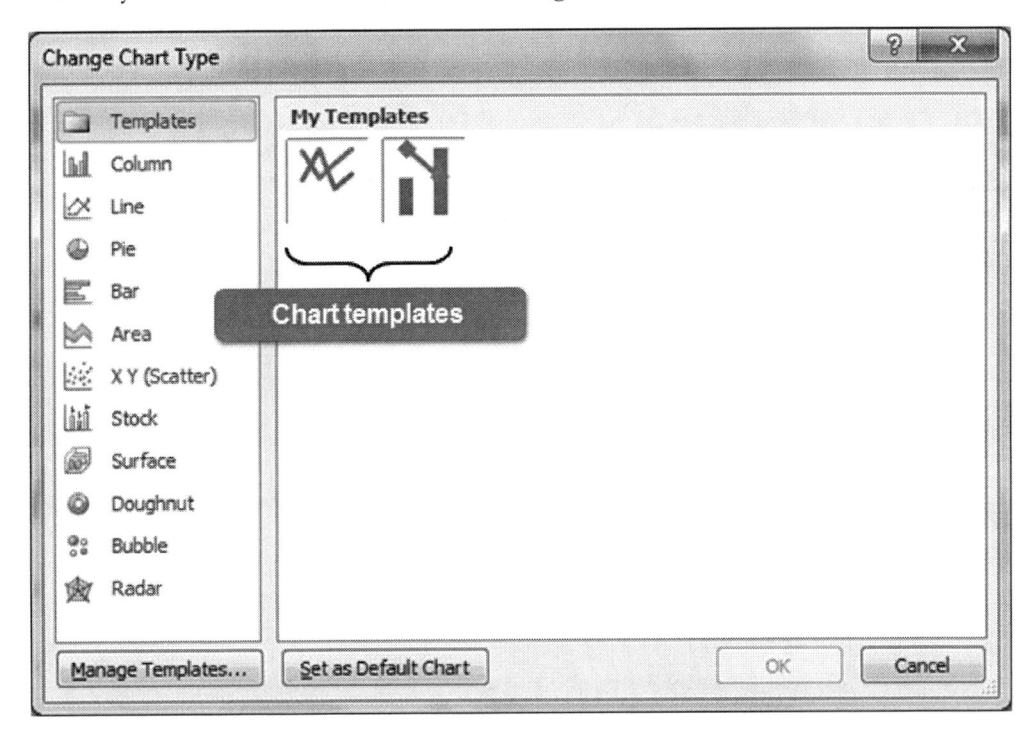

Figure 7-4: Chart templates available for use in the Change Chart Type dialog box.

> Access the Checklist tile on your LogicalCHOICE course screen for reference information and job aids on **How to Create and Use Chart Templates**.

ACTIVITY 7-2
Creating a Chart Template

Before You Begin
The my_book_sales_dashboard_07.xlxs workbook file is open.

Scenario
You like the overall look and feel of the chart you created to forecast earnings and unit sales. Additionally, you know you'll be creating similar charts for other sales periods and fiscal years. Instead of adding trendlines and formatting your charts each time you create them, you decide to create a chart template from the chart that you can apply to future datasets.

1. Ensure the chart on the **Sales_Trends** worksheet is still selected.

2. Create a chart template from the chart.
    a) From the **Chart Tools** contextual tab, select **Design→Type→Save As Template**.
    b) In the **Save Chart Template** dialog box, ensure that the **Charts** folder is selected.

    \AppData\Roaming\Microsoft\Templates\Charts

    > **Note:** Remember that Excel will automatically display chart templates saved in the **Charts** folder as chart types in the **Insert Chart** and **Change Chart Type** dialog boxes. You will find them in the **Templates** folder in the left navigation pane when you create charts or change chart types.

    c) In the **File name** field, type *Trendline Chart Template*
    d) In the **Save as type** drop-down menu, ensure **Chart Template Files(*.crtx)** is selected, and then select **Save**.

3. Verify Excel saved the chart as a template.
    a) Select the range A1:N3, select **Insert→Charts**, and select the dialog box launcher.
    b) In the **Insert Chart** dialog box, in the left navigation pane, select the **Templates** folder.
    c) In the **My Templates** section, select the **Trendline Chart Template** icon and select **OK**.

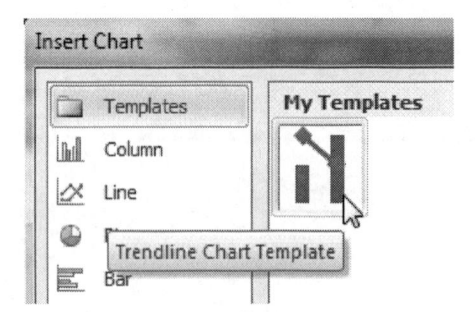

    d) Verify that Excel created a chart with the appropriate formatting that includes the trendlines.

4. Delete the new chart and save the workbook.

TOPIC B

Create Sparklines

Although charts and trendlines can be convenient ways to graphically display data, trends, and relationships to worksheet viewers, they aren't always practical. For example, imagine presenting a chart that displays the sales trends for 2,000 sales reps throughout your organization. The chart would be so dense and cluttered, no one would be able to make sense of the information you're presenting. It would be nice to give your sales managers an easy way to visually identify trends for any of their reps with just a glance. By taking advantage of Excel's handy data visualization functionality in sparklines, you can combine the benefits of storing massive amounts of data on very large worksheets with the ability to discern important information and identify trends with just a glance.

Sparklines

You can think of *sparklines* as a type of miniature chart that you can actually insert within worksheet cells. Unlike charts, shapes, images, or SmartArt graphics, sparklines are not objects that float above worksheet cells; they become the background image for the cells themselves. You can use sparklines to visually display relative values of cell data over time. Although you can insert sparklines into cells that contain text or data, it is often a good idea, for the sake of legibility, to insert them into empty cells near the data they represent.

You can apply pre-formatted styles to sparklines, or customize them to suit your needs. And, you can change the sparkline type for existing sparklines just as you can change chart types. Sparklines can be grouped together so you can apply formatting to large numbers of sparklines simultaneous. As is the case with other cell content such as formulas and functions, you can copy sparklines down a range of data by using relative references to quickly populate large ranges with sparklines. When you create ranges of sparklines all at once or you use the **fill handle** to copy sparklines, Excel automatically groups them together. If you copy and paste sparklines to new cells, Excel does not automatically group them together. You can access the commands for inserting sparklines in the **Sparklines** group on the **Insert** tab.

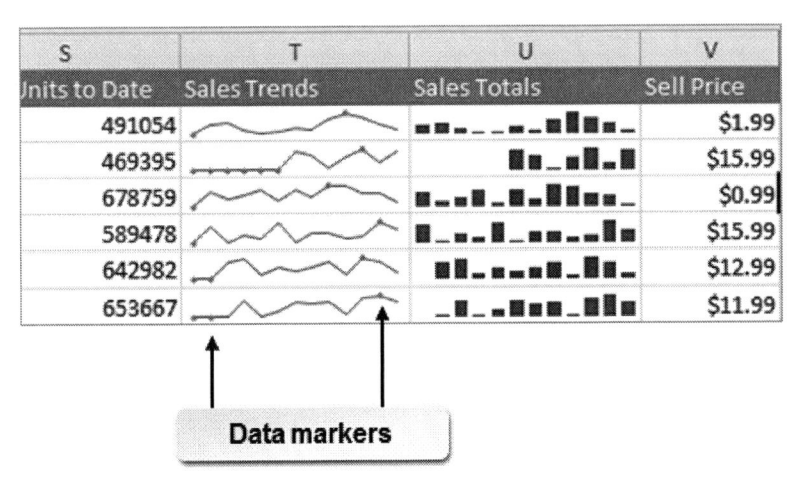

Figure 7-5: A worksheet displaying two different types of sparklines.

Sparkline Types

There are three types of sparklines available in Excel 2010: line, column, and win/loss. Each of these sparkline types is best suited to displaying particular types of relationships or trends. The following table describes each of these in some detail.

Sparkline Type	Image	Description
Line		This sparkline type is ideal for displaying trends in data changes over time. Line style sparklines can also display data markers, which are the points at which the sparkline represents a data entry in the data range.
Column		Columns are ideal for showing how the various values in a row of data relate to each other in terms of relative value.
Win/Loss		Use the win/loss sparkline type to show which entries are positive and which are negative. The win/loss sparkline does not show relative values among the data points, but which are positive and which are negative.

The Create Sparklines Dialog Box

You will use the **Create Sparklines** dialog box to add sparklines to your worksheets. From here, you can define the data range for a sparkline and select the cell you wish to insert it in. You can access the **Create Sparklines** dialog box by selecting any of the commands in the **Sparklines** group on the **Insert** tab.

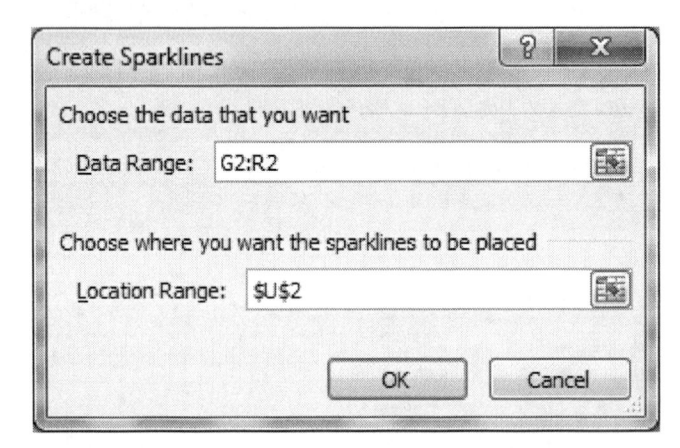

Figure 7-6: Use the Create Sparklines dialog box to add sparklines to worksheet cells.

The Sparkline Tools Contextual Tab

As with many other types of workbook elements, Excel displays the **Sparkline Tools** contextual tab when you select cells that contain sparklines. The **Sparkline Tools** contextual tab contains only one tab, the **Design** tab. The command groups on the **Design** tab display the commands and options you will use to work with worksheet sparklines.

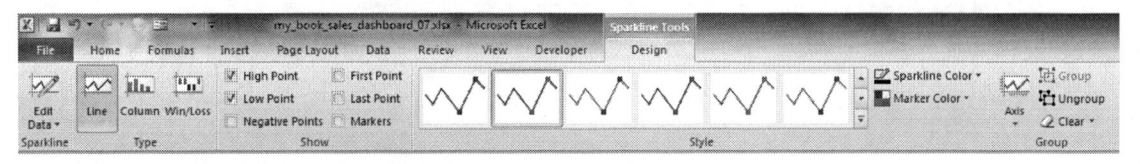

Figure 7-7: The Sparkline Tools contextual tab.

The following table identifies the types of commands you will find in the command groups on the **Design** tab of the **Sparkline Tools** contextual tab.

Design Tab Group	Contains Commands For
Sparkline	Changing the data range associated with sparklines and determining how sparklines handle empty cells in the data range.
Type	Changing sparkline types.
Show	Toggling the display of data markers on and off.
Style	Applying pre-formatted styles or custom formatting to sparklines.
Group	Grouping or ungrouping sparklines, modifying sparkline axes, and removing sparklines from worksheets.

Access the Checklist tile on your LogicalCHOICE course screen for reference information and job aids on How to Create and Modify Sparklines.

ACTIVITY 7-3
Creating Sparklines

Before You Begin
The my_book_sales_dashboard_07.xlsx workbook file is open.

Scenario
Given the large number of titles that Fuller and Ackerman (F&A) publishes, you've received a request from some of the sales managers for an easy way to quickly assess the sales history for any particular title. You realize that charts wouldn't be effective for visually displaying information for such a large number of individual items. You decide to add a column to the **Raw_Book_Sales** worksheet that you will use to add sparklines. You first believe that Column sparklines would work best, but after adding them, you realize the Line style will work far better.

1. Select the **Raw_Book_Sales** worksheet.

2. Add a new column between the **Total Units to Date** column (column S) and the **Sell Price** column (column T), and label it *Sales Trends*. Ensure that Excel formats the column label the same as the others.

3. Add a Column sparkline for the first title on the worksheet.
   a) Select the range **F2:R2**, and then select **Insert→Sparklines→Column**.
   b) In the **Create Sparklines** dialog box, in the **Data Range** field, ensure that **F2:R2** appears.
   c) In the **Location Range** field, enter *T2* and select **OK**.

4. Copy and paste the sparklines into the remaining cells in the **Sales Trends** column.
   a) Verify that cell **T2** is selected and press **Ctrl+C**.
   b) Use the **Name Box** to select the range **T3:T1737**.
   c) Press **Ctrl+V** and verify that Excel added the sparklines to all entries.

   > **Note:** You are using the copy and paste method here because double-clicking the fill handle does not work with this feature.

5. Group the sparklines so you can edit them simultaneously.
   a) Select the range **T2:T1737**.
   b) On the **Sparkline Tools** contextual tab, select **Design→Group→Group**.

6. Change the sparklines from Column sparklines to Line sparklines.
   a) Select any one cell containing sparklines.
   b) On the **Sparkline Tools** contextual tab, select **Design→Type→Line**.

c) Verify that Excel changed the style for all sparklines.

491054		$1.99
469395		$15.99
678759		$0.99
589478		$15.99
642982		$12.99
653667		$11.99
1102064		$11.99
526065		$9.99
585271		$15.99
548769		$15.99
1441961		$12.99
640108		$3.99
594242		$0.99
549727		$15.99

7. Format the sparklines.
   a) Ensure one of the sparklines is still selected.
   b) Select **Design→Style→More** button.
   c) From the **Style** gallery, select a shade of red.
   d) In the **Show** group, check the **High Point** and the **Low Point** check boxes.
   e) Verify that Excel applied the formatting to all of the sparklines.

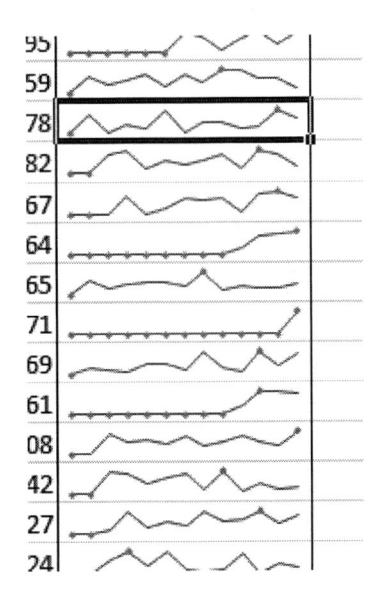

8. Save and close the workbook.

Summary

In this lesson, you used advanced charting features and sparklines to convey complex or large datasets graphically. Taking advantage of Excel's data visualization functionality will enable you to instantly make a connection with your audience and give workbook viewers instant insight into even the largest datasets.

What uses will you have for Excel's advanced charting features in your current role?

What is the main benefit of using sparklines over charts or other visual methods to convey meaning from data?

> **Note:** Check your LogicalCHOICE Course screen for opportunities to interact with your classmates, peers, and the larger LogicalCHOICE online community about the topics covered in this course or other topics you are interested in. From the Course screen you can also access available resources for a more continuous learning experience.

Course Follow-Up

Congratulations! You have completed the *Microsoft® Office Excel® 2010: Part 3 (Second Edition)* course. You have successfully worked with a number of different workbooks simultaneously, collaborated with colleagues to develop workbooks, automated a variety of tasks, and constructed highly complex formulas and functions to get Excel to perform tasks that there are no existing functions or features to perform.

Remaining competitive in today's market requires constant vigilance and a continual effort to look forward, which means you can't let distractions get in the way. You can't afford to get bogged down in continuous review cycles or back-and-forth communications. You don't have the time to constantly perform repetitive, low-value tasks just to maintain your workbooks. When problems arise, you need to solve them quickly. By letting Excel do this kind of heavy lifting for you, you will free yourself from time-consuming tasks that keep your focus off of analyzing your data to help organizational leaders make informed, beneficial decisions.

What's Next?

Microsoft® Office Excel® 2010: Part 3 (Second Edition) is the final course in this series. As such, you are encouraged to continue building upon your Excel knowledge and experience by seeking out available information to hone and expand your skill set. Participate in online forums and user groups to discover new ways to construct Excel formulas and functions to tackle difficult tasks. Research available add-ins and other support tools to help you get the most out of your Excel experience. And search for online videos and tutorials that demonstrate how to resolve common issues users experience. You are also encouraged to explore Excel further by actively participating in any of the social media forums set up by your instructor or training administrator through the **Social Media** tile on the LogicalCHOICE Course screen.

A | Cube Functions

Excel 2010 includes a set of functions called cube functions that you can use to query data stored in certain databases. Cube functions are designed to work with Online Analytical Processing (OLAP) databases. OLAP databases differ from relational databases such as Microsoft Access, in that they store data, relationships, and hierarchies in multidimensional structures know as cubes instead of in two-dimensional tables. Using data from OLAP database sources speeds up the process of querying data because the server hosting the database, not Excel, does a lot of the processing for you. When you import data into a workbook from an OLAP database, Excel brings it in as a PivotTable or a PivotChart.

> **Note:** An in-depth discussion on OLAP databases and cubes is beyond the scope of this course. For more information on these topics, please visit **office.microsoft.com**.

Excel 2010 includes seven cube functions you can use to query data stored in OLAP databases.

Cube Function	This Function	Syntax
CUBEKPIMEMBER	Returns a key performance indicator property and the name of the indicator in a cell.	=CUBEKPIMEMBER(connection, kpi_name, kpi_property, [caption])
CUBEMEMBER	Will help identify whether or not a particular member belongs to a cube.	=CUBEMEMBER(connection, member_expression, [caption])
CUBEMEMBERPROPERTY	Takes the CUBEMEMBER function one step further and returns a specified property value for the specified member if it exists in the cube.	=CUBEMEMBERPROPERTY(connection, member_expression, property)
CUBERANKEDMEMBER	Returns the specified ranked members of a cube set. This can be useful for identifying top- or bottom-performers from within the database.	=CUBERANKEDMEMBER(connection, set_expression, rank, [caption])
CUBESET	Defines a calculated set of members.	=CUBESET(connection, set_expression, [caption], [sort_order], [sort_by])
CUBESETCOUNT	Returns the value of the number of items in a set.	=CUBESETCOUNT(set)

Cube Function	This Function	Syntax
CUBEVALUE	Returns a single or combined value from the cube.	=CUBEVALUE(connection, [member_expression1], [member_expression2], ...)

B | Import and Export Data

Appendix Introduction

Although Excel is quite handy for entering and analyzing vast amounts of data, entering data you already have readily available in another source is, quite frankly, a waste of time. Copying or re-entering data from Excel worksheets to external applications or databases is a waste of time as well. Excel 2010 enables you to import data to or export data from your workbooks. Doing so can not only save you incredible amounts of time and effort, but can also help eliminate errors that can be introduced by manually transferring information.

TOPIC A

Importing and Exporting Data

In this topic, you will learn about methods for importing and exporting data between various applications and in various formats.

Importing and Exporting

Importing is the process of bringing information or data into an application or database from an outside source. Exporting is the process of sending information out of an application or database to another. Excel 2010 enables you to import data from and export data to a number of other applications and database types. You can access the commands for importing data from outside sources in the **Get External Data** group on the **Data** ribbon tab. You can access the commands for exporting data in a number of different formats by selecting **File→Save & Send→Change File Type**.

There are several sources from which you can import data into Excel. The following table describes the three most common ones.

Data Source	Description
Access databases	Excel enables you to import data from any of the tables in Microsoft Access databases that you have access to.
The web	Web queries enable you to import data from pages on the World Wide Web. One of the key benefits of this feature is that, as the data updates on the web sites, Excel automatically updates the information in your workbooks as well. You can use web queries to import a specific table, multiple tables, or all of the text on a given page.
Text files	This option enables you to import data from simple text files that are delimited in a variety of ways.

There are also four common formats for exporting Excel data for use in other applications. These are described in the following table.

Export Option	Description
Text (Tab delimited) (*.txt)	Exports Excel data as a tab-delimited text file. In these files, individual entries are separated by pressing the **Tab** key.
CSV (Comma delimited) (*.csv)	Exports Excel data as a comma-delimited text file. Individual entries are defined by placing a comma between them.
Formatted Test (Space delimited) (*.prn)	Exports Excel data as a space-delimited text file. These are similar to tab-delimited text files but the use a single space between characters to define individual entries.
PDF/XPS document	This option doesn't technically export Excel data, but rather saves documents in either the PDF or XPS format so they can be opened and viewed in other applications, such as Adobe Acrobat and Adobe Reader.

Methods of Importing Text Files

There are two methods you can use to import data from text files into Excel. You can either open the text file within Excel or you can import the data from the text file as a data range. If you open the file directly in Excel, you do not need to create a link to the text file. If you import the data, you will need to link the workbook to the text file in order for changes to the text file to reflect in the Excel workbook. Not all text file formats are directly compatible with Excel, so you may not be able to open all text files directly in Excel.

The Text Import Wizard

You will use the **Text Import Wizard** to configure the importation of data from text files. The **Text Import Wizard** walks you through a three-step process in which you identify the type of data the file contains and where you would like to start the import; select the type of character that separates entries in delimited files; and then select the desired cell formatting options for the columns that will contain the data after importing. Each step of the wizard displays a preview of what the imported text will look like given the current selections and settings. You can access the **Text Import Wizard** by selecting **Data→Get External Data→From Text**, and then selecting the desired text document from the **Import Text File** dialog box.

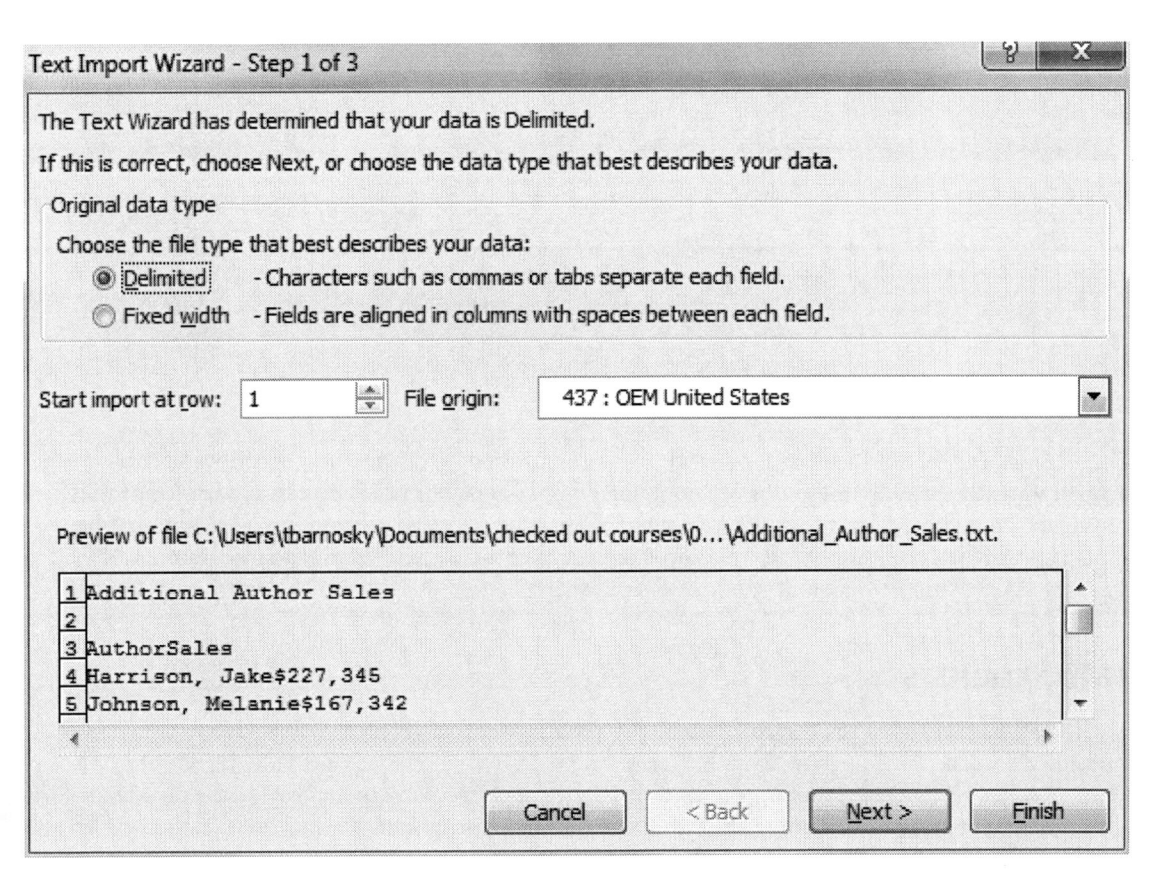

The New Web Query Dialog Box

When you import data from the web, Excel opens the **New Web Query** dialog box. From here, you can navigate to the web page from which you wish to import data and select the specific data you wish to import. Selecting the yellow and black arrow icons selects either particular tables or screen elements, or the entire page for importation. You can access the **New Web Query** dialog box by selecting **Data→Get External Data→From Web**.

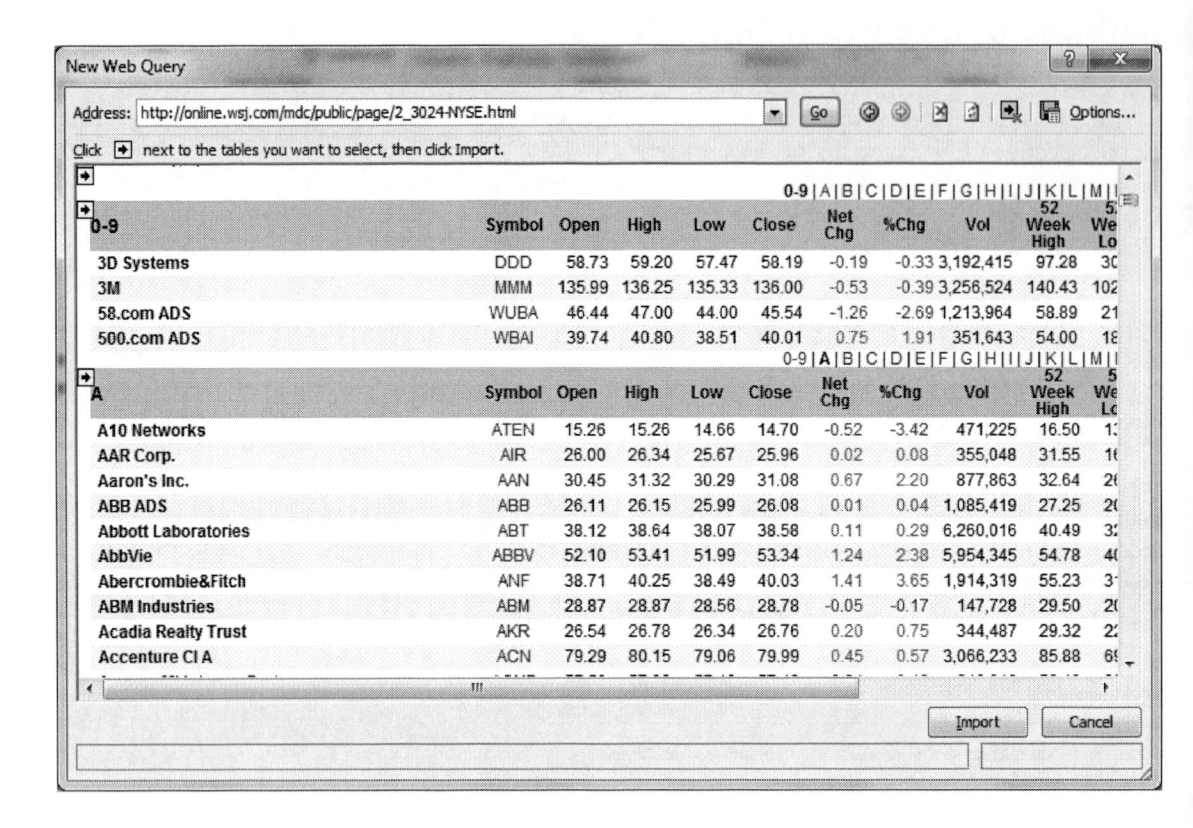

Access the Checklist tile on your LogicalCHOICE course screen for reference information and job aids on How to Import and Export Data.

XML

The eXtensible Markup Language, or XML, is a programming language that describes data by using structured text files. XML elements are contained within tags that hold the actual data. Once these tags have been defined, data can be moved and exchanged between and among XML-compatible applications. XML commonly uses markup language that is compatible with a large number of applications, making it an ideal format for data exchange.

XML Schemas

An XML schema establishes the rules and structure for other XML files. You must set out the data type and allowable attributes of XML files in a schema. One schema can provide the structure for multiple other XML files. Schemas can outline a particular structural hierarchy for the data in an XML document as well as defining the types of data that exist within the document. Schema files are saved with the .xsd file extension.

You use XML tags to define the data types that exist within a schema. For example, in the source XML file that you want to import, your data entries might contain tags that look like this: <LastName>Smith</LastName>, <FirstName>Bob</FirstName>, and <MiddleInitial>L</MiddleInitial>. In your XML schema file, you would include these tag sets to define data types the schema will recognize. Once you have these data types defined for your entries, which is the text inside the tags, you can create column labels on the target worksheet to match: Last Name, First Name, and MI. Then you simply need to tell Excel which data type goes in which column for the import. This process is knows as mapping.

XML Maps

You create maps in Excel to tell it where to put particular data types from an XML document in your worksheets. Excel uses the structure defined within the XML schema file to identify where entries should be placed. Each unique data type, as defined by the schema tags, appears as a separate element in XML maps. To tell Excel where to place entries for that particular element, you simply drag the map element to the desired spreadsheet location. The cells you map the content to represent the starting points for particular types of data to import to. Typically, this would be the first cell in a particular column below the column label.

One of the key things to remember about XML schema files you are using as maps is that the schema file does not contain the data you will ultimately import into Excel. The data will be contained in a separate XML file that uses the tags defined in the schema file to identify data types. Wherever you map a particular data type to on a worksheet is the cell that entries contained within the same set of tags in the data source document will begin populating during the import. Subsequent entries within the same tags will populate down the column by default.

The XML Source Task Pane

You can use the **XML Source** task pane to map elements of an XML schema to the desired worksheet cells. From here, you can add XML schema files to a workbook to use as maps, set mapping options, and map schema elements to the desired locations. For the currently selected map, the **XML Source** task pane displays all unique elements, which you can manually drag to the cell you want that data type to start importing to. You can access the **XML Source** task pane by selecting **Developer→XML→Source**.

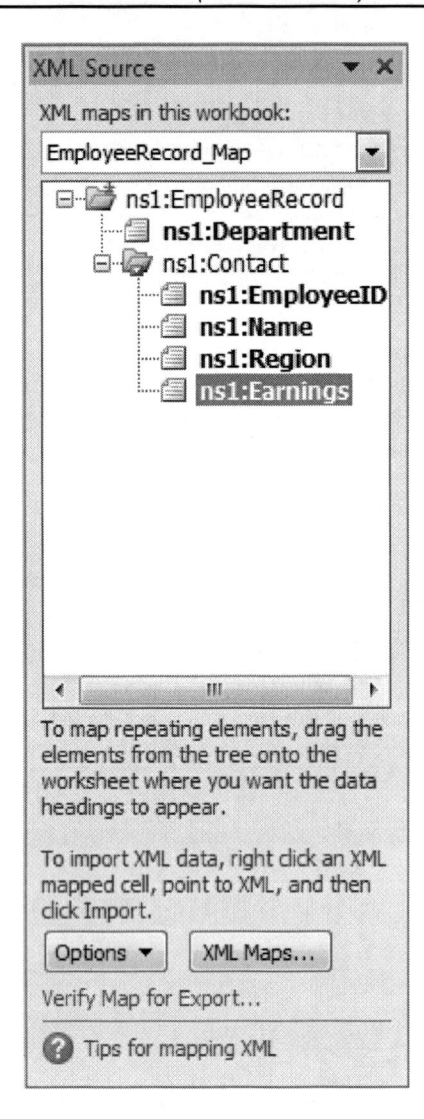

The XML Maps Dialog Box

You can use the **XML Maps** dialog box to add, delete, or rename XML maps in your workbook files. The **XML Maps** dialog box displays a list of all maps attached to the currently selected workbook. You can have more than one XML map attached to a workbook file simultaneously. To access the **XML Maps** dialog box, select **XML Maps** from the **XML Source** task pane.

[XML Maps dialog box screenshot]

Name	Root	Namespace
EmployeeRecord_Map	EmployeeRecord	http://MyEmployeeData/EmployeeRecord.xsd

Access the Checklist tile on your LogicalCHOICE course screen for reference information and job aids on How to Import and Export XML Data.

C Microsoft Office Excel 2010 Exam 77-882

Selected Logical Operations courseware addresses Microsoft Office Specialist certification skills for Microsoft Office 2010. The following table indicates where Excel 2010 skills that are tested in Exam 77-882 are covered in the Logical Operations Microsoft Office Excel 2010 series of courses.

Objective Domain	Covered In
1. Managing the Worksheet Environment	
1.1 Navigate through a worksheet	
1.1.1 Use hot keys	Part 1
1.1.2 Use the name box	Part 1, Part 2
1.2 Print a worksheet or workbook	
1.2.1 Print only selected worksheets	Part 1
1.2.2 Print an entire workbook	Part 1
1.2.3 Construct headers and footers	Part 1
1.2.4 Apply printing options	
1.2.4.1 Scale	Part 1
1.2.4.2 Print titles	Part 1
1.2.4.3 Page setup	Part 1
1.2.4.4 Print area	Part 1
1.2.4.5 Gridlines	Part 1
1.3 Personalize the environment by using Backstage	
1.3.1 Manipulate the Quick Access Toolbar	Part 2
1.3.2 Customize the ribbon	
1.3.2.1 Tabs	Part 2
1.3.2.2 Groups	Part 2
1.3.3 Manipulate Excel default settings (Excel Options)	Part 2
1.3.4 Import data to Excel	Part 3, Appendix C
1.3.5 Import data from Excel	Part 3, Appendix C
1.3.6 Manipulate workbook properties	Part 1

Objective Domain	Covered In
1.3.7 Manipulate workbook files and folders	Part 1
1.3.8 Apply different name and file formats for different uses	Part 1
1.3.9 Using save and save as features	Part 1
2. Creating Cell Data	
2.1 Construct cell data	
2.1.1 Use paste special	
2.1.1.1 Formats	Part 1
2.1.1.2 Formulas	Part 1
2.1.1.3 Values	Part 1
2.1.1.4 Preview icons	Part 1
2.1.1.5 Transpose rows and columns	Part 1
2.1.1.6 Operations	Part 1
2.1.1.7 Comments	Part 1
2.1.1.8 Validation	Part 1
2.1.1.9 Paste as a link	Part 1
2.1.2 Cut, move, and select cell data	Part 1
2.2 Apply AutoFill	
2.2.1 Copy data using AutoFill	Part 1
2.2.2 Fill series using AutoFill	Part 1
2.2.3 Copy or preserve cell format with AutoFill	Part 1
2.2.4 Select from drop-down list	Part 1
2.3 Apply and manipulate hyperlinks	
2.3.1 Create a hyperlink in a cell	Part 1
2.3.2 Modify hyperlinks	Part 1
2.3.3 Modify hyperlinked cell attributes	Part 1
2.3.4 Remove a hyperlink	Part 1
3. Formatting Cells and Worksheets	
3.1 Apply and modify cell formats	
3.1.1 Align cell content	Part 1
3.1.2 Apply a number format	Part 1
3.1.3 Wrap text in a cell	Part 1
3.1.4 Use Format Painter	Part 1
3.2 Merge or split cells	
3.2.1 Use Merge & Center	Part 1
3.2.2 Merge Across	Part 1
3.2.3 Merge cells	Part 1

Objective Domain	Covered In
3.2.4 Unmerge Cells	Part 1
3.3 Create row and column titles	
3.3.1 Print row and column headings	Part 1
3.3.2 Print rows to repeat with titles	Part 1
3.3.3 Print columns to repeat with titles	Part 1
3.3.4 Configure titles to print only on odd or even pages	Part 1
3.3.5 Configure titles to skip the first worksheet page	Part 1
3.4 Hide and unhide rows and columns	
3.4.1 Hide a column	Part 1
3.4.2 Unhide a column	Part 1
3.4.3 Hide a series of columns	Part 1
3.4.4 Hide a row	Part 1
3.4.5 Unhide a row	Part 1
3.4.6 Hide a series of rows	Part 1
3.5 Manipulate Page Setup options for worksheets	
3.5.1 Configure page orientation	Part 1
3.5.2 Manage page scaling	Part 1
3.5.3 Configure page margins	Part 1
3.5.4 Change header and footer size	Part 1
3.6 Create and apply cell styles	
3.6.1 Apply cell styles	Part 1
3.6.2 Construct new cell styles	Part 1
4. Managing Worksheets and Workbooks	
4.1 Create and format worksheets	
4.1.1 Insert worksheets	Part 1
4.1.2 Delete worksheets	Part 1
4.1.3 Copy worksheets	Part 1
4.1.4 Reposition worksheets	Part 1
4.1.5 Copy and move worksheets	Part 1
4.1.6 Rename worksheets	Part 1
4.1.7 Group worksheets	Part 1
4.1.8 Apply coloring to worksheet tabs	Part 1
4.1.9 Hide worksheet tabs	Part 1
4.1.10 Unhide worksheet tabs	Part 1
4.2 Manipulate window views	
4.2.1 Split window views	Part 1

Objective Domain	Covered In
4.2.2 Arrange window views	Part 1
4.2.3 Open a new window with contents from the current worksheet	Part 1
4.3 Manipulate workbook views	
4.3.1 Use Normal, Page Layout, and Page Break workbook views	Part 1
4.3.2 Create custom views	Part 1
5. Applying Formulas and Functions	
5.1 Create formulas	
5.1.1 Use basic operators	Part 1
5.1.2 Revise formulas	Part 1
5.2 Enforce precedence	
5.2.1 Order of evaluation	Part 1
5.2.2 Precedence using parentheses	Part 1
5.2.3 Precedence of operators for percent vs. exponentiation	Part 1
5.3 Apply cell references in formulas	
5.3.1 Relative references	Part 1
5.3.2 Absolute references	Part 1
5.4 Apply conditional logic in a formula	
5.4.1 Create a formula with values that match your conditions	Part 3, Topic 4-B
5.4.2 Edit defined conditions in a formula	Part 3, Topic 4-B
5.4.3 Use a series of conditional logic values in a formula	Part 3, Topic 4-B
5.5 Apply named ranges in formulas	
5.5.1 Define, edit, and rename a named range	Part 2
5.6 Apply cell ranges in formulas	
5.6.1 Enter a cell range definition in the formula bar	Part 1
5.6.2 Define a cell range using the mouse	Part 1
5.6.3 Define a cell range using a keyboard shortcut	Part 1
6. Presenting Data Visually	
6.1 Create charts based on worksheet data	Part 2
6.2 Apply and manipulate illustrations	
6.2.1 Clip Art	Part 2
6.2.2 SmartArt	Part 2
6.2.3 Shapes	Part 2
6.2.4 Screenshots	Part 2

Objective Domain	Covered In
6.3 Create and modify images by using the Image Editor	
6.3.1 Making corrections to an image	
6.3.1.1 Sharpen or soften an image	Part 2
6.3.1.2 Changing brightness and contrast	Part 2
6.3.2 Use picture color tools	Part 2
6.3.3 Change artistic effects on an image	Part 2
6.4 Apply Sparklines	
6.4.1 Use Line, Column, and Win/Loss chart types	Part 3, Topic 7-B
6.4.2 Create a Sparkline chart	Part 3, Topic 7-B
6.4.3 Customize a Sparkline	Part 3, Topic 7-B
6.4.4 Format a Sparkline	Part 3, Topic 7-B
6.4.5 Show or hide data markers	Part 3, Topic 7-B
7. Sharing Worksheet Data with Other Users	
7.1 Share spreadsheets by using Backstage	
7.1.1 Send a worksheet via email or SkyDrive (As of this writing, SkyDrive has been re-branded as OneDrive.)	Part 3, Topic 2-A
7.1.2 Change the file type to a different version of Excel	Part 1
7.1.3 Save as PDF or XPS	Part 1; Part 3, Topic 2-A
7.2 Manage comments	
7.2.1 Inserting comments	Part 3, Topic 2-A
7.2.2 Viewing comments	Part 3, Topic 2-A
7.2.3 Editing comments	Part 3, Topic 2-A
7.2.4 Deleting comments	Part 3, Topic 2-A
8. Analyzing and Organizing Data	
8.1 Filter data	
8.1.1 Define filters	Part 2
8.1.2 Apply filters	Part 2
8.1.3 Remove filters	Part 2
8.1.4 Search filters	Part 2
8.1.5 Filter lists using AutoFilter	Part 2
8.2 Sort data	
8.2.1 Use sort options	
8.2.1.1 Values	Part 2
8.2.1.2 Font color	Part 2
8.2.1.3 Cell color	Part 2
8.3 Apply conditional formatting	

Objective Domain	Covered In
8.3.1 Apply conditional formatting to cells	Part 1, Topic 4-F; Part 2
8.3.2 Use the Rule Manager to apply conditional formats	Part 2
8.3.3 Use the IF function to apply conditional formatting	Part 2; Part 3, Topic 4-C
8.3.4 Icon sets	Part 2
8.3.5 Data bars	Part 2
8.3.6 Clear rules	Part 2

D | Microsoft Office Excel 2010 Expert Exam 77-888

Selected Logical Operations courseware addresses Microsoft Office Specialist certification skills for Microsoft Office 2010. The following table indicates where Excel 2010 skills that are tested in Exam 77-888 are covered in the Logical Operations Microsoft Office Excel 2010 series of courses.

Objective Domain	Covered In
1. Sharing and Maintaining Workbooks	
1.1. Apply workbook settings, properties, and data options	
1.1.1. Set advanced properties	Part 1
1.1.2. Save a workbook as a template	Part 1
1.1.3. Import and export XML data	Part 3, Appendix C
1.2. Apply protection and sharing properties to workbooks and worksheets	
1.2.1. Protect the current sheet	Part 3, Topic 2-B
1.2.2. Protect the workbook structure	Part 3, Topic 2-B
1.2.3. Restrict permissions	Part 3, Topic 2-B
1.2.4. Require a password to open a workbook	Part 3, Topic 2-B
1.3. Maintain shared workbooks	
1.3.1. Merge workbooks	Part 3, Topic 2-A
1.3.2. Set Track Changes options	Part 3, Topic 2-A
2. Applying Formulas and Functions	
2.1. Audit formulas	
2.1.1. Trace formula precedents, dependents, and errors	Part 3, Topic 5-A
2.1.2. Locate invalid data or formulas	Part 3, Topic 5-B
2.1.3 Correct errors in formulas	Part 3, Topic 5-C
2.2. Manipulate formula options	
2.2.1. Set iterative calculation options	Part 3, Topic 6-C

Objective Domain	Covered In
2.2.2. Enable or disabling automatic workbook calculation	Part 2
2.3. Perform data summary tasks	
2.3.1. Use an array formula	Part 2
2.3.2. Use a SUMIFS function	Part 2
2.4. Apply functions in formulas	
2.4.1. Find and correct errors in functions	Part 3, Topics 5-B, 5-C
2.4.2. Apply arrays to functions	Part 2
2.4.3. Use functions	
2.4.3.1 Statistical	Part 1, Topic 2-B; Part 2
2.4.3.2 Date and Time	Part 2
2.4.3.4 Financial	Part 2
2.4.3.5 Text	Part 2
2.4.3.6 Cube	Part 3, Appendix C/D?
3. Presenting Data Visually	
3.1. Apply advanced chart features	
3.1.1. Use Trend lines	Part 3, Topic 7-A
3.1.2. Use Dual axes	Part 3, Topic 7-A
3.1.3. Use chart templates	Part 3, Topic 7-A
3.1.4. Use Sparklines	Part 3, Topic 7-B
3.2. Apply data analysis	
3.2.1 Use automated analysis tools	Part 3, Topics 6-A, 6-B, 6-C, 6-D, 6-E
3.2.2 Perform What-If analysis	Part 3, Topics 6-A, 6-B, 6-C
3.3. Apply and manipulate PivotTables	
3.3.1 Manipulate PivotTable data	Part 2
3.3.2 Use the slicer to filter and segment your PivotTable data in multiple layers	Part 2
3.4. Apply and manipulate PivotCharts	
3.4.1. Create PivotChart data	Part 2
3.4.2. Manipulate PivotChart data	Part 2
3.4.3. Analyze PivotChart data	Part 2
3.5. Demonstrate how to use the slicer	
3.5.1. Choose data sets from external data connections	Part 2
4. Working with Macros and Forms	
4.1. Create and manipulate macros	
4.1.1. Run a macro	Part 3, Topic 3C
4.1.2. Run a macro when a workbook is opened	Part 3, Topic 3C

Objective Domain	Covered In
4.1.3. Run a macro when a button is clicked	Part 3, Topic 3C
4.1.4. Record an action macro	Part 3, Topic 3C
4.1.5. Assign a macro to a command button	Part 3, Topic 3C
4.1.6. Create a custom macro button on the Quick Access Toolbar	Part 3, Topic 3C
4.1.7. Apply modifications to a macro	Part 3, Topic 3C
4.2. Insert and manipulate form controls	
4.2.1. Inserting form controls	Part 3, Topic 3B
4.2.2. Set form properties	Part 3, Topic 3B

Lesson Labs

Lesson labs are provided for certain lessons as additional learning resources for this course. Lesson labs are developed for selected lessons within a course in cases when they seem most instructionally useful as well as technically feasible. In general, labs are supplemental, optional unguided practice and may or may not be performed as part of the classroom activities. Your instructor will consider setup requirements, classroom timing, and instructional needs to determine which labs are appropriate for you to perform, and at what point during the class. If you do not perform the labs in class, your instructor can tell you if you can perform them independently as self-study, and if there are any special setup requirements.

Lesson Lab 1-1
Working with Multiple Workbooks

Activity Time: 15 minutes

Data Files

C:\091020Data\Working with Multiple Worksheets and Workbooks Simultaneously\sales_totals.xlsx

C:\091020Data\Working with Multiple Worksheets and Workbooks Simultaneously\Q4_sales.xlsx

C:\091020Data\Working with Multiple Worksheets and Workbooks Simultaneously\product_prices.xlsx

Scenario

You are the national sales manager for a food service supply company. Senior managers have asked you for data on the sales performance of some of your company's herbs and spices. You already have the sales data for the first three quarters entered in your sales totals workbook, but you still need to add the fourth quarter figures. As quarterly sales, overall sales, and product pricing information are saved in separate workbooks, you realize you'll need to use formulas with external links to pull all of the required information into one workbook.

The specific questions company leaders have asked are:

- What are the total quarterly sales for each spice across all regions?
- What are the average quarterly sales for each spice across all regions?
- What is the highest sales total for each spice in each quarter out of all of the regions?

As you need to generate summary information on the products, you feel that including 3-D formulas and data consolidation in the workbook will be the best way to generate the answers to these questions.

---

1. Open the **sales_totals.xlsx**, the **Q4_sales.xlsx**, and the **product_prices.xlsx** workbook files.

2. Use external references in formulas or functions to calculate the fourth quarter sales figures for each spice in each region.
   a) In the **sales_totals.xlsx** workbook, on the **North** worksheet, calculate the fourth quarter sales for each spice in the northern region by multiplying the sales totals on the **North** worksheet in the **Q4_sales.xlsx** workbook by the prices listed in the **product_prices.xlsx** workbook.
   b) Repeat the calculations for the southern, eastern, and western regions.

3. On the **overall_sales_totals** worksheet in the **sales_totals.xlsx** workbook, use formulas or functions with 3-D references to sum together the total sales of each spice per quarter across all regions.

4. Use data consolidation to return the average sales totals for each spice below the overall totals. Use cell A17 as the top leftmost cell for the consolidated data range.

5. Use data consolidation to return the highest sales total for each spice in each quarter out of all of the regions. Use cell G17 as the top leftmost cell for the consolidated data range.

6. If desired, format the consolidated data ranges to match the sales total figures.

7. Save the workbook to the **C:\091020Data\Working with Multiple Worksheets and Workbooks Simultaneously** folder as *my_sales_totals.xlsx* and close all workbooks.

Lesson Lab 2-1
Using Collaboration Tools and Protecting Excel Files

Activity Time: 10 minutes

Data File
C:\091020Data\Sharing and Protecting Workbooks\sales_totals_02.xlsx

Scenario
You are the VP of sales for a major food service supply company. Your national sales manager has handed off the final sales figures for portions of your herb and spice line for your approval. As you notice that some of the initial figures are inaccurate, you decide to make the corrections with change tracking enabled before handing the figures back to the national sales manager so she can include the figures in other reports. Despite some of the data errors, you're confident the formulas on the **overall_sales_totals** worksheet are correct, so you decide to lock the cells on that sheet to prevent users from revising them and to hide formulas and functions from view. You will need to protect the worksheet cells before enabling change tracking because worksheet and workbook protection is disabled in shared workbooks.

1. Open the **sales_totals_02.xlsx** workbook file and select the **overall_sales_totals** worksheet.

   > **Note:** As turning on change tracking will automatically save the workbook, a backup copy of the **sales_totals_02.xlsx** workbook file has been included in the **solutions** folder for this lesson. Because of this, the actual solution file for this lab is named **sales_totals_02_solution.xlsx**. If you would like to repeat this lab for additional practice, copy the backup version of the data file back to the **C:\091020Data\Sharing and Protecting Workbooks** folder to overwrite the version that is saved when you enable change tracking.

2. Apply worksheet protection to the **overall_sales_totals** worksheet that allows users to select only cells and that hides all formulas and functions.

3. Select the **North** worksheet and add a comment in cell **H1** that indicates you have found some errors and are making corrections with change tracking enabled.

4. Enable change tracking for the workbook to mark up worksheets for all changes made by all users.

5. Make the necessary corrections to the workbook data.
   a) Change the value in cell **B7** to *$5,789*
   b) Change the values in cells **C13** and **D13** to *$2,344* and *$3,423* respectively.
   c) On the **South** worksheet, change the following values:
      - B13 = *$2,332*
      - C13 = *$3,372*
      - D13 = *$2,472*

6. Save the workbook to the **C:\091020Data\Sharing and Protecting Workbooks** folder as *my_sales_totals_02.xlsx* and close the workbook.

Lesson Lab 3-1
Automating Workbook Functionality

Activity Time: 15 minutes

Data File
C:\091020Data\Automating Workbook Functionality\inventory_form.xlsx

Scenario
You own a chain of bowling establishments with pro shops that are located throughout Greene City and the surrounding area. You are currently performing your quarterly inventory, which you track in Excel workbooks. While you enter inventory counts, it occurs to you that much of your data entry is highly repetitive; after all, your bowling centers all stock pretty much the same equipment (balls, shoes, towels, and so on) and many of these items come in standard sizes and weights. You decide to create a macro that will fill in most of the text labels and apply most of the formatting you need to record your inventory. You would like to be able to use this macro in any workbook as you will create a new workbook for each fiscal year. And, because items such as bowling shoes and bowling balls come in standard sizes and weights, you decide to include data validation criteria in the macro that allows only for particular entries for these items.

---

1. Open the **inventory_form.xlsx** workbook file and select the **Sheet2** tab.

2. Rename the **Sheet2** tab as *Q2 Counts* and, if necessary, select cell **A1**.

3. Begin recording a macro named *AddInventorySheet* that you will save in the personal workbook, that will run when users select the keyboard shortcut **Ctrl+Shift+I** and that uses absolute references.

4. Record the macro steps.
    a) In cell **A1**, enter the text *Inventory Counts*
    b) Select the range **A1:H1** and merge the cells by using the **Merge Across** option.
    c) Apply the **Title** cell style to the merged cells.
    d) Select cell **A2** and enter the text *Item*
    e) Continue entering the following text labels in the following cells:
       - B2 = *Location*
       - C2 = *Count*
       - D2 = *Size (I/A)*
       - E2 = *Weight in Lbs. (I/A)*
       - F2 = *Color (I/A)*
       - G2 = *Value/Unit*
       - H2 = *Total Value*

    > **Note:** The *(I/A)* text in the labels stands for "if applicable."

    f) Adjust column widths as necessary.
    g) Apply the **Heading 3** cell style to the range **A2:G2** and the **Total** cell style to the cell **H2**.

h) Select the range **B3:B100** and apply data validation so the cells contain a drop-down list that enables users to select one of the locations in the range **D2:D5** on the **Colors_Sizes_Weights** worksheet.
i) Select the range **D3:D100** and apply data validation so the cells contain a drop-down list that enables users to select one of the sizes in the range **A2:A39** on the **Colors_Sizes_Weights** worksheet.
j) Select the range **E3:E100** and apply data validation so the cells contain a drop-down list that enables users to select one of the ball weights in the range **B2:B7** on the **Colors_Sizes_Weights** worksheet.
k) Select the range **F3:F100** and apply data validation so the cells contain a drop-down list that enables users to select one of the colors in the range **C2:C10** on the **Colors_Sizes_Weights** worksheet.
l) Select cell **A3**.

5. Stop recording the macro.

6. Run the macro on the **Sheet3** worksheet to ensure it works as expected.

7. Save the workbook as a macro-enabled workbook to the **C:\091020Data\Automating Workbook Functionality** folder named *my_inventory_form.xlsm* and close the workbook.

Lesson Lab 4-1
Applying Conditional Logic

Activity Time: 15 minutes

Data File
C:\091020Data\Applying Conditional Logic\employee_list.xlsx

Scenario
You're preparing a dashboard worksheet that the people in the human resources department can use to look up particular information for company employees. Specifically, you want users to be able to look up employee names, departments, salaries, and regions simply by selecting the desired employee ID from a cell. Additionally, you would like users to be able to determine each employee's annual bonus when they select the employee IDs. Your company determines bonuses based on employee region because the cost of living varies from one part of the county to another. As you already have the employee information and a bonus table entered into a workbook, you can now simply add lookup functions and a nested formula to add the desired functionality. You have created a defined name, **Emp_Info**, for the employee information dataset on the worksheet.

You have also received a request from the human resources director to highlight the name and employee ID for anyone who earns $100,000 or more a year. You realize you will have to use a formula to apply conditional formatting to fulfill this request.

---

1. Open the **employee_list.xlsx** workbook file.

2. Add lookup functions to return the desired employee information in the range **B5:E5** when a user selects an employee ID in cell **A5**.
    a) Use a VLOOKUP function in cell **B5** to look up employee names based on the selection in cell **A5**.
    b) Use a VLOOKUP function in cell **C5** to look up employee departments based on the selection in cell **A5**.
    c) Use a VLOOKUP function in cell **D5** to look up employee earnings based on the selection in cell **A5**.
    d) Use a VLOOKUP function in cell **E5** to look up employee regions based on the selection in cell **A5**.

3. Enter a nested formula in cell **F5** that contains the MATCH and INDEX functions as nested elements of the expression. For the employee whose ID is selected in cell **A5**, the formula should look up the bonus rate in the Bonus Table and multiply that by the employee's earnings.

4. Select several employee IDs in cell **A5** to confirm the dashboard works as expected.

5. Use conditional formatting to highlight in red the name and employee ID for any employee in the **Emp_Info** dataset who earns $100,000 or more a year.

6. Save the workbook to the **C:\091020Data\Applying Conditional Logic** folder as *my_employee_list.xlsx* and then close the workbook.

Lesson Lab 5-1
Auditing Worksheets

Activity Time: 15 minutes

Data File
C:\091020Data\Auditing Worksheets\sales_and_discounts.xlsx

Scenario
You manage all of the sales regions for your organization and you use Excel workbooks to track and analyze sales for a variety of purposes. One of your regional managers is reporting issues with the sales and discounts workbook you use to track sales and calculate customer discounts. Specifically, he says Excel returns a #DIV/0! error message when he tries to look up discounts for certain customers. Your organization gives a 10-percent discount to customers who have more than $1,000,000 in sales for any given year and more than $250,000 in sales for the second quarter, which had previously been your slowest. Otherwise, your customers receive an 8-percent discount if their annual purchases are more than $800,000 or a 5-percent discount if their annual purchases are less than or equal to $800,000. You suspect someone modified one or more of the formulas involved with calculating the discounts, so you plan to use trace arrows and formula evaluation to resolve the issue.

Further, the regional sales manager says the figures for two of your customers don't match the figures he has on a separate tracker. He believes invalid data is the culprit and has asked you to see if you can isolate the issue. You decide to use the Watch Window to monitor cells calculating sales for the two customers as you hunt down the invalid data to ensure your changes are, in fact, resolving the issue.

1. Open the **sales_and_discounts.xlsx** workbook file and ensure that the **Sales_Summaries** worksheet is selected.

2. Check the **Sales_Summaries** worksheet for errors and verify that Excel flags cell **C24** as containing a #DIV/0! error.

3. Continue checking the worksheet to verify there are no other formula errors.

4. Use the **Trace Precedents** command to determine where cell **C24** is getting its data.

5. Verify that the zero (0) value in cell **C23** is causing the error and then clear the trace arrows.

6. Correct the formula in cell **C24** to *F21*C23* because total sales should be multiplied by the discount, not divided by it.

7. Verify that changing the formula resolved the error.

8. As all customers should receive some discount, evaluate the function in cell **C23** to determine why Excel is returning a value of zero (0) for customer 1001's discount.

9. Resolve the issue by revising the function to return a discount of 5 percent for customers who are not eligible for the higher discounts.

10. Verify that the function works correctly; customer **1001** should receive a 5 percent discount and have adjusted sales of **$9,727.95**.

11. Add the cells calculating the sales totals for the customers with incorrect sales totals to the Watch Window, so you can monitor them as you scan the workbook for invalid data.
    a) Open the **Watch Window** and, if necessary, pin it to the Excel user interface above the **Formula Bar**.
    b) Add cell **M12** to the **Watch Window** to monitor customer 1010's sales total.
    c) Add cell **M13** to the **Watch Window** to monitor customer 1011's sales total.

12. Switch to the **Raw_Data** worksheet and scan the worksheet for invalid data.

13. Verify that Excel circled three cells for containing negative values.

14. While monitoring the **Watch Window**, change the values in cells **E5**, **G9**, and **H18** to positive values.

15. Verify that the value in cell **M12** updated to **$1,386,192.00** and the value in cell **M13** updated to **$630,388.00**.

16. Save the workbook to the **C:\091020Data\Auditing Worksheets** folder as *my_sales_and_discounts.xlsx* and close the workbook.

Lesson Lab 6-1
Using Automated Analysis Tools

Activity Time: 15 minutes

Data File
C:\091020Data\Using Automated Analysis Tools\sales_and_discounts_06.xlsx

Scenario
You are working on sales projections for your company for the coming fiscal year. Senior managers have set a target growth goal of 6 percent in overall sales, but they would also like to see the figures for a variety of other possibilities. First, they would like to see the sales projections for a variety of growth rates. They are also interested in the net sales projections once customer discounts are considered. As customers receive different discounts based on particular sales goals, the average customer discount varies depending on who buys what. Company leaders would like to see how a variety of average discount figures affects net sales at a variety of different gross sales amounts. Finally, they would like to know how much of a percentage of growth the company needs to experience to meet the stretch goal of $18.5 million in sales for the coming year. You realize you will need to use a variety of what-if analysis tools to give company leaders the information they're seeking. You have already added formulas and labels to the **Sales_Summaries** worksheet to begin the analysis.

1. Open the **sales_and_discounts_06.xlsx** workbook file and ensure that the **Sales_Summaries** worksheet is selected.

2. Create a one-variable data table out of the range **P7:Q17** that adjusts next year's sales projections based on the possible growth figures already entered.

3. Use the data in the range **S3:T6** to create scenarios by using the following values to calculate net sales after customer discounts at a variety of growth and discount rates: 5-percent sales growth and an average discount of 6 percent, 5.5-percent sales growth and an average discount of 6 percent, 6-percent sales growth and an average discount of 6.5 percent, and 6.5-percent sales growth and an average discount of 6.75 percent.

    > **Note:** Remember to also include a scenario with the original values, as Excel will convert formulas to values when you create the scenarios.

4. If the **Scenario** command is not on the **Quick Access Toolbar**, add it. Use the **Scenario** command to show and view the various scenarios.

5. By using the data in the range **P19:R22**, use the Goal Seek feature to determine the necessary sales growth to achieve $18.5 million in total sales.

6. Save the workbook to the **C:\091020Data\Using Automated Analysis Tools** folder as *my_sales_and_discounts_06.xlsx* and close the workbook.

Lesson Lab 7-1
Presenting Data Visually

Activity Time: 10 minutes

Data File
C:\091020Data\Presenting Your Data Visually\sales_and_discounts_07.xlsx

Scenario
You have finished the analysis work you've been performing in the sales and discounts workbook. As you have to present your findings to company leaders at an upcoming meeting, you decide to add some visual elements to make the data easier to interpret. First, you'd like to add a dual-axis chart displays both the total quarterly sales and the average quarterly sales per rep. And, as you think it's important to get a sense of how customer sales are tracking over time, you also decide to add sparklines to the **Sales by Customer** dataset to get a better sense of relative sales figures for your customers. You have already added a new column to the dataset for the sparklines.

1. Open the **sales_and_discounts_07.xlsx** workbook file and ensure the **Sales_Summary** worksheet is selected.

2. Use the data in the range **A2:E4** to create a dual Y-axis column chart with the average sales per rep on the secondary axis. Change the chart type for the average sales per rep to the **Line** chart type. The scale of the primary axis should be millions and the scale for the secondary axis should be thousands. Format the chart as you wish and place it below the data on the **Sales_Summaries** worksheet.

3. Add **Line** style sparklines to the range **M3:M22** that display relative values for the quarterly sales figures.

4. Group the sparklines together and format them in a red color with the **Hight Point** and **Low Point** data markers turned on.

5. Save the workbook to the **C:\091020Data\Presenting Your Data Visually** folder as *my_sales_and_discounts_07.xlsx* and close the workbook, and then close Excel.

Glossary

3-D references
References to the same cell across a range of worksheets.

ActiveX controls
Type of control that is far more flexible and customizable than form controls. ActiveX controls can execute VBA code authored by users or developers.

change tracking
Excel feature that adds page markup to workbook changes, making it easy for users to identify revisions.

circular reference
A reference, either direct or indirect, that points to the cell containing the reference.

comments
A type of worksheet markup that allows workbook users to convey information to one another.

constraints
In Excel, conditions that limit the values that can appear in changing cells for optimization models.

control properties
Control settings that assign specific functionality to controls, configure visual formatting options, define the linked cells, and determine how controls interact with the associated worksheet.

controls
Objects that users can add to worksheets that help other users perform certain tasks, such as entering data.

data consolidation
The process of summarizing data from a variety of datasets that aren't necessarily laid out in the same fashion.

data tables
Excel what-if analysis tool that enables users to replace one value in one or more formulas or functions, or replace two values in a single formula or function to determine a set of possible outcomes.

data validation
Excel feature that enables users to restrict data entry to particular specified criteria.

dependent cells
Cells that are fed by the data in other cells.

developer tab
Ribbon tab that users can add to the Excel ribbon in order to access the commands and tools for adding new functionality to Excel.

external links
Links to cells in other workbooks.

external references
References in formulas or functions to cells in other workbooks.

forecasting
The process of using the trends that exist within past data to predict future outcomes.

form
Either a physical or an electronic document that is organized for the purpose of collecting information.

form controls
Controls that add functionality to Excel worksheets without the need for writing VBA code.

formula evaluation
The process of breaking down Excel formulas or functions into component parts to determine how Excel is performing calculations.

internal links
Links to cells within the same workbook.

invalid data
Data entries that do not conform to the data validation criteria applied to a cell or range.

iterative calculations
Repetitive mathematical operations that approach the approximate solution to a problem by using the output of the previous calculation as part of the input for the subsequent calculation.

linked cells
Cells that are connected to the data in other cells. The data in a linked cell appears as the original data and behaves much like a standard data entry. The data in linked cells updates when the original data is updated.

macro
A series of steps or instructions that users can execute by using a single command or action.

modules
Containers for storing VBA code.

nesting
The process of using a function as an argument in another function or as part of a formula's expression.

one-variable data tables
Type of data table that replaces only a single variable in a formula or function. Users can determine possible outcomes for multiple formulas or functions by using one-variable data tables.

personal workbook
Hidden Excel workbook that users can use to store macros for use in other workbooks.

precedent cells
Cells that feed data into other cells.

shared workbook
An Excel workbook with certain collaboration features enabled. Shared workbooks enable multiple users to contribute changes to a workbook file that can then be merged together in the master copy of the workbook.

sparklines
Data visualization tools that exist within worksheet cells and display the relative values of entries in the defined dataset.

trace arrows
Worksheet markup that visually identifies relationships among worksheet cells.

two-variable data tables
Type of data table that replaces two variables in a formula or function to determine a range of possible outcomes.

Visual Basic Editor
Development tool used for creating and editing VBA code.

Visual Basic for Applications
The programming language developers use for Microsoft Office applications and other related add-ins, macros, and applications.

Watch Window
Excel feature that enables users to view the contents of specified cells regardless of their location on a worksheet.

what-if analysis
The process of calculating possible outcomes by replacing particular formula or function values with a set of variables.

Index

3-D references
    defined *2*
    summary functions *3*, *4*

A

Accept Changes dialog box *25*
Active X controls *54*
Add Constraint dialog box *140*
Add Scenario dialog box *127*
Analysis ToolPak *144*, *145*

B

black dashed-line trace arrow *101*
blue trace arrow *101*

C

cells, linked *8*
change tracking *23–25*
chart templates *159*
Circle Invalid Data command *107*
circular references *133*
comments *22*
Compare and Merge Workbooks command *28*
conditional formatting
    cell references *92*, *93*
    custom rules *90*
Consolidate dialog box *15*
constraints *137*
control properties *54*, *55*
Create Sparklines dialog box *162*

D

data
    consolidation *15*
    invalid *107*
    validation *42*
    validation, criteria *43*, *44*
Data Analysis dialog box *144*
Data Table dialog box *122*
data tables
    defined *120*
    one-variable *121*
    two-variable *122*
dependent cells *100*
Developer tab *52*
document exchange format *29*
dual-axis chart *152*

E

Edit Links dialog box *10*
Error Alert tab *45*
Error Checking command *107*, *108*
error types *108*
Evaluate Formula dialog box *112*
external references *11*

F

forecasting *153*
Format Trendline dialog box *154*, *155*
form controls *52*
forms
    defined *49*
    types of *50*, *51*
formula evaluation *112*
functions

HLOOKUP 78, 79
INDEX 81
Lookup 76
MATCH 79, 80
VLOOKUP 77

G

Goal Seek feature 132
Go To dialog box 102

H

Highlight Changes dialog box 24, 25
HLOOKUP function 78, 79

I

INDEX function 81
Input Message tab 44
invalid data 42, 107
iterative calculations 132–134

L

linked cells
    defined 8
    editing 10
    syntax 9
Lookup functions 76

M

Macro dialog box 66
macros
    defined 62
    names 67
    recording 64
    security settings 62, 63
MATCH function 79, 80
Microsoft OneDrive 27
modules 64

N

nesting
    defined 85
    function syntax 85, 86

O

OneDrive 27
one-variable data tables 121
online file storage 27

P

PDF file format 29
PEMDAS 112
personal workbook 67
precedent cells 100
protecting workbooks 33–35
protection formatting 127
Protect Sheet command 34
Protect Workbook options 35, 36

R

recording macros 64
Record Macro dialog box 64
red trace arrow 101
Remove Arrows options 102

S

Save & Send options 26, 27
Scenario command 128
Scenario Manager dialog box 125, 126
scenarios
    adding 127
    defined 125
    managing 125
    protection formatting 127
Scenario Values dialog box 127
security settings 62, 63
shared workbooks 23
Solver Parameters dialog box 138
Solver Results dialog box 141
Solver tool 137, 139
sparklines
    defined 161
    types of 162
Sparkline Tools contextual tab 162
summary functions
    3-D references 3, 4

T

trace arrows 101
Trace Precedents/Dependents command 100
tracking changes 23–25
trendlines
    defined 153
    types of 154
two-variable data tables 122

U

Use Relative References command *65*

V

VBA *63*
VBE *64*
Visual Basic Editor, *See* VBE
Visual Basic for Applications, *See* VBA
VLOOKUP function *77*

W

Watch Window *111*
what-if analysis *120*
workbook protection *33–35*
workbooks
    comparing and merging *28*
    personal *67*
    shared *23*

X

XPS file format *29*